The
Leadership
Manual

The
Leadership
Manual

Your Complete Practical Guide to Effective Leadership

**Hilarie Owen, Vicky Hodgson
and Nigel Gazzard**

PEARSON
Prentice Hall
BUSINESS

London • New York • Toronto • Sydney • Tokyo • Singapore
Hong Kong • Cape Town • Madrid • Paris • Amsterdam • Munich • Milan

PEARSON EDUCATION LIMITED

Edinburgh Gate
Harlow CM20 2JE
Tel: +44 (0)1279 623623
Fax: +44 (0)1279 431059
Website: www.pearsoned.co.uk

First published in Great Britain in 2004

ISBN-10: 0-273-67551-6
ISBN-13: 978-0-273-67551-8

British Library Cataloguing-in-Publication Data
A catalogue record for this book is available from the British Library.

Library of Congress Cataloging-in-Publication Data
A catalog record for this book is available from the Library of Congress

10 9 8 7 6 5 4 3
08 07 06

Typeset in 11.25pt Minion by 30
Printed and bound in Great Britain by Bell & Bain Ltd, Glasgow

The publisher's policy is to use paper manufactured from sustainable forests.

Contents

General introduction

On a warm summer day 500 managers congregated in a London hotel to take part in a debate on leadership. These individuals ranged in the areas and fields they worked in, spanned three decades in age and were both male and female, from diverse backgrounds.

We wanted to know: what were their questions, concerns or issues around 'leadership'? What kept them awake at night and what did they struggle with in their lives and their organisations. More than 50 issues and questions were raised and recorded.

The Leadership Manual has captured those questions and issues as representative of what most leaders, or would-be leaders, would like to know or understand or find guidance on. Using our knowledge and experience as practising leaders and researchers, and that of others, we now offer practical answers to those questions to help the millions of individuals working in a multitude of environments. This manual will try and help you through the daily challenges you face and encourage you to take the journey from manager to leader. It will help you understand others and enable you to develop their leadership potential too.

Leadership isn't always easy. In many ways it's much easier to manage than to lead, as management is largely about tasks and procedures. Leadership is as much about who you are and how you express that as it is about what you do. But good leadership well practised is powerful beyond belief and can elicit results from people that straight management never can.

Leadership is sometimes made harder by the organisations we work in, and the thinking of people around us. In particular, the present hierarchical structure of most organisations (even more flattened ones) results in cultures based on most power at the top rather than distributed power. If you feel powerless, it's hard to express much leadership.

What is required is true transformation. This does not mean we need more vision statements and direction from CEOs, Directors, Permanent Secretaries, Presidents, Prime Ministers, Head Teachers or senior managers. **The challenge of transformation requires us all to take responsibility and participate**. The answer we seek is not 'out there' it is within each one of us. Transformation begins with the self and this requires leadership from all of us – managers, teachers, civil servants, nurses, prison officers, care assistants, young and old, men and women, black, brown, white and yellow.

This manual is intended to provide guidance to anybody, to help us all feel sufficiently powerful to become leaders, whatever our role in work and life.

Never before has there been so much attention paid to the concept of leadership while at the same time we are more disheartened and mistrustful of our so-called leaders. To deal with this paradox, a major shift in our thinking is required, and we believe that we stand on the edge of a huge shift. Our thinking, beliefs and behaviours as human beings and leaders have the wings to carry us over the edge to a different place. If we stay where we are the issues facing us at work and on a global scale will never be resolved.

What form does this new thinking take? Having studied leadership for over twenty years in the fields of politics, business, education and social contexts we have developed four basic truths about leadership. We have researched and tested these truths and share them with you.

1. Every single person has some leadership potential. We need to recognise that leadership is not the preserve of those at the top of the hierarchy. We are all leaders and followers at different times. We must take responsibility for ourselves.

2. No two people express leadership the same so it can't be placed in a single model that does not tolerate a diversity of leadership. Rather the focus must be to enable each individual, each one of us, to understand, know and express our own leadership. We must take responsibility for both ourselves and each other.

3. Developing leadership requires a lifelong learning approach that consistently develops throughout a career using a mix of knowledge, experience, reflection and action learning. Leadership is not something you acquire on a week's training programme. We must take responsibility for ourselves, each other and our learning.

4. To encourage and sustain leadership in organisations they need freedom and democratic transformation throughout. We must each take responsibility for ourselves, for each other, for our learning and our environment, cultures and structures. No matter where we are in an organisation, we can influence it by having the courage to transform some part of it.

Where do we begin? *The Leadership Manual* is a good place because it deals with the real issues faced by the majority of people at work today. We have tried to avoid jargon where possible and take theory to an end outcome where you can put your knowledge into practice. Therefore, we wrote this manual to help, support and encourage individuals in their daily work. We know from research that the best way to develop leadership is to relate it to real work and we will encourage you to do this.

The Leadership Manual is a practical book that you can dip into time and time again. We live in a fast-changing world and with this comes the need for quick, practical information that will achieve results to be successful while remembering that leadership is as much about who you are as it is a set of skills. As much about how you do things as what you do.

In this context *The Leadership Manual* is the first practical reference guide for busy people that addresses finding your authentic self and how you express this at work. It is for anyone wanting to develop their own leadership potential in a work situation including busy professionals, managers and entrepreneurs. It provides fast, practical information with suggestions, ideas and steps to encourage you the reader to use your leadership potential in every situation you face at work. Finally, *The Leadership Manual* addresses the transformation required in organisations and shows how you can participate in this transformation regardless of your role.

The structure of the book is set out in the diagram on page xix enabling you to dip in and out of it for years to come. Therefore this is a lifelong learning resource (Diagram 1). What this is not is a book on management that has just changed the title to leadership. The focus here is on leadership which is very different to management and requires a few moments each day for thinking and reflection. Leadership also requires action and therefore *The Leadership Manual* will encourage this. Good luck and we hope the issues you want to resolve are here with advice that will support and help you.

The Institute of Leadership

The Institute of Leadership is a not-for-profit independent organisation set up to be a global think tank and network for those interested in learning and practising leadership. To find out more, visit our website at www.ifo.org or www. instituteofleadership.com. Alternatively, contact hilarie.owen@iofl.org.

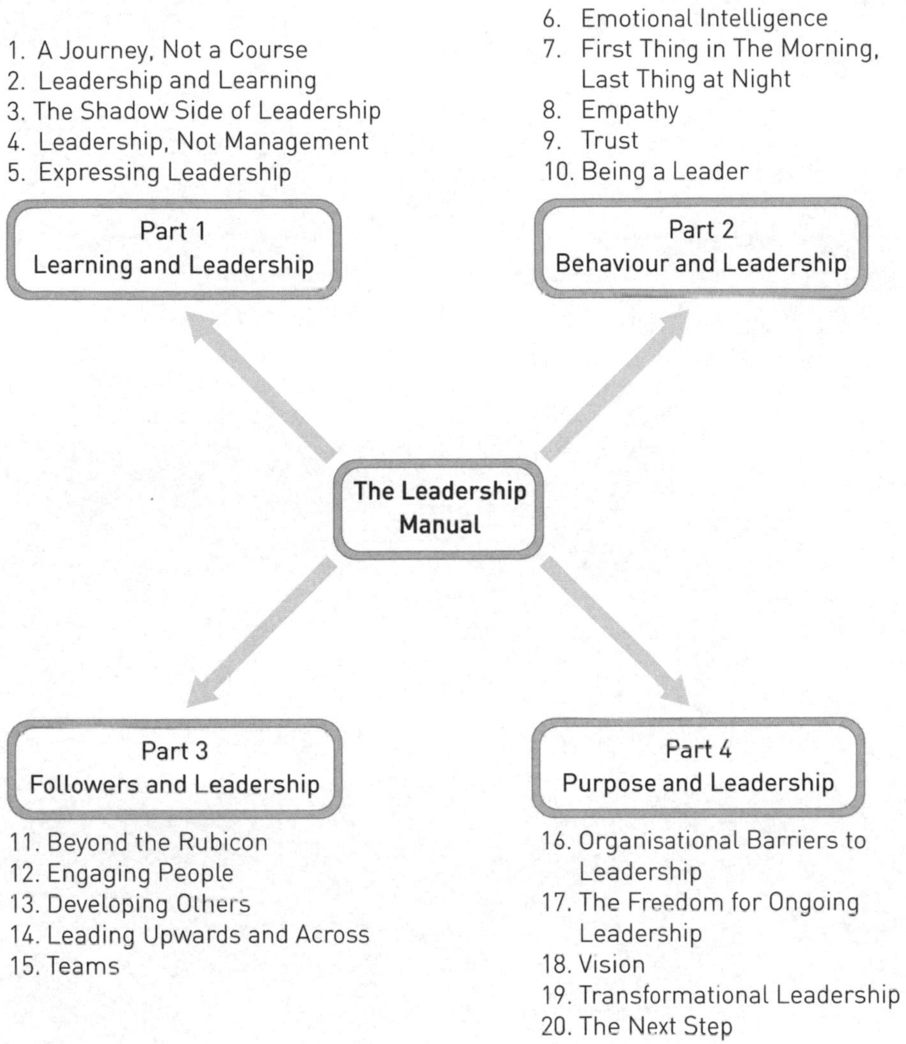

1. A Journey, Not a Course
2. Leadership and Learning
3. The Shadow Side of Leadership
4. Leadership, Not Management
5. Expressing Leadership

6. Emotional Intelligence
7. First Thing in The Morning, Last Thing at Night
8. Empathy
9. Trust
10. Being a Leader

Part 1
Learning and Leadership

Part 2
Behaviour and Leadership

The Leadership Manual

Part 3
Followers and Leadership

Part 4
Purpose and Leadership

11. Beyond the Rubicon
12. Engaging People
13. Developing Others
14. Leading Upwards and Across
15. Teams

16. Organisational Barriers to Leadership
17. The Freedom for Ongoing Leadership
18. Vision
19. Transformational Leadership
20. The Next Step

Diagram 1. Route Map

Part

1

Learning and Leadership

1

A Journey, Not a Course

Chapter guide:

- realising that leadership is not about position but is inherent in every human being to some degree;
- knowing that leadership requires ongoing learning and development;
- needing to understand that developing leadership is more like a journey than a training course.

Contents:

Introduction

You've just had a memo from the HR department saying that leadership development is a priority for the next six months and that you have to attend a week's course in the Lake District next month. How do you feel about it?

This scenario happens in organisations every day. What hasn't been realised is that leadership development is not achieved on a training course alone – no matter how good or how much fun. Developing your leadership potential is a lifelong learning process. It began before you went to school and will continue indefinitely.

Our tendency in life today is to look for the 'quick fix'. Developing certain skills on a training course can contribute to learning as long as the individual can then practise what they have learned. The difference with leadership is that it is as much about *who you are* as what you do and how you do it. Therefore the process is ongoing – and it's never too late or too early to begin.

In this part we explore learning and leadership and explain why we take the approach we do throughout the *Manual*. First, there are two things about learning we need to clarify:

1. Learning doesn't just happen as a single, specialised function of the brain. Learning involves the whole brain, including thinking, feeling and perceiving.
2. Learning involves the creation of meaning from past and current events that serves as a guide for future behaviour. Therefore to change behaviour involves 're-wiring' the brain, including some of the beliefs we hold.

Likewise, leadership is more than a single function, involving thinking, feelings, perceiving and behaving. These thoughts and feelings are based on past and present events and experiences, making leadership a personal expression of the way one relates to the world. The way you express your leadership will differ from that of everyone else. The mistake made by many of those in teaching or training is the belief that a single model or tool will create a similar result in everyone. Instead, try to see learning as a journey that will take you to a place not yet experienced.

If the process is a journey rather than a training course, then try and see this *Manual* as your guidebook. If we travel to Italy we buy a guidebook to help us understand the country's geography, its culture, some key words and the highlights. However, your visit will still remain unique to you and so it is with leadership. We can map out some of what you may learn here and even mark the highlights, but the journey will be yours alone. You will need some things to take with you on this leadership journey. The first is a 'suitcase'.

There are two types of suitcases in the book that will be useful for us to open at various points on the journey:

- one for practising leadership;
- one for reflecting for a moment.

The reflective suitcases are to be opened where you stop and convert what you are reading into learning for yourself. Reflective learning is different to the process of gathering information and knowledge. It includes thinking, asking yourself questions and making your own mind up about your own learning. It can include questions such as: 'What have I learned today?', 'How am I going to use that learning?', 'How successful was that project?', ' How could it have been done differently to improve the outcome?', 'Why did I react like that?', and ' What else do I need to learn?' In doing this you are taking responsibility for yourself and your behaviour – this is vital in developing your leadership.

These suitcases are ideally to be opened at a quiet moment and the reflection shouldn't be rushed. The practising suitcase will challenge you to put leadership learning into action and will encourage taking responsibility for yourself, taking responsibility for each other, taking responsibility for learning, and taking responsibility for the environment, culture and structure where you work.

To give your leadership a different perspective, there are mentors you will meet on this learning journey – people who offer guidance and different examples of how to put leadership into practice. Some of these are people you will have heard of – others not. These mentors reflect the diversity of worldwide leadership and include men and women of black, Asian and white cultures.

'Knowledge Banks' occur throughout the book and can be visited anytime during the journey to enable you to use knowledge as your currency. Don't be a miser and cling to all the knowledge you have but rather share it with colleagues and your team. You will also need 'Route Maps' (←/→) and these will also be provided as the terrain becomes complicated. They will link related topics so that you can return to specific sections.

The next section will explain how we should think about leadership in the 21st century and put it into practice. Let's explore the whole notion of leadership with an open mind and how you express it today at work.

The essence of leadership

When they look at leadership many people begin by asking, 'What is it?' for thousands of years philosophers and writers on leadership, and latterly behavioural scientists have tried to answer this question. The result is a multitude of answers, each contributing to the debate in some way. These range from Distinguished Professor Warren Bennis, political scientist, researcher and writer, saying that leadership is like beauty – hard to define, but you know it when you see it, to Ken Blanchard, researcher and writer, asserting that leadership is about going somewhere rather than wandering aimlessly. But what is the essence of leadership that will help you to understand it and practise it?

Let's explore some of the things we have learned about leadership and establish their contribution to developing our understanding of it. Some of the most revealing and profound learning about leadership is actually in ancient texts, especially those of Confucius, the Chinese philosopher. One of the most valuable lessons from these old writings is the belief that an individual who can express the best of themselves through leadership will encourage and influence others to do so. If a leader is good it is more likely that those who follow will also be good. If a leader is selfish so will the followers be selfish and so on. So we can ask, who are the people around you? What are they expressing in their leadership? Where has it come from?

Confucius regarded education as a transformational process that takes place within an individual but does so through others. He said that in order to establish oneself, one has to establish others. In other words, *the journey of leadership is not so much an isolated one for the individual as one that exists only in a set of relations with others.*

Modern ideas on leaderships

During the 20th century interest in understanding leadership began to grow. In the early 1900s it was believed that leaders were born and studies focused on traits identified mainly by psychologists. After many years no difference was found in leaders compared to other persons. During the 1950s and 1960s behaviourists focused on what leaders do. One of the well-known US studies was undertaken by Robert Blake and Jane Mouton, who developed a grid divided into two areas based on whether an individual was employee-centred or task-centred. This tool was used to give feedback to managers that resulted in slight positive outcomes but not much change overall. However, it did open up the belief that leadership could be taught and in the UK John Adair was using his action-centred model at Sandhurst to develop leadership in the army.

During 1969–70, researchers Paul Hersey and Ken Blanchard put leadership into a situational context based on the skill and motivation of the employee and how an individual should lead. The results were still limited and unimpressive but training was taking off and trainers liked the model because they could use it. Also in the 1970s the psychometric tool Myers Briggs Type Indicator based on the work of the Swiss psychoanalyst Carl Jung was developed and used to explain personality differences, but it did not explain leadership effectiveness. So after 75 years of studies from psychologists and behaviourists nothing changed very much in understanding leadership except that the fast-growing training industry had tools they could use.

The real pioneers of understanding leadership

Others with a different perspective *did* contribute to our understanding of leadership. They were the political scientists. The first was Mary Parker Follett an American political scientist who, in a series of papers written for business education during the 1920s and 30s, set out views of leadership that were to influence others. She began by criticising psychologists who viewed leadership as aggression and domination. Follett believed leadership could come from anywhere, regardless of the leader's position. She believed that leadership was about grasping the total situation and the ability to organise everyone to serve a common purpose. This, she said, meant that instead of personal power there was 'group power'. In addition, Follett said that leadership required a pioneering spirit that would challenge and blaze new trails by seeing possible new paths. That is, leadership took us to new places because it required courage. Her contribution to our understanding of leadership included her ideas about followers who she did not believe were passive but actively helping the leader to stay in control of a situation. In other words, *the success of the team enabled the success of the leader, not the other way around.*

This reality has huge implications for you in the workplace. If leadership is to be unleashed in organisations then followers have a role to play and should be included in the learning and development process. The role is dynamic, not passive, sitting back and waiting for 'the leader' to decide what to do. Each one of us (employees, customers, suppliers, directors, shareholders, managers, civil servants, ministers, doctors, nurses, teachers, solicitors and accountants) have to take responsibility for leadership to be effective.

This links us to the ancient Chinese writings: *the journey of leadership is not so much an isolated one for the individual as one that exists only in a set of relations with others.*

Another political scientist, James MacGregor Burns, made a fundamental discovery in the notion of the actions of leaders that he called 'transformational leadership' and published his findings during the 1970s. He found that leadership involved transforming people and organisations rather than motivating employees to exchange work for pay. The latter he called 'transactional leadership' and is the basis of management today.

An important part of Burns' concept of transformational leadership was that it had a moral side to it and involved the example of an individual in relation to others in achieving transformation that could extend to societal change. If this concept is valid, then transformational leadership will be important for our future as we struggle with the leadership paradox (← p. xvi). We will therefore explore Burns' work fully in Part Four when we look at transforming organisations (p. 309 →).

In the early 1980s Warren Bennis used qualitative research in the form of interviews with many individuals that identified the actions of leadership as:

attention to vision;

communicating the vision;

building trust;

respecting self and others and risk-taking.

But the questions remained – how do you teach or develop trust or respect? Will we ever know all the answers? Will you know everything about leadership by the time you finish this *Manual*?

Bennis will be our first mentor on the journey, for he can answer that question. He wrote recently: 'The arc of events that have shaped my intellectual passions … language, thought, feelings, community, change, human advancement, and a promising future … still remain obscure to me, perhaps easier to describe than understand' (2001). But he also wrote: ' … it's much easier to express yourself than to deny yourself. And much more rewarding, too' (1989).

The key to understanding leadership is to accept that no-one will ever know everything. This *Manual* should help you to express the leadership you have within you, but you yourself must find the courage to use it. With that in mind, let us carry on with the journey through 20th century knowledge on leadership.

In the 1980s Jim Kouzes and Barry Posner, researchers and writers on leadership, focused their research on the actions and behaviours involved in leadership. They found five key actions, each of which contains two behaviours. They are:

1. challenging the process – requires the behaviours of searching for opportunities, experimenting and taking sensible risks;

2. inspiring a shared vision – requires the behaviours of constructing a future vision and building follower support;

3. enabling others to act – requires the behaviours of fostering collaboration and supporting followers in their personal development;

4. modelling the way – requires the behaviours of setting an example and focusing on step-by-step accomplishments;

5. encouraging the heart – requires the behaviours of recognising followers' contributions and celebrating their achievements.

Kouzes and Posner developed psychometric tools to measure these actions and again trainers loved this because they could use the tools. However, leadership is more than actions and behaviours. Training courses that have focused on these tools have not changed much in workplace behaviour and leadership ability. That is why we include other central issues involved in leadership including power, emotions, beliefs, thinking and the environment where leadership is expressed. But first, what have we learned so far? If we take all the written works on leadership from ancient times to the present and summarise them in one sentence we can say the essence of leadership is:

The full, authentic expression of an individual working towards a purposeful goal that affects positive transformation involving collaborative relationships with others resulting in collective action.

Knowledge Bank

According to the dictionary, the word essence means 'most important feature of something which determines its identity'. The key words in the sentence are 'authentic', 'purposeful', 'positive transformation', 'relationships' and 'collective action'. Together they pull together the important features that determine leadership. Being authentic and your best means you have to **know yourself** and express this without ego or status falsifying the truth. This takes **honesty** and openness. When actions are purposeful and bring about positive transformation they often have to be accompanied by **courage** to overcome inertia or power. Leadership is also a **relationship** with others that has an **outcome** and in creating it **enables others** to express leadership also.

Within this sentence is the richness of what can be achieved through human endeavour and shows why leadership is so vital to not only our organisations but to the world. It also shows clearly that being a leader is not about being bossy, controlling, loud or arrogant. Expressing leadership is not based on position or power but rather on **trust** and **relationships**.

Reflective Suitcase

You can start to think about packing your first suitcase by exploring the answers to these questions.

How is leadership perceived in your organisation?

How is leadership perceived by your team or colleagues?

Do people expect to be told what to do or participate in deciding their future?

You will see how our beliefs really do result in behaviour and until beliefs change, behaviour remains unchanged. Changing beliefs and understanding, let alone practising, leadership isn't easy, and that's why it's simpler to fill our day with tasks or measure an individual's performance rather than their learning.

Learning is a fundamental process to developing leadership and we found it central in our research on how people cope and use their leadership in a fast-changing, demanding work environment. Those who were constantly learning could not only cope but achieved excellent results and were regarded by others as leaders. While some individuals picked up concepts on courses or postgraduate study and uttered the words, they were not translated in their everyday behaviours and actions. Learning involves more than acquiring knowledge and repeating it. Learning has to be internalised, interpreted and incorporated into our wider beliefs to challenge and develop them.

Nothing will change if we continue to do what we've done before. Developing leadership begins with you.

Reflective Suitcase

What does leadership mean to you?

The journey you will travel

The leader you want to be is achievable. The only person stopping you is yourself and how you think about yourself, the world and leadership in it. To become the leader you want to be will require more than a training course. It will require exploration of your deepest beliefs, values, fears, purpose and emotions as an ongoing learning process. Instead of developing a list of skills, the focus in the *Manual* will be on knowing and developing *you*, who you can become and how to express this in your work and life.

Your leadership is important because of the huge challenges facing us today. Let's go back to the paradox we mentioned at the start of this book. We live in a world wanting to understand leadership but at the same time we have never felt so mistrustful of our leaders. What has happened to bring this about?

Practising Suitcase

What do you think of the leadership in your organisation?

What do you think of leaders in the business world?

What do you think of leadership in the civil service and government departments with their 'experts' and advisers?

What do you think of political leaders around the world?

How does this make you feel?

Pinpoint what it is they are doing that you feel is wrong.

What is it they do that you think is right?

You are now beginning to identify what you think about leadership as you see it every day. What has this to do with your work? Your head is picking up on all the examples around you and this influences how you see leadership in the world today. At work it will surprise you how much we emulate and copy what we see elsewhere.

Reflective Suitcase

Take a moment to consider yourself in relation to the paradox.

How would you like to use your leadership?

What do you need to do to realise this?

If you are not, why aren't you?

Leadership isn't about achieving more targets or improving bottom line figures, as important as these may be. Leadership begins with having the courage to become all you can be. When you do this achieving targets or improving performance will follow. If you express your leadership others will notice. It will encourage them to use their leadership potential. Therefore see the challenge as throwing a pebble in the pond. The ripples move across the pond until all the water has been stirred. Be a pebble and begin a stir. What is it inside you that is stopping this? Write it down as we will come back to it.

On our leadership journey we are going to meet our next mentor, Nelson Mandela. He is one of the few individuals in the world today who is regarded as a wise leader but he will be the first to admit that he wasn't always so. He talks about his leadership journey in his biography, *The Long Walk to Freedom*.

Mandela tells of how as a child he considered himself to be free until he became a young man. At first, he says, he wanted freedom for himself to do as he wanted, as most young people do, but gradually he realised that all black people lacked freedom to become what they desired and he wanted freedom for all his people. He turned from being a lawyer to an outlaw fighting for what he believed to be just.

In prison, Mandela spent time talking with other prisoners and some of the guards. He then realised that his oppressors must be free too – free from prejudice. For Mandela the road to freedom and leadership was a journey of learning about who he was and how best to use that knowledge in working with others to achieve their common goal.

Throughout this example you can see the process of learning that enabled Mandela to be the person he is today. The learning cycle we will use here is from Kurt Lewin, theorist of experiential learning, and has four stages (Diagram 2):

1. experience,

2. observation and reflection,

3. forming abstract concepts and generalisations, and

4. testing the implications of the concepts in new situations.

Mandela experienced apartheid as a young man and observed that this was the reality for all his people. Upon reflection he decided to resist and through the generalisation that all white people were the enemy of his people he at first was a strong rebel. This was *tested* and he was arrested by whites. While in prison he experienced that many

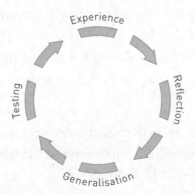

Diagram 2 Learning Cycle – developed by Levin and later Kolb

white men supported him and through this further reflection he formed new concepts and generalisations and so on. So here is an example of learning and its relevance to developing leadership. Now try this cycle out using your own life.

Do you believe you have leadership potential? Do you believe you are a leader in something? Do you want to develop your leadership potential? Do you believe leadership is a positive attribute? If your answers are 'yes' then we can progress through this first section. If you are unsure, then ask 'why' and reflect on the answer.

On this journey you will have baggage with you, and during the experience it will be a good idea to get rid of some of the old baggage and replace it with new things. This is where the suitcases help. You will also need a passport as a means of identifying yourself. What does the passport picture look like? Is this what you really look like? Could it be better? What experiences and places have you recorded in the passport? (Where have you been? What have you done there? What did you learn?) How have they contributed to your leadership potential?

Reflective Suitcase

Before we continue you have to know your destination – or at least some idea of it. To do this there is a very important question to ask yourself. *What sort of leader do you want to be?* Take five minutes now to answer this because you need to know your destination on this journey. Keep this information beside you as you read because we will refer to it from time to time.

Is leadership down to genes?

One of the big questions often raised when learning about leadership is whether genes affect who has leadership potential? There is no doubt that genes are powerful and pass on more than physical attributes, but other factors also come into play such as environment, parents' values and the influence of peers. However, the truth is that we are all free to choose who we want to be, but to do so is not encouraged in many aspects of our education or workplaces. When some organisations say they want leadership what they really mean is compliance – they want workers to fit in and not rock the boat and so they test us with psychometric tests and when we join an organisation we 'learn' to fit.

There is also a perception of leadership as only being something for those in positions of power and everyone else feels degrees of powerlessness in the organisation. From this perspective there is a tendency to sit back, not take responsibility and expect the person at the top to 'fix' everything, often justified by the fact that the top individual earns much, much more than the rest of the organisation.

Knowledge Bank

Seeing the world as a hierarchy is a view we inherited in the western world from the Greeks and, in particular, Aristotle. Greek society was made up of the elite who originated in Athens, workers who were Greek, slaves who came from other parts of their empire, and women, who were considered below men. Only those in the elite class could be considered leaders and participate in their 'democracy'. Aristotle put all life into a hierarchy and ever since his time this is how we tend to see the world. It is *a* reality but not necessarily *the* reality. We build hierarchical structures and equate leadership with position and power. This perception limits us.

Practising Suitcase

Try sitting down with some colleagues and ask them how they feel about the word 'leader'. Collect their views. What does this tell you? Can we ever distinguish leaders from those who hold the power?

Hierarchies are built on power: those at the top will have more power than those below them. Those at the bottom often feel powerless. That does not mean that those in senior positions are expressing leadership. In fact, if we look at many of them we see a shortage of leadership practice. Therefore, it is our *expectation* of certain individuals to express leadership that is an issue because we perceive them as being in a position to do so. The problem is that when they do not know their leadership potential or how to use it, the result is ineffective organisations because they have been focusing on gaining power and status for their own reasons rather than developing leadership that is meaningful and transforming. Why does this happen?

If certain individuals regard the world as a place where survival is based on the fittest, strongest, wealthiest, etc. then their motivation is to become stronger and wealthier than others. This is particularly true of many men for whom work has replaced the role of hunter. They prove their 'hunting success' with the car they drive, the size of house they live in and the skins they wear, including possession of items such as an MBA to prove how good at 'hunting' they are. Does this enable these individuals to be leaders? It doesn't.

This takes us back to the question that has been a debate for a long time – is leadership genetically programmed in only a few individuals? Again there has been influence from the Greeks, who wrote tales of heroes to inspire others, but not all. Plato, who was a student of Aristotle, said that there were those who could lead and those who could not. This notion that there are a few remarkable people who can lead was reinforced in the UK by the class system and remains today with the 'great man' theory.

Although the 'great man' theory is dying out there are still expectations that certain individuals will come along and fix the world whether in business or politics. This expectation fuels the belief that the majority of people do not have the genes, talent or abilities to express leadership, with the result that the majority of us don't take any responsibility for the world we live in because we don't believe we can make a difference and we've learned to keep our heads down and just focus on those close to us. Is this belief true, or can we all make a difference through expressing our leadership?

Knowledge Bank

On 13th March 1996 Thomas Hamilton walked into a school in Scotland and indiscriminately shot children and a teacher, killing most with a handgun before shooting himself. Small children dropped to the floor in pools of blood while others screamed and tried to escape. Parents around the UK were shocked that such an incident could happen. Yet a few months earlier another man had gone crazy shooting people in Hungerford, England. But it was the image of small children being shot as they sat in school that led to three women from Scotland who also had children to begin The Snowdrop Campaign to rid the UK of handguns so that this tragedy would not happen again. A few years on we traced one of the women who explained how a group of people fought to change the law through organised protest.

'Firstly, I must say that we probably would not have had the national support without the media, especially the *Daily Record* in Scotland who kept the story going when other papers had stopped. So the media are important in such campaigns. The other significant support was from our husbands who took over the washing, ironing, shopping and chores while we focused on what became a huge responsibility. Every day there were letters to reply to, phone calls to deal with and Saturdays we spent getting signatures for the petition we decided to take to the House of Commons.

The petition was where we started, using a wallpaper pasting table. People came from all around Stirling and beyond to sign it. It was about 11 weeks later we took the petition with around three-quarters of a million signatures to Parliament. However, we were not allowed to see Prime Minister John Major, only the parents of children who had died were given that option. Instead we were left alone inside the Parliament building with a cup of tea.

We didn't know "the rules of the game" so we just did what we did by instinct and I think this worried some politicians. We just knew that what we were campaigning for – to get rid of the private possession of guns – was right. I believe we need more people to get their heads out of "soaps" and get interested in the world around them.

In Scotland no Tory MP signed the petition but Alex Salmon (SNP), Jim Wallace (LibDem) and Martin O'Neil (Lab) did sign after hearing the arguments. We also had the support of someone who knew all the technical aspects of guns who helped us enormously in understanding this side of what we were doing and saying.

The law changed when Labour were elected in 1997. There was a free vote in Parliament and it was passed that no private individual could own or possess a handgun though people can still have shotguns and rifles with a licence.'

We asked her about children being killed by guns in other western countries such as the US. She added: 'The US needs to realise that the enemy is within. They said during the Kosovo Crisis that they would do everything to avoid one body bag coming back to the US yet more children are killed in the US than soldiers killed in Vietnam' (one of the Founders of the Snowdrop Campaign).

What can we learn from this story?

1. People care about things and will be moved to action when it touches them.

2. Making change happen requires support from others and a focus of activity.

3. Expressing leadership to transform something requires taking responsibility, courage and the will to act.

How can we apply this learning to work situations?

When leading change do you identify what people care about as part of the new outcome you want to achieve?

Do you gain people's support for the change?

Do you focus the activity on the end result but identify ways to reach it?

Do you take responsibility for the outcome?

Do you use your courage to ask for more from people?

Do you act to ensure success?

Follow these questions at work when you want to bring about change and you can make a difference just as the three women in Scotland did.

Today, with an educated workforce, leadership is an opportunity for many to make a difference. We can see the change coming through the rise in people protesting on a global scale. Our limitations are self-inflicted rather than caused by genes. We still build organisations that are hierarchical in structure and power-based for the few. Within these organisations have you heard yourself or others mutter: 'I work in a hierarchy, what can I do?' or 'I can't influence anything.'

The evidence in recent years shows that the person at the top will not resolve everything and so we criticise and replace them for another who perhaps is attracted to power, status and challenge, and so it goes on. Self-esteem may be more important than genes. Self-esteem or how we perceive ourselves is based on our own and others' expectations of who we are. *Self-esteem affects leadership*. At the Institute of Leadership we found children with low self-esteem had a parent and other family members with low self-esteem. Low self-esteem means they do not have a positive view of themselves and their capabilities. Whether it can be put down to genes or learned behaviour is difficult to answer. What we do know is that you can change your perception of self-esteem because leadership requires a healthy self-image.

Our view is that leadership may be influenced by genes but leadership is more greatly influenced by many other factors and our *potential* for leadership is *not* related to genes. As Follett said 'Leadership can come from anywhere' (1995).

Who can be a leader?

The truth is that every human being has leadership potential. For some this will be small and for others the potential will be huge. In between will be where most of us lie, but you definitely don't have to be a manager to be a leader.

Inside each of us is leadership potential that may not be acknowledged or put into practice. What does this tell you about those you work with? Do you see this potential in their everyday work? If not, why not? Did they have this potential before they were recruited?

There is a need to shift our expectation of leadership for the few to one where each person has some potential. The problem is that most don't know they have this potential and have never had the opportunity to develop it for the benefit of their organisation, community or the world at large.

Everyone has leadership potential

- What are the implications for this truth?
- How does this impact on you and where you work?

You have unique leadership potential that you can use to achieve all sorts of things. If you work with other people, you also need to acknowledge that they also have the same quality. There's John down the corridor who does what he's asked to do but no more. There's Michelle who is intelligent but never says anything at the monthly meetings. Each of these individuals has leadership potential but either they don't believe they have or say they don't want leadership responsibility because they are fearful. More often individuals feel deep inside that they do have leadership potential but don't know how to develop it. How will this affect you and your performance? Let's put you in a scenario.

Practising Suitcase

You are team leader and it is your responsibility to achieve certain targets by achieving certain results. You look at your team and you give the important, stretching responsibilities to the couple of team members who you know from experience are capable and won't let you down. The problem is that these two will end up with so much work they may eventually feel they cannot cope and begin to hate coming into work.

What about the rest of the team? They will plod on and experience no learning or personal growth. What should you do?

The answer is that you should give the rest of the team stretching projects too, but at first do some of the work with them or support them through the process. Here you have to balance helping and encouraging them without it developing into a dependency relationship. So now think about how you develop leadership potential in your team. Don't use the excuse of lack of time to do this – when you develop your team you end up with more time for what you really need to focus on.

Being a leader does not mean you control things all the time. When individuals are only used to control they learn to play helpless and risk-averse. Can you change this? You can if you follow this procedure.

Practising Suitcase

When an individual comes to you for help ask them how they think something should be done at the beginning. Don't take over but encourage them to work things out for themselves. There is nothing wrong with saying: 'Go back and try to do this yourself and if you still can't by the end of the day come and see me in the morning.'

It's amazing how many times most will do the work themselves and feel great for doing something they didn't think they could do. This will lead to confidence and realising that they have more potential than they believed, including leadership potential.

Meanwhile, if you have someone who comes back in the morning and you believe they are capable of working things through for themselves but are playing helpless then ask them some questions about the work that may clarify where the blockage is. Doing this results in *both* of you learning: you, about what support and help they need and they, about what they can do. You can then send them away again saying that you really think they can do it themselves. If they still can't do the work then do it with them but do not take over. Make a suggestion but allow them to decide how to achieve the work. They must find their own leadership potential.

Does this mean the end of followers?

When we say leadership can be expressed by everyone it does not mean that there will be no followers. The reality is that each of us is a leader and follower at different times – the key is to recognise when. In addition, leadership will look different at different times and with different people. However, some managers will regard themselves as the leaders and the rest followers because they want to maintain hierarchy and control and regard an alternative as anarchy and a threat. Do not let this distract you from developing your own authentic leadership potential or that of others.

Think of two people you know who express leadership. How does each come across? How do they apply leadership? Is one better than the other or do they just have different styles?

Each individual must find out who *they* are as a leader. No two people will express leadership the same way and so to try and fit everyone into a model or framework is actually stifling the quality. The problem is that many organisations want people to fit into a box and be similar. We call this 'leadership in a box'. Instead we should be valuing the differences. It's time for another look in the suitcase.

Reflective Suitcase

Now, if everyone in the organisation felt they not only had leadership potential but knew what it was and how to use it in a meaningful way, how would they feel?

In addition, suppose individuals – regardless of their role – could express their leadership towards achieving positive change that resulted in more than bottom line results, would things begin to be different?

Leadership is complex, but if we think about leadership in the following way our journey will take us to new worlds and be fun.

Message 1. Leadership is not based on position but potential in every human being.

Action   Accept that everyone has some of this potential;

Do not allow a hierarchy to make you feel helpless or prevent you from expressing your leadership.

Message 2. Developing leadership is a journey of continuous learning.

Action   Look at your journey so far and reviewing what you have learned;

See every day as an opportunity to learn more about leadership;

Make it a habit to keep an open mind and identifying mentors who can help you.

Message 3. We are all leaders and followers at different times.

Action   Develop the leadership potential around you;

Don't be the leader all the time by encouraging others to take that role at meetings or presentations, etc;

Make it clear to others that the role of followers is important and dynamic.

Message 4. **No two people express leadership in the same way.**

Action   Accept and celebrate the diversity of leadership;

Promote individuals who are different to you.

---

2 Leadership and Learning

Introduction

How does learning impact on leadership?

Knowledge Bank

These are the words from the autobiography of one individual who learned how to express his leadership through the many hours of study he undertook as a young man.

'... capitalism is always in danger of inspiring men to be more concerned about making a living than making a life. We are prone to judge success by the index of our salaries or the size of our automobiles, rather than by the quality of our service and relationship to humanity ... My reading of Marx also convinced me that truth is found neither in Marxism or in traditional capitalism. Each represents a partial truth. Historically capitalism failed to see the truth in collective enterprise and Marxism failed to see the truth in individual enterprise ... Through studying Hegel's philosophy his analysis of the dialectic process helped me see that growth comes through struggle ... I thought the only way we could solve our problem of segregation was an armed revolt. I felt that the Christian ethic of love was confined to individual relationships. I could not see how it could work in social conflict ... Then one Sunday afternoon I travelled to Philadelphia to hear a sermon by Dr Mordecai Johnson, president of Howard University ... he spoke of the life and teaching of Mahatma Gandhi. His message was so profound and electrifying that I left the meeting and bought a half-dozen books on Gandhi's life and works ... As I read I became deeply fascinated by his campaigns of non-violent resistance. I was particularly moved by his Salt March to the Sea and his numerous fasts ... As I delved deeper into the philosophy

of Gandhi, my scepticism of the power of love gradually diminished, and I came to see for the first time its potency in the area of social reform … Love for Gandhi was a potent instrument for social and collective transformation. It was … the method for social reform I had been seeking. The intellectual and moral satisfaction that I failed to gain from the writings of the utilitarianism of Bentham and Mill, the revolutionary methods of Marx and Lenin, the social contracts theory of Hobbes, the "back to nature" optimism of Rousseau, the superman philosophy of Nietzsche, I found in the non-violent resistance philosophy of Gandhi … My study of Gandhi convinced me that true pacifism is not non-resistance to evil, but non-violent resistance to evil. Between the two positions, there is a world of difference.'
Dr Martin Luther King (1999), American civil rights activist.

The relationship between leadership and learning

It is through learning that our leadership can develop and be expressed. It includes understanding ourselves, others and the world we live in. Those who have written about learning conclude that it is about being human. However, let's not get carried away with our arrogance – all life learns to adapt and survive. As humans it is through learning that we can re-create ourselves or become the best we can be.

For Peter Senge at MIT, learning gives us the capacity to create and he wrote in 1990 that learning organisations differ from others in their ability to create their future. So how can learning help you in your quest to be a good leader?

Wherever you work in an organisation leadership includes two things:

knowing what you want to achieve – your goals, and

knowing the reality as it is.

One of the most common faults of those at the top of organisations is their inability to correctly assess the present reality. For some reason they tend to believe things are better than they actually are.

Our mentor for this part of the journey

On this part of our journey our mentor is Gandhi. When he arrived in India after studying law in London and working for a short time in South Africa, he travelled around his home country seeing the reality of life for millions of people. Other Indian activists were based in the cities and lived comfortably and, like the British, decided what was best for people without knowing their reality. This is one of the reasons why Gandhi was such a good leader of transformation – he listened to his people, he felt both their pain and their love. By understanding the reality it is possible to decide on the right actions to take to achieve transformation.

So what are the realities in your organisation? These are the things you must learn before using leadership to act. The only way to do this is to spend time walking around, talking to people and listening. An even better way is through a process called 'dialogue' that goes beyond conversation.

Dialogue

Dialogue explores our values – what is important to us; our emotions – how we feel about things; our thought processes – how we think; and our memory and culture, and in doing so, questions our assumptions and identity. Dialogue provides a way of understanding our reality, what it is to be human and how leadership can be liberated in our organisations.

Through dialogue we can begin to unravel our reality and build a learning community within a group of individuals. It goes beyond regular meetings and becomes a process of learning and transforming our consciousness. Through this process of deep learning we discover our own leadership uniqueness and the reality of our organisation. It is then, and only then, that we can go on to set goals and a wider vision.

Practising Suitcase

Seven steps to encourage simple dialogue to improve meetings:

1. In a group explain how we all bring with us unexpressed differences and perspectives. Encourage the group to recognise this (for example, how Marketing see things, how Finance see things).

2. Encourage the group not to hide these differences but allow them to be explored.

3. Identify shared beliefs, assumptions and intentions.

4. Discourage people from defending their differences and instead focus on patterns of how they feel and see things.

5. Next, establish which of these patterns of assumptions are true and which are false.

6. Conversation will take a different form and learning will be collective.

7. From this new understanding you can begin looking at the problem/issue from a new perspective without people defending their territory.

While activists were talking of the withdrawal of the British from India, Gandhi learned that the people's first concern was food and to stop paying impossible amounts of money to the British landlords. Hunger and staying alive was their reality and this came before 'freedom'. Martin Luther King's reality was the indignity of segregation as much as the right to vote. In both cases the larger vision was achieved, but dealing with the reality of the people was the first step.

Practising Suitcase

Gather information and enter into dialogue to establish the reality for the majority of employees in your organisation. This is much more than sending questionnaires around but can begin with these, followed by group feedback. What is the best way forward to transform the reality? p. 218 →

It is through learning that leadership will be given a chance to succeed. But what does learning really mean and is it just an extension of what we did at school?

Understanding learning

In old Chinese writings two characters represent learning. One means 'to study' and is composed of two symbols. The first means 'to accumulate knowledge' and is above a symbol of a child in a doorway. The second character means 'to practise constantly' and shows a bird developing the ability to leave the nest. This symbol represents flying while the other symbol stands for youth. In this translation learning is perceived as ongoing study and constant practice as a way of self-improvement, as well as knowledge and understanding of the world.

The English word 'learning' originated from the Indo-European noun 'leis' meaning track. Therefore 'to learn' meant 'to walk along a track (to which there is no end) that will take each of us to a different place'. This gives us a visual dimension to learning and makes it a lifelong activity, not something that stops at a certain age.

Understanding learning was the basis of the work of Kurt Lewin and later David Kolb (theorist of experiential learning). The result of their study was a process that involved having an experience, reflecting, forming abstract concepts and generalisations and finally testing the concepts in new situations (Diagram 2). ← p. 14.

In a work situation we are so busy *doing* things that there is no opportunity to reflect and without it, little learning. With little learning, developing leadership is kept to a minimum. It is through learning that we become more self-aware while at the same time more aware of the problems around us affecting the behaviour of our colleagues.

To be an effective leader requires courage to face feelings and assumptions, to re-think and to act. These are often difficult and it is amazing how we find excuses not to do any of this. 'I'm too busy to think,' 'I don't have time for feelings.' Learning includes addressing our feelings and this is explained fully in Part Two (p. 81 ➜). In the meantime, work through this exercise to experience learning as part of being an effective leader.

Practising Suitcase

Think of a situation or project that went really well. Write down what it involved. How did it feel? What did you learn from it? What would you do again? What would you change?

Now think of a situation or project that didn't go as well as expected. Write down what was involved. How did it feel? What assumptions did you make? What did you learn? What would you do again? What would you change?

Learning allows our leadership potential to develop and become all it can be. Living a totally active life sometimes covers up a fear of addressing past experiences, reflecting and learning from them. To become the leader you are capable of being you must learn. This is more than reading or studying. It can be achieved on your own or with others. Finally, you must test the learning – put it into action.

From our reflections we construct future action as part of the learning process. Through reflecting we should gain a new way of understanding an experience and through this we can decide *different* actions and *new* behaviours. This is where performance and leadership is enhanced and improved. You can see that when some-one remarks: 'I've 20 years' experience of this job', it doesn't equate with whether they are effective or not. When we stop learning we stop developing and growing to become the best leader we can be.

One of the best ways to learn leadership is to work through this cycle of experience, reflection, forming concepts and generalisations and testing these with a small group or 'action learning set'. Research has found this a really effective way to develop leader-ship as it is both a learning and a supportive experience. Action learning follows the process with the intention of getting things done. In addition, an individual not only learns from their own reflections but through those of others by working on real prob-lems. Therefore both action and learning are the outcomes. It involves a group of people working together for a concentrated time with a focus on one individual and their learning in dealing with an issue. Therefore it is a supportive experience.

Action learning also holds the underlying belief that whatever the context there is some-thing that can be done and that includes deciding *not* to act. This is important because there is a shift from looking for someone to blame to taking individual responsibility for our own issues/problems. By doing this the individual, with support of the group, can decide what they can do to move forward. This is crucial in leadership because without action nothing changes and one of the key differences between leadership and manage-ment is *transformation through action*. Therefore the relationship between learning and leadership is crucial.

Learning for 21st century leadership

The 21st century should be an opportunity to develop self-learning individuals who are responsible for their own development. This will be difficult when work is still per-ceived as 'doing' while reflecting and learning at work is seen as wasting time. It seems that the founder of scientific management, Frederick Taylor's words: 'You are here to work, not think', are still part of the reality of too many people.

Training, or teaching, is often believed to be synonymous with learning. It is not. Training in organisations is a small part of learning and not particularly effective in developing leadership. The emphasis for training in work organisations is to improve performance, reduce costs, develop a competitive edge, innovate and improve productivity. However, training alone will not accomplish these without ensuring employees have the right tools to do their job and work in a healthy environment (physically and mentally), while also encouraging feedback and learning.

While many organisations undertake training they do not go beyond that to instil learning into the culture. Training departments will have to reinvent themselves as part of a wider transformation of organisations which will come this century. Part of this process will be to question what we mean by learning and its significance in developing leadership throughout organisations. When we realise that leadership is not position, other assumptions will also have to topple and you may have a role to play in this.

Practising being a learning leader for the rest of your life

Practising Suitcase

As we said in the beginning, leadership is a journey – a lifelong learning journey. On it you should discover who you are, the world around you and the people you encounter. However, there is another part to this journey and that is to establish a purpose for your life and leadership. To discover this you have to be open to every opportunity to learn, every challenge that comes your way and see life as giving you the opportunity to experience, reflect, learn and act.

A good way to do this is to keep a 'learning log'. In it record your experiences, how you feel, what you've learned from these and how you will change your behaviour and plan new actions.

However, do not gather learning as a possession but rather see it as a path to your true self. To learn is not to *have* in the form of qualifications or certificates – learning is to *be*.

Like any journey this one begins with the first steps. Buy an exercise book with a cover that reflects something about you – it could be the colour, a pattern or a picture. If you can't find this, take a blank cover and glue a picture from a magazine or a photograph that has some meaning to you onto the cover. Then take five minutes every evening or morning, travelling on the train or having five quiet minutes alone before putting on the TV when you get home. Follow the learning model we have shown you and try to do this every day for three weeks. Then you will have formed a new habit – a learning habit that will help you become the leader you desire to be and are capable of being. Learning should be experienced as personal transformation.

Message 1. **Leadership involves lifelong learning.**

Action   Make learning part of your day;

Suggest learning be part of your team's objectives;

Take time to reflect and record your learning;

Enjoy and have fun while learning.

Message 2. **It is through learning we become more self-aware, more aware of our world and the real problems around us.**

Action   Use your learning log to record how you feel as well as what you do;

Read a quality newspaper;

Talk to people about what concerns them.

Message 3. **'You are here to work, not think' does not apply today.**

Action   Encourage others to think and learn;

Speak up at meetings about what you've learned as well as what you've achieved;

Reward others for doing this and encourage them to discuss what they think.

Message 4. **Learning should be experienced as personal transformation.**

Action Record how learning has changed you in different ways;

Encourage others to use learning to change their behaviours;

Try to make courage and taking personal responsibility part of your personal transformation;

Let others see how you are changing and expressing your leadership.

3

The Shadow Side of Leadership

Chapter guide:

- understanding that each of us has a dark side that we should not ignore;
- knowing the difference between a good and bad leader;
- realising that being a leader doesn't mean being any more lonely than in the rest of our life;
- recognising that what prevents us from being the best is fear;
- knowing how to transform fear;
- understanding the difference between a dictator and leader.

Contents:

Introduction

Within all of us, no matter who we are, there are negative impulses that lead us to actions that seem outside our normal personalities. This shadow is made up of all the unpleasant bits of ourselves that we hide such as jealousy, hate, or aggression. As children we quickly learn what is frowned upon by parents and teachers. We learn guilt and shame and we repress our negative impulses below the surface of consciousness in the hope of approval from others. The shadow side, if denied, limits our leadership potential. How does it do this?

Example 1   The HR department spent a great deal of money to find a good Sales and Marketing Director and felt pleased when Sandra Yeats joined the company. They were impressed with her product knowledge and understanding of the marketplace. However, within a month two of the sales team hand in their notice and now HR are wondering what has happened. They arrange a meeting with the sales team and discover that the new director is very efficient but has a terrible temper that is making the team dread coming into work and in particular attending the weekly sales meeting on a Monday morning when she had twice exploded.

The HR Director decides to speak to Sandra on her own and when he does she admits that she has had problems with her temper in the past but really tries to control it. He asks her how long has she had a problem with her temper and Sandra admits that ever since she was a child she felt she was competing with her brother for her father's attention. At first she hated feeling so jealous so she learned to cover it up by shouting to get the attention she craved. Now shouting has become a way to get attention from other people.

Everything within us that we dislike, hate, deny, resist or disown undermines our feelings of worthiness. By not allowing parts of ourselves to exist we spend energy keeping them hidden. The problem is whatever we refuse to recognise about ourselves has a way of rearing its head and making itself known when we least expect it. For example, you may spend months building trust with colleagues and then you say or do something that destroys that trust in seconds. If we are insecure about who we are and have low self-worth it affects the relationships we have with others.

Leadership has to be the expression of the authentic self and this requires self-awareness and self-knowledge. It means accepting all of who you are. When you know your whole self you no longer need a shell for protection and when you show your whole self you connect with others. In transforming yourself to become a leader you do not become a different person but let the real you be seen instead of an image or persona.

In this chapter we are going to explore the shadow side of leadership and ways of opening it out and using these shadows positively. But we begin with clarifying the difference between a 'good' leader and a 'bad' leader.

The 'good' leader

We are often asked to differentiate between a 'good' and 'bad' leader. There is no easy answer but there are clues that show the difference. The first is that a good leader serves a purpose rather than themselves. Now some may argue that to begin with Hitler was serving a purpose – bringing the nation together and rebuilding its pride, but it was based on the destruction of others. His fear became a nation's fear which was then replaced with control and hate. You could say that fighting a war serves a purpose but also destroys some people. Therefore is any war justified? Does the purpose have to have a moral element? Does serving a purpose make good leadership?

There are those in the public sector and the military who regard themselves as having taken a decision to *serve* because of the type of organisation in which they work. However, this is not necessarily true. Within these places there is as much ego, politics and self-interest as other organisations. The problem arises when those who lack ability and serve themselves are 'rewarded' with advancement because this gives a message to others that the way to get on is to promote yourself, play politics or make sure you are alright and to hell with everyone else.

How do we change this? What is needed are good people with educated consciousness to liberate their leadership potential in all walks of life and organisations. This does not mean creaming off the Oxbridge graduates to take leadership positions. In fact, it is this very action that has caused problems in some public organisations because our formal education system propagates a certain way of learning, of passing exams and problem solving that isn't always effective in other situations. These individuals may have a high IQ but can be severely lacking other skills that are needed for leadership.

What is required are individuals who are constantly learning, who have common sense and practise good leadership. This isn't something that can be measured, put into a competency framework, or judged by educational attainment. Rather it is a state of being that is authentic in its nature and courageous in its actions.

Leadership as 'being'

When we acknowledge leadership as 'being' rather than position then character, integrity, learning, courage, self-awareness, service and responsibility in behaviour and action will be the hallmarks of a leader rather than egos with power and money. We will also realise that what matters is what we do now, today and every day.

We hear you saying: 'This sounds good on paper but how do I do it in everyday work, especially when it is my boss who needs to read this and change?'

Practising Suitcase

OK, let's get real. Do you believe that as an individual you can make a difference at work? Is it our feelings of powerlessness that make us put responsibility elsewhere – with a boss, for example? You are only responsible for yourself and how you behave – not how your boss behaves. But by expressing your authentic leadership you can change your boss because you can change the relationship.

When talking, stand firmly on both feet and your boss will sense your power. Body language gives more away than words. Challenge your boss with examples and show real alternatives with explanations. Talk firmly but without raising your voice. This is especially important for women who can shriek when raising their voice. Instead lower it slightly and you will sound stronger.

Express your power and you will find the relationship will change.

Finding your courage

Go back to what you wrote down about the leader you want to be (← p. 15). What is stopping you? The structure and management systems don't help but another barrier is you – your beliefs and your fears. A 'good' leader acts from the heart, from authenticity, from self-knowledge and becomes what they are capable of being. This requires courage and courage comes from within.

Leadership isn't an easy road and sometimes fear or laziness prevents individuals from expressing their untapped potential. Do you want to become the leader you desire? Why? It's the 'why' that will help you overcome the barriers. One of the barriers we often hear of is being alone as a leader.

Coping with loneliness

While we see leadership as 'position' it does appear to be a very lonely place at the top of a hierarchy. This stops many wanting to take more responsibility and instead they 'play safe' with what they know. Is this perception correct? Is loneliness a state of mind or a position?

There is no doubt that in an organisation that is very hierarchical, where politics among senior managers and directors is rife and where mistakes are not tolerated, a senior role can seem isolated. This is why executive coaching has become so popular. However, much of coaching is like taking medicine for a cold – it helps with the symptoms but the illness has to take its course and medicines do not address the cause, how long it lasts or how it affects each individual differently. A hot toddy can make us feel better – and this is something you can make yourself!

Knowledge Bank

When practising leadership there is something important to remember. There is a myth that the best achievements are down to the individual. When you look closer, whether it's beating a record in sailing, climbing Everest, turning around a failing school or expanding a business, you will see that teamwork and cooperation are big factors in the success.

Leadership does bring its moments of loneliness. One of the best examples is from Sir Ernest Shackleton who said that leadership was a fine thing, but it had its penalties. And the greatest penalty was loneliness. Undoubtedly, there will be moments of difficult decision-making and moments of feeling huge responsibility. But the courage and wisdom to deal with these is within us if we have spent time connecting to inner wisdom and courage.

Trusting self

The key to dealing with loneliness is to trust yourself, know your values and be true to yourself. Yet in public life we see the opposite more often and this results in a cynical society. When we trust ourselves we trust others. Then there is no need for tight controls, the most recent example being the new clocking-in system for BA staff. The ill-feeling it caused was huge and the damage will be long lasting.

When we know our values we appreciate that others have different ones that drive them. For one person it may be freedom to be creative, for another it may be family and security. When we begin to realise the diversity among us we recognise that to treat all employees as wanting the same things is folly.

Finally, if we are true to ourselves, listen to our inner voice and intuition, we will make the best decision for us, at that particular time, knowing what we know. You cannot do more. The worst scenario is when an individual procrastinates and refuses to make a decision. Then they are allowing fear to run their life.

Dealing with your fears

The biggest thing that stops us from being our true, authentic selves and expressing our full leadership potential is fear. Our fear tells us not to take risks. Our fear tells us that we cannot achieve our dreams. Our fear can keep us in relationships that are unhealthy. Our fear keeps our lives limited. Through fear we create situations in our lives that act to prove to ourselves that this self-imposed limitation is appropriate.

Reflective Suitcase

There are two ways we look at the world:

as a scary place where we have to play safe and build a reservoir of savings, do our job and no more, ask for nothing but focus on ensuring the family is the focus of everything and the rest of the world will take care of itself, change isn't something we relish as much as the desire for security; or

as a place of adventure, excitement, continual learning and challenges that will stretch us, where children are given the skills to be independent and encouraged to explore and try new things, perhaps we are self-employed and find it hard to separate work from who we are, the world is connected to us and so we should share our knowledge and skills to contribute in some way.

Which way do you see the world?

Most of us will come somewhere between these two examples but we will tend toward one more than the other. How we perceive the world will depend on whether we live from fear or love. When we live from fear it limits our leadership potential. Fears can range from fear of looking a fool to fear of failure or even success.

Everyone has experienced fear at some point in their life but there is a difference between someone confronting their fear and dealing with it and someone who avoids issues or things and allows fear to dictate their life. Once we embrace our fear we can choose not to be afraid anymore.

When we begin to confront the shadow causing fear we can discover that some of the things we have learned to suppress it can actually be useful if channelled properly. For example, the positive side of anger is energy and energy can be used for doing something constructive about the situation that made us angry. Think back to Sandra the Sales Director who had a problem with anger. She was also successful in that she had energy to achieve. What she needed to do was confront her need for attention and realise that she could give this to herself. Sandra could spend an hour a day doing yoga, having a relaxing bath by candlelight, or writing down what she had done that day and reflecting on her achievements.

Confronting the shadows that result in fear

Listed below are things to do to learn what your shadows are and to confront them so you can express your leadership fully. Work through the questions with a notebook and take time to get a positive effect. Do not be afraid of your feelings but acknowledge them.

What resentments, old wounds or regrets do you carry with you?

Who in your life have you been unwilling to forgive?

What do you need to do to forgive yourself and others?

Make a list of people you need to forgive and write a short letter to them.

Write a forgiveness letter to yourself.

Who are the three people you admire the most from the past or present?

What are the three qualities you admire in each of them?

How can these qualities help you?

Now let go and decide to live through the person you really are and not to allow any more fear stopping you being the leader you are meant to be.

Fear at an organisational level

At an organisational level fear hinders energy, creativity, initiative, trust and leadership throughout. In managers it can show itself as aggressiveness and even bullying. Over time, fear can even create what we wanted to avoid. Avoidance tactics are sometimes learnt as children and by the time we are adult we are not conscious of them. For others, we join an organisation looking forward to having a career and quickly learn that to 'survive' the culture it is best to keep your head down and that new ideas are not welcome.

Facing fear

Would fear prevent you from racing to a frightened child being threatened by a dog? Would fear stop you facing a burglar who was threatening your partner or child?

Example   Alex had spent years sailing and was an experienced skipper. Her biggest challenge came when she was accepted as skipper on a boat in the BT Global Challenge Yacht Race. She was the last to get sponsorship but set off with her team against the elements. Alex finished first in the first part of the race and celebrated the success in Auckland, New Zealand.

Starting the next heat they could see a boat ahead that they were set to collide with. It was her responsibility to give way so she guided the boat to avoid the other. For the first time in her life she made a wrong calculation and hit the other yacht, damaging both in the process. Both had to return to Auckland to spend weeks being repaired. Alex was devastated but grateful no-one was hurt.

Alex decided that she should resign and against the advice of others did so. She sat on a beach trying to come to terms with what had happened. Emotionally she beat herself up until she realised she could either carry on doing so or get on with life. She decided on the latter and still works with the race team helping others succeed. Her fear was seeing others in the sailing world after such a mistake in front of the world's media but she has faced that fear and learned so much.

Overcoming these obstacles gives us the greatest learning opportunities. It was George Bernard Shaw who said that we can blame circumstances but ultimately it is how we deal with them that makes us who we are. It is through learning from life that our leadership develops and we must never lose sight of what is important to us and makes us passionate.

Practising Suitcase

 What was the worst thing you had to face at work? How did you deal with it? What did you learn?

Reflective Suitcase

If we care about something we find it easier to find courage and overcome fear. When we care enough about our future, the planet, other people or animals – something that truly matters to us – we overcome our fears. That is why someone who values themselves will not tolerate being treated badly by a boss, partner, colleague or organisation. But when we live from fear and do not value ourselves we do nothing or ascribe blame or make excuses. *We are not victims but co-creators of the world as it is.*

Leader or dictator?

When we ask people whether they are a leader the majority will say 'no'. They will explain this by saying that being a leader means being in charge and telling people what to do and this is either a negative view of themselves or too much responsibility and hard work.

There are those few individuals, however, who relish being in charge and controlling the lives of millions. Are they leaders or dictators? The difference between them is that a dictator acts solely to serve themselves and has to use force to keep their power rather than legitimate authority. In addition, a dictator has to use more and more power and fear to keep control and in doing so becomes more likely eventually to be overthrown, replaced or killed. We are now facing the darkest side of leadership and we should not forget this or ignore it.

We also see this pattern in workplace organisations. All three of us have at some time worked for a 'bully', but remember bullies are usually the biggest cowards so don't be afraid to stand up to them – even if that bully is your boss. Bullying, like sexual harassment, is about power and using power *over* another. It is up to us as to whether we allow it.

Power can have a negative effect on some individuals and we can sometimes see this when some people put a uniform on. The uniform gives them power and while many will treat power with respect, others will abuse it. In other circumstances a manager's fear of being exposed as not as good as they try to pretend they are can lead to aggressive or bullying behaviour. People use power when they are fearful themselves.

Dealing with a bully

Remember your body language –

- stand evenly on two feet;
- keep your hands to your sides;
- look them straight in the eye;
- speak calmly but firmly;
- use your own power to deflect theirs.

Knowledge Bank

 Remember that each one of us has some element of a 'shadow side' that is judgemental, frightened, resentful, guilty, blaming, cynical, arrogant, jealous, controlling, perfectionist or greedy. We see these shadows when we react to something and are driven by fear. It can result in plotting or scheming. In organisations it is seen in different ways, ranging from lack of trust to plotting for a course of action to fail because it wasn't that person's idea. Be aware of this.

A dictator will regard people as being of little value and there to be herded, controlled, lied to and manipulated. A leader should regard people as basically good, creative, trustworthy and wanting to do work of which they are proud.

Recent studies have found that the high-profile, charismatic leader gets attention but in fact the quiet, humble leader actually achieves more. In the US much focus has been on individuals such as Jack Welch, past chief executive of General Electric, when in fact lesser known chief executives and managers are better examples of leadership. In many large corporate organisations you can succeed if your 'face fits' or your behaviour reflects the culture. In other words, you conform to what is considered 'successful'. This maintains a culture and status quo, but do these organisations have a long-term sustainable future?

When exploring the spectrum from leader to dictator it is not only businesses that suffer from dilemmas. Ambitious civil servants and executives in the public sector are known to have problems with the right balance. However, the biggest concern is when we look at politics. Here, leaders choose themselves and put themselves forward for election. They then campaign hard against others who also seek office. The danger is that our present democracy contains 'self seekers' who have a strong need for power. Once elected part of their job is to keep power, no matter what the cost.

True leadership is about developing others to express leadership so that they bring about the transformations necessary to improve the lives of many. Does politics enable the voters to express leadership? Do the people who have more positional power in your organisation enable the rest to express leadership? Do you find opportunities to develop leadership in others?

Message 1. **We all have shadows to face and they shouldn't be ignored because left unchecked they can limit our leadership potential.**

Action   Identify and accept your shadow side as part of you;

Use your shadow side in a positive way.

Message 2. **A good leader serves a purpose, not themselves.**

Action   Identify the purpose of your work;

Establish what you bring to your work;

Explore how you can make your work more meaningful.

Message 3. **The key to dealing with loneliness is to trust yourself, know your values and be true to yourself.**

Action Learn to trust your abilities and value them;

Identify the most important things in your life;

Be yourself, not what others expect or demand.

4

Leadership, Not Management

Chapter guide:

- understanding the difference between leadership and management;
- recognising when leadership matters;
- being able to experience what leadership looks and feels like when you are doing it.

Contents:

Introduction

During the last few years there has been much debate on the difference between management and leadership. Many confuse the two, offering programmes called 'Strategic Leadership' that turn out to be 'Management' in their content, or bolt leadership onto management as an extra. Yet studies by some academics have differentiated the two quite clearly. Warren Bennis thinks of the differences as being between 'those who master the context and those who surrender to it' (1989). From the debate a list has emerged to help differentiate the two:

- the manager maintains; the leader develops;

- the manager focuses on systems and structure; the leader focuses on people;

- the manager administers; the leader innovates;

- the manager accepts the status quo; the leader challenges it;

- the manager relies on control; the leader inspires trust;

- the manager imitates; the leader originates;

- the manager has a short-range view; the leader has a long-range perspective;

- the manager is the good soldier and complies; the leader is their own person and uses their values to guide them;

- the manager asks how and when; the leader asks what and why.

How would this be realised in your department? If people were underperforming, had no spark and a general view that their work was just a job, how would a manager respond? How would a leader respond? A manager is likely to tighten control by setting targets and implementing performance management systems. A leader would get everyone together and listen to how the employees feel about their work and what would enable them to get fired up and give more meaning to it. The leader would then work with the group to realise their requests as far as possible.

This is a broad picture of the difference between managers and leaders but the most comprehensive research was undertaken by Abraham Zaleznik at Harvard University:

Knowledge Bank

Managers view themselves as conservators and regulators of an existing order that they personally identify with and from which they gain rewards. They worry more about people's roles than the people themselves. They enhance their self-worth by perpetuating existing processes and orders. To maintain controlled, rational structures, managers generate red tape and display little warmth. Managers do not ask for the hearts and minds of people only their performance and targets. Problems are looked at one at a time using calculation and compliance and a great deal of politics. The managerial mind is programmatic and greatly resistant to change. It has the ability to turn a blind eye to errors of omission that result in the slow death of an organisation or further and further cost cutting.

Leaders adopt a personal and active attitude towards goals and attempt to adopt fresh approaches to problems. They worry about ideas and how they will affect people while relating to people in intuitive and empathetic ways. They actively seek change as they wish to profoundly alter human, economic and political relationships. Leaders do not depend on work titles or roles for their sense of identity and even promote organisational structures that may appear turbulent and even disorganised but often produce results beyond those expected. Leaders are not bound by a process but challenge it to produce creative actions.

This chapter will focus on these differences and how you can recognise them in yourself or others.

Example   A company in the aerospace industry identifies nine individuals who have potential for promotion to director level. They pay a consultant to run a six month leadership programme for them to develop their capabilities. It is agreed that at the end of that time the nine will decide on a project to carry out in the company that will add value and enable them to practise their leadership potential. Keen to use their leadership to bring about improvement, they put forward the outline of a project that is dismissed by the managing director, who offers an alternative. The alternative is not what they want to do but they begin. After a few days they are told to forget the project as they don't have time to do it and to get back to their work as before.

What has happened here? Would the nine be allowed to express their leadership? What would you have done if you had been one of them? Is this management or leadership? Was the managing director showing leadership or management?

Are managers the product of organisations or types of people?

The answer is both: hierarchical organisations require more and more managers to maintain them, while at the same time many of our schools, colleges, universities and workplaces encourage a myth about control through the way we are educated and work.

Management is a way of bringing order and control to hierarchical organisations, however, the reality is another paradox. Management is simultaneously in control and not in control. What preoccupies most managers is the need to adapt to situations of uncertainty. Yet within management thinking, to be out of control or to lose control is to be perceived as incompetent, resulting in managers either trying to assert greater control or trying harder to appear in control. To deal with this paradox many in management avoid change and tend to maintain the status quo as this avoids risk.

Leadership is about human endeavour to challenge and bring about transformation. However, many of those who have leadership positions based on power often talk about leadership but in fact want management. In other words, they may talk about transformation but actually want to maintain control.

Practising Suitcase

Ask the managers and directors in your organisation to identify their greatest personal fear.

For the last 60 years there has been much emphasis on management and developing managers, with business schools offering MBAs. Research has shown a gap between MBA students' skills and those required for organisations today. The schools themselves reinforce management control and the status quo in how they are run or through the programmes they offer. Moreover, there is confusion between 'leadership' and 'management', with the terms used interchangeably. This makes it really difficult for individuals to express leadership rather than management. Why is this such an issue?

As a concept, leadership has been studied and written about for thousands of years, mainly as an example of how to behave and how to accomplish change. On the other hand, management has grown with the industrial and technological revolutions to deal with order and control at work, and political administration. Time for some more knowledge currency.

Knowledge Bank

In the 20th century we created thousands of large, hierarchical organisations across the world that required more and more managers to run them. Frederick Taylor, one of the first champions of management, created the subject as an efficient way to turn the human body into a mechanism – it was all about control. Even as a child, Taylor forced his friends to use strict rules in their games and couldn't understand why many didn't want to play with him. He believed that people and the workplace should be treated as machines.

Today there still is a belief that, if reengineered, organisations will run like a machine and in doing so will improve productivity and profit. In practice this has not been the case, and low productivity is still an issue in the UK. With control comes passivity and compliance but, most of all, lack of trust, innovation, initiative and creativity that over time develops a culture of risk aversion and blame. Many have tried to change this and a few have succeeded to some extent. How many times have you been sold poor services or products? Why are so many workplaces inefficient for customers and stressful for employees? There are two reasons: the first is that there is evidence that managers tend to prefer to be in control than to be effective; and the second is that they identify culture as their biggest challenge but perceive it as a separate thing from the people whose behaviour it describes. This is not a criticism but an observation and leadership involves making sense of what we see and experience without becoming defensive. This need for control extends to most professions, including human resources.

The general view is that reflected by Californian writer Alan Briskin, who wrote on modern management: ' … what began as a method of control for managers to motivate and channel their workers' productivity became instead a failed psychological contract.' He continues: 'Human relations was perched on a contradiction: advocating for personal development and democratic principles on the one hand, and on the other serving in a subordinate role to the increasingly bureaucratic and mechanized workplace' (1998). In other words, human resources is limited by its management approach and environment. Information technology has the same problem in that its applications are limited to its management thinking as well as environment.

Therefore, if management is about control and maintaining the status quo, then leadership is about liberating your own and others' potential to achieve extraordinary things and new possibilities. Does this difference matter? Work through the questions below:

Reflective Suitcase

 How many changes have you seen in organisations during the last 5–10 years?

What was the outcome?

How many were effective?

How many are still in place today?

What impact did this have on everyone?

Suppose individuals, regardless of their role, could express their leadership towards achieving positive change that resulted in more than bottom line results – would things begin to be different?

Example   A high-tech company was set up in the south of England by two individuals driven by clear values such as openness and equality. They recruited people as more and more work came to them. The company grew to over 200 people but maintained its democratic ethos. Individuals from large corporate companies such as IBM and Compaq were working alongside this small business and witnessed a totally different way of working. They saw people coming in very early in the morning, people being treated with respect regardless of their role, the directors making tea or coffee for others when it was their turn.

The most significant difference the corporate employees noticed was that people were allowed to make decisions and get on with their work, asking for help or support when needing it but not controlled by managers as they were. The small business became very successful and all employees were also involved in community projects and raising funds for charities. Every employee felt they could and did express leadership, including the young school leaver on her first job.

The directors decided it was time to take on a 'professional managing director' to grow the business further and allowed him to make changes while they remained on the board. One of the first things he did was put in a management structure creating a hierarchy. He sold equity in the business to a venture capitalist who insisted on high returns that were even greater than the soaring success they already had achieved. Targets were introduced.

The company missed the targets by a small gap but enough for the VC to demand redundancies for the first time since the company formed, even though the profits were huge. The impact was detrimental and people felt they had lost something greater than people – they had lost their energy and drive because of the way the business had developed. The founders sold the business and many employees left.

It is a myth that increase in size requires the latter measures. What was implemented was a remnant of the industrial world still operating in the UK and US (where it was most successful). That world wasn't just about machinery and large-scale production, it was a way of seeing, thinking and believing that has to be transformed in the next few years if people's health and quality of life is to improve on a global scale. We are now adapting this industrial approach to other sectors of society. Very soon there will be a backlash as people realise that leadership cannot be stifled or controlled with a management approach of measurement and control.

Does it matter?

Does it matter if we have management rather than leadership in organisations today? It matters greatly, for when the focus began on management nearly 60 years ago we were recovering from a devastating world war and the emphasis was on rebuilding. In the UK this included a health service, education for all and work for those who could offer a trade or skill. Management is excellent in a fairly stable world and market environment. But the world has changed dramatically. Today most of those skills and trades have disappeared and been replaced with technology. We face a crisis point in healthcare and prisons, while schools and the police struggle to match our expectations. In 10 years we have seen the internet revolution, mass media communications and global business change how we connect with the rest of the world.

To cope with this 'new' world the emphasis should not be on building but on transforming and ensuring that all benefit from change, not only the well off. What is required now is leadership. We need to challenge, ask big questions and change our thinking and understanding of the world – we need to take huge leaps into the unknown, to a new place. We need leadership from the many, not the few.

Where leadership is required

Reflective Suitcase

You are now taking a two hour journey in a car. You can be the driver or passenger. The radio is on and for an hour you listen to the news. You hear stories of people dying in Ethiopia because of hunger and drought, children becoming orphans in Rwanda and Liberia because of war, women in Africa dying of Aids after being raped, children losing legs after stepping on land mines, elderly people in the UK afraid to go out of their homes because of fear of being mugged, almost half of American youngsters leaving school with no qualifications and feeling they have no future, the company you used to work for squandering the pensions of the employees, hospitals in the UK sending patients to France to get treatment because they are unable to cope, and the local school having been closed because of arsonists setting it on fire.

At the end of the hour, how do you feel?

What do you do at the end of the broadcast? Do you turn over to listen to music or sit and reflect on what you've heard? Do you feel angry? Powerless? Sad? Do you do something – write an article, join a volunteer group? It is *action* that separates those who feel powerless and those who may feel powerless but still try to do something. It is action that enables leadership to be shared and seen. Some individuals feel scared or powerless but still take action. Why do they? Are they different from the rest of us? The difference is that they recognise that we all have responsibility for the world we create and live in and want to challenge others to do the same.

Leadership that is purposeful is infectious.

Leadership is required everywhere.

The transition from manager to leader

How do you begin to express your leadership?

The first step is to believe that you have leadership potential. The key word here is 'believe'. Your beliefs give you permission to do things but they also limit what you believe you can do. What are your beliefs about the universe and religion? What are your beliefs about work and your contribution? What are your beliefs about family and love? What are your beliefs about yourself?

The second step is to try to establish what that potential is. This can be done through 360 degree feedback (that is, from all around and all levels) for example, but to do this you need to add something important. At the beginning of the *Manual* you were asked to answer the question: What sort of leader do you want to be? (← p. 15) What did you answer? Now look at what you have written. That is coming from your heart – the leader you aspire to be. You need to know what result you want and this is it.

This is your benchmark: feedback is a way of knowing where you are in relation to it. However, many training organisations use someone else's benchmark and tell you that you need to develop your potential as a figurehead or as a negotiator, for example. These are someone else's version of leadership, not your own, and being a figurehead isn't part of who you are as a leader. In fact, 'figurehead' is one of the management roles identified by Henry Mintzberg that is now part of classic *management* theory. As soon as someone tries to mould you into something you are not they are trying to control you and this comes from the management paradigm. It begs the question – what do these people really know about leadership?

Reflective Suitcase

Reflect on these words and consider their relevance to you.

'"Know thyself" means separating who you are and who you want to be from what the world thinks you are and wants you to be.' (*On Becoming a Leader*, Bennis, 1989)

As a manager you are asked to set objectives and goals. You are challenged to make them 'smart' objectives – specific, measurable and so on. In doing this you are thrown into tasks – doing. Compare this to the above answer, the leader you want to be. This is more about who you are – your being. Instead of a rigid 12 month plan, leadership entails constant learning and shifting as you grow into you as a leader. The most you can plan for is the next 6 months.

The third step is to ask, Who are you now? Many who have studied leadership write about the importance of self-awareness. One of the most poignant comments follows.

Knowledge Bank

'… Like the physician, it is important for the leader to follow the maxim "know thyself" so that he can control some of the pernicious effects he may create unwittingly. Unless the leader understands his actions … [h]e may be the carrier rather than the solver of problems.' (Warren Bennis and Philip Slater, 1999)

This is why 360 degree feedback is good if it's honest and given with good intent.

The fourth step is to identify your authentic self, meaning that not only are you self-aware but that you express your genuine self to the world, which requires self-acceptance. This in turn requires confidence and courage.

Around the age of five we develop the ability to empathise. We also realise that different people have expectations of us. We begin to project a 'persona', an image we believe is acceptable. An image that will get us praise or recognition. Over time, this persona becomes 'us' and we lose touch with our unique being; instead we use energy to maintain our persona. Confidence and courage is required to be authentic because we do not seek praise or recognition.

The fifth step is to do with our uniqueness. Each one of us is different and the only person who can express leadership exactly like Churchill or King was Churchill and King. We can learn from them but we can never be them. Instead, focus on you. What is unique about you? What drives you? What do you care about? Role models can help you identify parts of yourself but it is *your* leadership you will express in the world.

This takes you to *the final step*. Decide how you want to use your leadership potential not only at work but in every aspect of your life. What would you like to achieve with the work you do? Are you achieving this at present? Will you ever achieve it in your present work? Where else can you express leadership?

A big issue is that so many do not know how to use their leadership potential. People end up 'doing a job' but never become the leader they are capable of being. To live an honest life requires us first to be honest with ourselves. Are we doing what we should be doing with our lives?

Now you can see how difficult this journey is and how it begins with ourselves. The transition from manager to leader is about more than changing a title. It is about changing our thinking, understanding ourselves and others, and changing what we do and how we do it. Transformation begins with *you*.

When leadership matters most

Knowing when you need to express your leadership is important. The key point is to know whether transformation is required. This can range from changing how your team works to totally rethinking a business strategy on a global scale or challenging an unfair policy.

The first thing to understand is that there is a huge difference between change and transformation. If you take a glass of water and freeze it you will see it change to ice. Yet put back in its original environment and it reverts to water. How many training courses have you seen follow that process? How many change initiatives have been like this?

Now take a file of papers and set them alight. They will burn to ashes and can never again be paper. This is transformation – when change creates a permanent, irreversible difference.

We have all seen American films of wagon trains crossing the new world to make new settlements. Often people didn't know what to expect when they arrived, only that the journey was risky and that life would never be the same again. For all those making the journey it required courage, honesty, authenticity, integrity, being open with people, listening to concerns and fears, and instilling trust and inspiration for the future. It required some to know where they were heading and for others to trust them to achieve the task. It required leadership not just from one person but rather from many.

Leadership matters most when transformation is required.

How leadership looks and feels

How do you know when you are expressing leadership? Is it because you have a clear goal? It is actually more than that. The goal becomes a strong desire, not to prove something or gain recognition, but because inside you the goal is important and has purpose. You know what the goal looks like so you'll recognise it when you reach it. You feel responsible for your own behaviour and actions and encourage others to feel responsible too. You will be excited but keep your feet on the ground and deal with realities and difficulties. You will discover your courage as you do this and put actions into place.

You will become more and more aware of who you are and your capabilities. You will connect with others when they see your true self and feel connected too. You will be honest and face your fears knowing that, although risky, you will succeed in the end.

Finally, you will ensure that ego doesn't emerge and fool yourself into thinking you are great. You will acknowledge that you are a unique human being who has learned so much but still has much more to learn. You will be challenged but also satisfied. Is this how you feel at work? Is this how your colleagues feel?

Ten steps that will transform you from manager to leader:

1. Listen to people more and empathise.

2. Don't get hung up on process and control.

3. Be clear about your purpose rather than just focusing on goals.

4. Generate value in your work rather than just achieving targets.

5. Don't fear risk but embrace it.

6. Take fresh approaches to long-standing problems (which will result in new options).

7. Challenge work rather than accept mundane and safe practice.

8. Develop emotional attachments to people rather than detached ones.

9. Enhance and trust your intuition.

10. Find a mentor, role model or great teacher who can help you develop your leadership.

Message 1. **Develop a better understanding of the differences between leadership and management.**

Action   The 10 steps above;

Feel the difference when you change from one to the other;

Encourage others to take the 10 steps above.

Message 2. **Leadership matters most when transformation is needed.**

Action   Identify where transformation is required where you work;

Take action.

Message 3. **Leadership that is purposeful is infectious.**

Action   Find out what colleagues regard as their purpose;

Work together to achieve these and support each other.

5

Expressing Leadership

Chapter guide:

- how to begin using your unique leadership;
- how to 'walk the talk';
- dealing with the behaviours that get in the way of your leadership.

Contents:

Introduction

The expression of leadership takes many forms and in this chapter we are going to take the first step from learning to expressing leadership. We do ourselves a great injustice by believing that leadership is something expressed by a few who hold certain positions. A wonderful example of this is the suffragettes in the last century. There were women such as Emily and Sylvia Pankhurst who gave women a vision or goal – votes for women – however it was the thousands of women throughout the UK who courageously expressed their own personal leadership. They carried out their protest knowing that the outcome would be prison where they would refuse food and have to be held down and force fed. The purpose was to transform their lives, to be heard and to use voting as a way of improving the lives of many. An article in the *Newcastle Daily Chronicle* on 11th October 1909 described their endeavour: 'I have seen brave things done by men on the battlefield, among comrades, hot-blooded, flushed and excited. This was the rarer courage which does its deeds coldly and alone. What they were facing was the certainty of starvation, which may be followed by the torture of forcible feeding – a steel instrument between their teeth, the insertion of a gag, and outrage of the stomach-pump.'

It took courage for Sherron Watkins to challenge her boss Kenneth Lay at Enron in 2001 with the fact that the company was about to 'implode in a wave of accounting scandals'. Lay ignored her, believing she was unimportant. Today Watkins is setting up a not-for-profit organisation to advise on corporate governance which, she says, is more about the relationship between the board and management than a written document or set of procedures. Through her memos trying to persuade Lay to act, Watkins was expressing her leadership which today is enabling her to fulfil a unique purpose.

Expressing leadership at difficult times takes courage and commitment to do what you believe to be right. In the public sector and in the military we often hear of the incompetent being promoted, therefore we wanted to include a positive example of expressing leadership in this environment. One of the past team leaders of the RAF Red Arrows was concerned one year at the progression of a new pilot. He discussed it with others to gauge their feelings and decided that for the first time he would have to drop a pilot because he believed the lack of flying skills in this situation could endanger the team. However he wanted to ensure that this decision would not damage the pilot's career, as formation flying was very different to normal fighting combat flying. The team leader saw his superior officers and made his request. He could see they were wavering and so added that if the young man was not replaced he would resign as team leader. The senior offices realised that this was a serious decision and agreed to his request. It was the only time this team leader put his job on the line but it showed his commitment to the whole team. Today he is still considered one of the best team leaders in the history of the famous Red Arrows.

Expressing leadership

Leadership courage is being expressed in many parts of the world. An example is Aung San Suu Kyi, who is still struggling for freedom and democracy in Burma. She was two years old when her father, a national Burmese hero, was assassinated. After her education she spent 20 years raising a family in England, returning to Burma to look after her dying mother. While there a revolt occurred, challenging the political repression and economic decline. Aung San Suu Kyi founded a democratic party that won electoral victory in 1990 but in 1989 she had been put under house arrest (by the military junta) from where she is still fighting for democracy. In 1991 she was awarded the Nobel Peace Prize. The journalist Fergal Keene has spent time getting to know her and wrote: 'Chief among the attributes which make her a remarkable leader in our times is a deep humanity, a gift for understanding and embracing the pain of others as if it were her own' (1997). Empathy is an important part of leadership and we will explore this in depth in Part Two (p. 131 ➜).

What about you in your day-to-day work? Do you challenge unfair decisions? Do you support colleagues? Are you willing to make unpopular decisions? How do you express your unique leadership potential at work?

Which of these are you at work?

> Energetic.
>
> Positive.
>
> Working to clear goals.

Always learning more.

Quick at making decisions.

Pragmatic.

Analytical.

Quiet.

Speak out at meetings if I disagree.

Support others.

Funny.

Creative.

Frustrated.

Risk taker.

Good listener.

Add value to the organisation.

Motivate self and others.

Humble.

Committed.

Clever.

Courageous.

Disciplined.

Which of these are you outside work?

Do the two differ?

Which is your true self?

Are both part of who you are?

If so, why do you only express part of you at work?

What part of yourself do you leave outside the workplace?

Sometimes the culture of an organisation influences how you behave.

Do you believe you have to be 'tough', loud or outsmart colleagues to be regarded as credible?

Do you like who you are at work?

Is this who you are or who you think you should be?

When you act from the heart you are sincere, inspirational and connect with others. So why is it so difficult?

Reflective Suitcase

 Draw a picture of your organisation? Is it broken up into parts or departments? This is something modern humans do – break things into parts to understand them. Now think of yourself. Do you see a working person, a home person, a sports or DIY person? Do you see yourself as a manager, a parent, a friend, a sibling? Again we break things up. This is not because it's what humans do – it's what modern humans do. In addition, the more parts we have in our lives the more stressful it feels.

Think of yourself as one whole person with the same values guiding you to be your true self regardless of what you are doing. This makes it easier to express your leadership.

How unique are you?

Every person is unique. What makes up that uniqueness? How are you different from your colleagues? Do you value this difference?

Psychologist James Hillman believes that it is our character and purpose that come into life when we are born. We believe that *each character and purpose is unique*. Being a leader involves knowing these two elements of yourself intimately and accepting them.

How do you get to know yourself? Some may begin by asking you to do a personal swot analysis on yourself. We will begin another way that is actually easier and is more to the point. Think of your family, your parents and siblings. In what ways are you like your mother? In what ways are you like your father? Write these down.

Do you have any brothers or sisters? How are you like them? Do you have aunts, uncles, grandparents, cousins, nieces or nephews? Are there things about you that you can see in them? Add these to your list.

Now, how are you different from all those above? What is it in your character that is different? What do you like to do that is different? Write these down and you will begin to identify your uniqueness. Take your time, for you may be discovering new things about yourself that you were not aware of before. You are special because everyone is, and it is 'specialness' that will differentiate your leadership from others.

Knowledge Bank

Most of us live our lives battling between our two selves: the one we were born to be, often called our true self, higher consciousness or whole self; and the self we have learned to be, called the ego or personality. The ego is a mask we wear to cover up the fact that we have lost connection with our true self. In organisations, ego is even extended to things such as a larger desk, a special parking slot or a very large office.

Psychoanalyst Carl Jung called the ego the 'persona', which comes from the Latin word for 'theatre mask'. Finding your unique self to express your leadership means removing this mask.

Be authentic

You will realise by now that much of leadership is self-awareness. Without authenticity others will not connect with you and you will eventually find yourself alone and your leadership potential redundant. Some rely on methods such as office politics to achieve success. Is this the sort of person you want to be?

Try completing the sentences below to find your authentic self. The best way to do this is to respond quickly. You may be surprised how your inner consciousness answers.

1. The five adjectives that best describe me are …
2. When I was growing up I dreamt I would be an adult who …
3. I feel at my best when …
4. I feel at my worst when …
5. The five greatest people I admire are …
6. My four great strengths are …
7. My four great weaknesses are …
8. I feel good when I think of …
9. I feel bad when I think of …
10. I perform my best in situations when …
11. I hold myself back when …
12. Most people think I am …
13. When I die I would like to be remembered for …
14. The most exciting thing I would like to do is …

Listen to what your true self is saying and learn from it. You are learning how to express your leadership.

> 'The perfect form lies concealed in the block of stone; all that is needed is to chip away until it is revealed.'
>
> *(Michelangelo)*

'Walk the talk'

A common criticism of individuals is that they don't 'walk the talk'. In other words, they say one thing and do another. So *how do you* walk the talk?

One of the best examples of this is Gandhi. On returning to India he listened to well-educated Indians plan and talk of getting rid of the British because they abused power and privileges, but not only did these Indians do the same, they offered no vision of what would replace British rule. Gandhi, on the other hand, listened, observed, and established what the people needed. He accomplished his goals by also living like the people.

In an organisational context walking the talk means that individuals should not hide in large offices, shut away with their secretaries and only meeting with their peers except when they are informing employees of what they plan to do. It means spending time each week walking around or joining people for lunch and listening to what they say needs to happen for the organisation to be successful.

Gandhi said that we must become the change we seek in the world. It's not enough to say that everyone is now going to do things differently, leadership is about living by example.

Walking the talk also includes understanding what people do at work and taking an interest. Ask questions such as: 'How do you see that fitting in with achieving objectives?' and 'What else do you think the strategy should focus on?' In this way you are showing a depth of understanding of what they do rather than just walking around and paying lip service.

In addition, many people should be involved in developing strategies rather than those who happen to hold a certain job title. The latter assumes that only those few know what the strategy should be and very often it is people at the sharper end who actually have a better grasp of this. There is nothing worse than dumping a strategy on people and then leaving for another promotion or role. Or creating a situation in work where people say: ' Hey, it's January, it must time for a new strategy.'

Words must be reinforced by example.

Be open

Expressing your leadership requires you to be open – sometimes a challenge in organisations – however there are huge benefits to be gained. The first is that when you are open people connect with you. They instinctively know they can trust you and will therefore follow. This involves disclosing things about yourself. This does not involve personal details but rather your hopes, your vision, your family, your interests. It's about opening your heart and being honest about how you feel and what you hope to achieve. This is difficult for some people and British culture does not always lend itself to this kind of behaviour. To be open is to be vulnerable, but it enables others to see our human side and that leads to trust. Being open is also infectious – others will feel safe to start being open and a team spirit is more likely to develop.

All employees should have access to the company's accounts and performance figures. Everyone is entitled to see what they contribute towards. Likewise, most people's work should be open, with opportunities to swap roles and learn what others do, and appreciate what happens elsewhere in the organisation. Often a fresh pair of eyes can resolve pesky problems. Being open at work is about much more than pouring your problems out – it is about consistently learning through new ideas and perspectives.

Earn the right to lead

Everyone has leadership potential and some will use that potential better than others. As we saw when looking at good and bad leadership, it all depends on an individual's guiding values, their perception of the world and what is in their heart.

Compare two people. The first individual has wealth and status as their important goals. They believe the world to be an unfriendly place and a battleground between the weak and strong. To be strong requires wealth and power as they do not want to be perceived as weak. This view has created a selfish character who treats everything and everyone (including those who love them) as a means to getting what they want. What sort of leadership would this person express? How long will they have credibility without seeing more people as 'the enemy' and therefore having to 'deal' with them. How long before they find themselves isolated with no-one *to* lead?

The second individual is very different. Driving this person is a desire to make a difference in some small, modest way. Freedom is important to them, not only to express their creative ideas but in respect for the freedom of others, too. For them the world is full of opportunity, wonder and interesting people. This person is strong and confident but speaks with a soft voice. They believe in being open and honest while listening and learning is second nature. They have a vision of how they can achieve something and a set of principles representing their values. Realising that changing things is difficult they build a strong internal side that keeps them determined and motivated because they know that they will one day succeed. What sort of leadership will they express? Do they deserve to lead? Will people want to work with them to develop a vision and use it to help them achieve their purpose?

Leadership requires courage but it also needs a positive motive. When an individual's heart is good their leadership will have beneficial outcomes and people will feel they earned the right to lead. Taking this notion even further is the work of Robert Greenleaf, who believed that a true leader is a servant first. Greenleaf developed his theory of servant leadership while an executive at AT & T. He subsequently lectured at MIT and Harvard. He believed that serving others enables an individual to then aspire to choose and develop their leadership. Greenleaf was inspired by the story of Leo, a character in Hermann Hesse's *Journey to the East*. The story tells of a group of men on a journey; Leo acts as their servant, seeing to their needs and doing their chores while sustaining them with his positive spirit and song. Then Leo disappears and the group falls apart, unable to complete their journey. For Greenleaf leadership was missing once Leo left because the rest of the group had not learned to serve each other first.

Servant leadership emphasises service to others at work where sharing of power in decision making and promoting a sense of community is a priority. This requires knowing and feeling comfortable with yourself. Learning is fundamental to this concept and that is why we began this *Manual* by explaining how learning and leadership walk hand in hand.

Knowledge Bank

Following in the footsteps of Greenleaf is Larry Spears who, as Executive Director of the Greenleaf Center for Servant Leadership, has identified 10 characteristics of the servant-leader. These are: listening, empathy, healing, awareness, persuasion, conceptualisation, foresight, stewardship, commitment to the growth of people and building community.

We will include some of these characteristics in the next section when we explore leadership capabilities. For now, take a moment to reflect on what you have learned in this section.

Reflective Suitcase

Do those you work with grow as people because of your leadership? Do they grow in wisdom and freedom, with responsibility and autonomy?

Message 1. **Each character and purpose is unique.**

Action   Understand your strengths and weaknesses;

Become positive about what makes you different;

Recognise what work you love to do;

Develop the skills and knowledge that build on your uniqueness;

Find your unique contribution to your organisation.

Message 2. **'The perfect form lies concealed in the block of stone; all that is needed is to chip away until it is revealed.'** (Michelangelo)

Action Practise your leadership talents at work;

Be authentic and real rather than what you think is acceptable;

Never stop learning about yourself and situations;

Discover the beauty and wisdom within you and allow others to see it.

Message 3. **Words must be reinforced by example.**

Action Become the change you wish to seek at work;

Live what you say;

Make sure management processes don't contradict each other.

Part

2

Behaviour and Leadership

6 Emotional Intelligence

Chapter guide:

- gaining knowledge of the concept of emotional intelligence and how it relates to leadership;

- understanding your own emotional intelligence and how you can grow and develop your capabilities;

- learning how to use emotional intelligence effectively to motivate yourself and others.

Contents:

Introduction

Emotional intelligence (EI) plays a significant role in developing leadership capabilities. According to academic research, it is suggested that leadership is at least 90 per cent emotional intelligence. Because EI is so important to leadership this chapter is in two parts. Part 1 focuses on understanding the concept of EI, recognising emotions and understanding how they influence behaviour. Part 2 deals with how EI relates to leadership, understanding how to use EI to change and enhance behaviour and when to use it to motivate and sustain behaviour change in others. Emotions are universal and are the prime reason why everyone has leadership potential and their own unique way of expressing leadership.

To inspire and guide us through this chapter we turn to Sir Ernest Shackleton as our leadership mentor.

On 30th August 1916 a group of men were rescued from the uninhabited Elephant Island in the Antarctic Ocean. It had been two years since they had set sail from Britain on their doomed expedition that had resulted in a race against time to escape from the perils of Antarctica. They owed their life to the leadership of one man, Sir Ernest Shackleton. Against all the odds for survival his energy, motivation, courage, integrity and empathy for his fellow men saved them. However, this rescue was not a single-handed venture, as Shackleton enabled others to develop leadership capabilities that allowed them to contribute to their own self-preservation and pull together to survive as a team.

Shackleton's leadership strengths of intelligence, marine knowledge and the ability to constantly be aware of the big picture were not the norm. What set him apart from other leaders and ensured the success of the rescue operation was his outstanding understanding and use of his emotional abilities, including his concern and care for his crewmembers. He inspired his men through his optimism, always addressing them in a positive way; he was fair, treating himself and each man alike, and when appropriate seeing to their individual needs; and he was confident, letting everyone know that he could be responsible, make decisions and focus on the future. Shackleton won their loyalty and devotion through his ability to lead by example, appoint and develop crew members who were competent in their roles, and his ability to lead in a crisis.

How was he able to develop these qualities? He was obviously blessed with a good ability to understand feelings and emotions. This ability was enhanced by his upbringing in a family that showed constant concern for each other's welfare and potential. His family background was in stark contrast to his early days at sea where he experienced brutal, negative sea captains who ruled their crews through fear, with little regard for their physical or spiritual well-being. It was the contrast between these two extreme situations and the realisation of how he needed to be treated in order to maximise his own motivation and abilities that contributed enormously to his knowledge of himself and his leadership capabilities.

This chapter will help you to understand the concept of EI and how the leadership qualities of people such as Shackleton are closely linked to emotional capabilities. It will show you how to understand your own emotional strengths and weaknesses, how they affect your self-confidence and outlook on life, and how they influence your behaviour.

This chapter will give you the opportunity to delve into the concept of EI and understand how:

- the emotional brain works;
- EI is connected to leadership;
- your own emotional strengths have developed;
- to develop your EI;
- to practise and sustain self-management;
- to effectively manage anger and stay optimistic.

Developing EI, like developing leadership, does not happen overnight – it takes time and continual practice and requires patience and perseverance. Sometimes this emotional journey can be disturbing, disconcerting or even terrifying. If at any time you feel overwhelmed then you will need to seek help. The nature of this help will depend upon the severity of disturbance experienced; coaching or mentoring or just talking things through with a close friend or colleague will normally be sufficient. If more extreme difficulties are experienced then professional counselling may be advisable.

Treat this chapter as your reference library of emotional knowledge and understanding. When appropriate, dip into the relevant sections to help you to continue your journey of emotional growth and understanding. Use this knowledge to help you relate your emotional capabilities to other areas of your leadership development.

Part 1: Understanding emotional intelligence

What is EI?

EI is the ability to understand our emotions and how they can work with us to increase our levels of *energy* and *motivation*. This understanding can also enhance our relationships with other people, enabling us to engage in a positive and energising manner.

The concept of EI is essentially a framework for understanding, balancing and connecting with:

- emotions and their triggers;
- emotions and cognitive thought;
- feelings and their resulting behaviour.

Effectively understanding and choosing how we think, feel and act can result in increased displays of:

- energy;
- authenticity;
- integrity.

These are all essential ingredients for developing leadership potential.

Knowledge Bank

Four essential components are interconnected in the concept of EI:

1. Being in tune with your emotions and feelings and understanding how they can influence your behaviour.

2. Using your emotional self-knowledge to manage behaviour and sustain energy levels and motivation.

3. Understanding the needs of others and using this knowledge to help them to become aware of their own development needs.

4. Being able to effectively interact with others and achieve results through effective communication, negotiation and synergy.

All four elements are essential to developing leadership capabilities and qualities and will be referred to throughout Section 2.

Understanding how emotions influence feelings and behaviour

First, let's look at what is meant by an emotion. Emotions are central to our existence; they come and go and vary in intensity. When emotions are initiated they allow our minds and bodies to communicate. At appropriate moments they provide us with signals and energy to quickly take action and at other times they help us 'feel' our way when making reasoned decisions. To know that you have experienced an emotion, to recognise the physical sensations that accompany it, and the feelings and behaviour that resulted from it, is an essential starting point for understanding the rudiments of EI.

Open the suitcase and reflect upon your emotional understanding:

Reflective Suitcase

 Think of two very different situations in your life, one where you feel happy and relaxed and one where you feel tense and uncomfortable. Write down how you physically feel in each of these situations and how your behaviour differs. Note how these feelings affect your optimism, energy and motivation.

Next, consider the following list of emotions and for each one note what physical feelings are triggered when it is experienced and how you usually behave.

Angry – Accepted – Acknowledged – Afraid

Bored – Blissful – Contented – Challenged

Delighted – Elated   Free – Friendly – Furious

Guilty – Hopeful – Independent – Irritated – Ignored

Loving – Motivated – Nervous – Optimistic – Pessimistic

Relaxed – Sad – Sympathetic – Tormented – Tense – Trapped

Notice how your behaviour contributes to your levels of optimism, energy or motivation.

To be able to enhance EI and develop leadership you need to be able to:

- recognise when you experience an emotion;
- understand your physical reactions to emotions;
- adapt your resulting behaviour accordingly, noting that your levels of optimism may need to be adjusted;
- use your emotional knowledge to increase your energy levels and motivation.

Taking responsibility and developing leadership depends upon acknowledging that sometimes your emotions may result in inappropriate behaviour. The challenge is to recognise this and adapt your behaviour accordingly.

Emotions trigger feelings, feelings influence thoughts and thoughts are responsible for our behaviour. This process is the result of the interaction of the emotional brain and the thinking brain. Your present levels of EI and leadership are the combined effect of these two parts of your brain. Your behaviour reflects not only your cognitive abilities but also your emotional reactions which are based largely upon emotional memories and behaviour you have learned in response to these memories. Emotions generated in your unconsciousness influence your conscious behaviour. Emotions are crucial to how you:

- make decisions;
- think creatively or critically;
- solve problems;
- present yourself;
- deal with others;
- work at an acceptable pace.

The brain and emotions

Essential to understanding your emotional self-awareness is knowledge of how the emotional brain is wired, how it deals with emotional inputs and why it is crucial that it connects with the cognitive or thinking part of the brain. Let's start by taking a look at the emotional brain:

The emotional centre of the brain is the *limbic system* (Diagram 3).

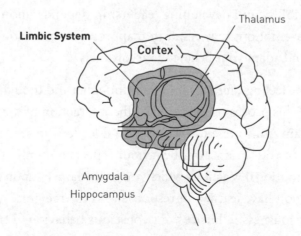

Diagram 3 The Emotional Brain

Knowledge Bank

The *limbic system* essentially contains the:

amygdala – stores emotional memories and constantly scans for danger

thalamus – constantly looks for information

hippocampus – compares present with previous information

Emotions, reasoning and logical thinking work together when links are made between the *limbic system* (emotional brain) and the *cortex* (thinking brain).

We react to emotions in different ways: information received initially by the amygdala causes a fast reaction as it works ahead and independently of the thinking brain. When the hippocampus, thalamus and cortex work together the emotional reaction is slower and allows us more time to think, feel and reason before we act. The amygdala acts as our 'guardian angel', constantly on the look out for signs of danger. It enables us to respond quickly to situations, aiding successful spur of the moment decisions or producing off the cuff remarks that get us into trouble and are regretted later. When behaviour results from this fast response the amygdala instantaneously captures the emotional stimulus, causing a reaction before the thinking brain has time to respond. During an amygdala capture you may experience emotional overload and:

- become angry;
- thump the table;
- utter verbal abuse;
- storm out of the room;
- withdraw – refuse to communicate;
- freeze – feel unable to take action;

- stamp on the car horn;
- lash out and strike;
- rush to help someone in danger;
- make impulsive decisions.

Whichever action you take will be the result of becoming overwhelmed by your emotions and acting spontaneously. The amygdala is continually scanning visual and auditory inputs while tapping into stored emotional memories. It is an ancient mechanism and always triggers an unconscious 'fight or flight' response. This response saved the lives of Neanderthal Man and although it exists to serve the same purpose today, being unaware of its function can get us into serious trouble. As thinking is absent when emotional responses are generated by the amygdala, a large percentage of these reactions result in negative behaviour. However, the positive side of this type of emotional reaction is that we can save ourselves and others from danger, and acts of heroism are largely due to quick reactions following an amygdala generated emotion.

Knowing your amygdala triggers and understanding how you respond is an essential part of developing your leadership. The following examples show how John behaves when his amygdala is overwhelmed.

Example 1 One weekend John witnessed a pedestrian knocked down by a car in his local high street. His instant reaction was panic and he fled from the scene as fast as possible. When he had time to reflect John felt ashamed as he remembered seeing other people running as fast as they could to the injured pedestrian to offer their help. He realised that all of his life he had avoided dealing with his irresponsible reactions to blood and medical matters; they had always induced him to turn or run away. John vowed to enrol as soon as possible on a First Aid course to try to overcome his inadequacies in dealing effectively with such incidents.

Example 2   John has an appraisal interview booked for first thing Monday morning. He is nervous about it and thinks the scheduling is not his best time to receive feedback, but he knows his interviewer is a positive, caring person so he is not too concerned. The interview starts well but at one point the interviewer points out to John that he lacks confidence. Although now a confident person, as a child John had often been told that he lacked confidence. John is an introvert and quiet, often mistaken by extroverts as a sign of lacking confidence. His instant reaction to this remark was to storm out of the room, back to his desk, and to ignore everyone around him. He sat very still, feeling angry and depressed. At lunchtime he took a walk and realised how foolish he had been. Plucking up courage he apologised to his interviewer and asked if the interview could be resumed the following day.

In both examples John's amygdala worked in a way that made him run away from situations. He took 'flight'. Awareness of what was causing his behaviour may have helped him to react in a more appropriate manner and instead to stay and 'fight'. Fighting appropriately in this instance would involve assertive behaviour.

Reflective Suitcase

 Now let's find out how you respond when your amygdala is overwhelmed. Think back during the last few weeks or months and recall several incidents where your behaviour was influenced by a sudden surge of emotions. For each incident note: What was the stimulus? How did you behave? What physical reactions did you experience? What were your thoughts an hour later or the next day?

Use the information you acquire from this exercise to become aware of when your emotions are producing inappropriate behaviour. Take action to make changes. Change will not happen overnight.

First be aware of the situation that triggers behaviour that you later regretted.

Then assess each situation and if necessary take advice and get appropriate help.

If later thoughts showed that your behaviour was appropriate then there is no need for change.

Emotional stimulus processed by the thalamus or hippocampus happens at a much slower rate and is tempered by reasoning and logical thought. Developing intuitive thought (where you listen to your heart as well as your mind) relies upon the memory capacity of the hippocampus and its ability to make comparisons and connect with the thinking brain.

Emotional triggers

Understanding what triggers your emotions is also an important aspect of developing your emotional self-awareness. Emotions can be triggered by any of the following:

- memories;
- visual input;
- auditory input;
- changing facial expressions;
- tone of voice – music – songs;
- imagination;
- touch – smell – taste.

Any one of the above can trigger emotions of varying intensity. Understanding your emotional triggers is just as important as knowing how you react and behave as a result of an emotion occurring. Realising how your emotions are triggered is essential in understanding how you can harness these emotions and modify your behaviour accordingly.

For instance, do you:

- form opinions about people from the way that they dress? If so, does this permanently influence your opinion of them?

- get annoyed when you consider that someone has an irritating voice? Does this impair your dealings with them?

- remember a television advert because of the music, song or visual stimulus? Are you more likely to seek out this product?

- imagine how you will behave in a forthcoming situation. Do you become fearful of the situation?

- do you get annoyed when people behave in a certain way, for example, are you irritated when people are obstinate?

- do you have days when your emotions are more likely to be triggered?

If you answered yes to most of these questions then chances are that you are unaware of how emotional triggers are affecting your behaviour.

Reflective Suitcase

Take one of the following stimuli of emotional triggers – memory, visual input, auditory input, imagination or the behaviour of other people. Spend a day concentrating on when that stimulus triggers an emotion. Notice your resulting behaviour. Look out for how these triggers may affect changes in energy or motivation. Do you need to make any changes?

Understanding that your own facial expressions and tone of voice can be triggers of emotions can help you to change how you feel and modify your behaviour. Try the following:

1. When you feel stressed or depressed, try smiling. Notice any changes in how you feel.

2. If you feel that other people are being irritable, try smiling at them.

3. Listen to your voice. You may sound more confident in some situations than others.

Your voice will sound more commanding and confident if your breathing is low down in the abdomen. If you find if difficult to change your breathing or voice according to the emotional triggers of various situations and events, then you could seek professional help. Working with a professional on your facial expressions and voice can help you to not only increase your emotional self-awareness but also make a start on modifying your behaviour.

Now that you have a basic knowledge of EI and understand the importance of recognising your own emotions and their consequences, the next section will show how emotional capabilities relate to leadership.

Part 2: **Emotional intelligence and leadership**

How EI relates to leadership

EI and leadership are intrinsically interlinked. EI provides the 'follow your heart' side of leadership and works in conjunction with cognitive abilities, technical expertise and strategic thinking. EI contributes to leadership when all four components (← pp. 87–8) are highly developed and work in unison. Emotionally-led leadership behaviour is beneficial whether you are guiding large numbers, a small team or yourself. Low levels of emotional intelligence are highly detrimental to leadership in any situation.

Developing leadership and EI go hand in hand and involve understanding your emotional self, being in tune with the needs of other people and using this knowledge to motivate them, not only to work effectively but also to develop their potential. Understanding how EI contributes to leadership will allow you to understand who you are as a leader. It is a more effective way of developing potential than looking at the traits of great leaders and trying to emulate their behaviour. Understanding how they behave is important, but it is even more important to know how and why they developed their leadership potential.

Let's look at the behaviour of leaders and the difference EI makes to leadership. Its influence can be explained by considering the behaviour of 'good' and 'bad' leaders. Good leaders almost always have high levels of EI. They may not always have large numbers of followers as they can be found at all levels in an organisation and in all walks of life. They will also be good at stepping out of the limelight when appropriate and allowing others to lead. Look out for leaders you consider to be good; their behaviour will almost certainly include many of the following traits:

- concern for high ethical standards;
- strong sense of integrity;
- attitude of continually learning – will admit immediately when they have a lack of knowledge or understanding;

- caring but tough attitude towards others – have a strong capability to help others develop;

- a noticeable sense of presence – they will stand out from the crowd in their views and actions;

- good, effective decision-making;

- self-confidence and a thorough understanding of their strengths and weaknesses;

- knowing when to lead and when to follow – take the lead when called for, regardless of position.

Make a note of any other behaviour your good leaders display. (These leaders may not always be at the top of organisations or in leadership positions.) In looking around at leadership behaviour you will undoubtedly come across 'bad' leaders. They may have excellent qualifications, experience and management capabilities but are likely to be low in EI. They tend to lead through fear, with a lack of integrity, ethical standards and sense of caring for others. Often they employ bullying tactics and will keep others down rather than motivate and help them to develop. Bad leaders emerge in leadership roles for a variety of reasons. They may:

- have deep fears of personal failure;

- take over 'weak' people;

- be brought into failing organisations to be tough;

- seek power above all else.

Bad leadership also refers to people working at any level who find it difficult to take responsibility for themselves or for others. These bad leaders are usually low in EI and can have a debilitating effect on organisations and those around them.

Reflective Suitcase

 Think about your own leadership. Would you class yourself as a 'good' or 'bad' leader? When you have considered this, think about whether you need to make changes?

EI makes a difference to leadership

Who you are as a person and as a leader are undeniably linked. If you fail to understand this then developing leadership will be an almost impossible task.

Understanding your strengths and weaknesses, knowing what you care about, realising how everyday events affect you and understanding your emotional reactions to the behaviour of other people are all crucial to becoming aware of how EI and leadership are intertwined. How you develop this awareness depends upon your determination to succeed and how deeply you are prepared to delve into your darkest thoughts. Looking inside yourself can be a painful process but it is the essential first step in understanding your responsibilities, knowing what prevents you from exercising them and, consequently, releasing your leadership potential.

Your emotional journey will now become more arduous as you realise which obstacles you need to overcome to understand your view of taking responsibility. Understanding *how* and *why* you take responsibility relies on knowledge of how your cognitive and emotional brains interact. You need to be aware of your emotional self, what you care about, and how and when you need to change your behaviour. Let's start with two very simple examples of how behaviour devoid of responsibility is constantly repeated.

Example 1 Every week a family place their dustbin bags outside their house the day before collection day. They allow their dogs to roam and open the bags in search of food and scatter the contents. After the bags are collected, litter is left on the verge. The litter is not picked up and blows into other people's gardens.

Example 2 Every month Tim, a project manager, calls a progress meeting and every month he is 5–10 minutes late for it. He is negative and grumpy if anyone fails to meet the targets set from last time and does not offer help with any problems that the team may be encountering. The result is that the team continually leaves these meetings demoralised and unmotivated. Because this manager is failing to take responsibility for himself he is also failing to encourage others to take responsibility.

We can only guess at why this family and Tim fail to change their behaviour and take responsibility. Perhaps they don't:

- notice what happens;
- think it's their responsibility;
- connect with their inner self and understand how their feelings affect their behaviour;
- believe that they have to take responsibility. Maybe they have always been in a hierarchical position either at school or at work, where taking responsibility was always for somebody else;
- think about their actions and consider changing their behaviour.

Whatever the reasons, these are excellent examples of people feeling that they have no need to or even no right to take responsibility.

Reflective Suitcase

Take a moment to think of situation in which you to failed or avoided to take responsibility. What thoughts and feelings did you have that made you decide not to take responsibility? What were the consequences of your failure to act? In what other situations have you failed to take responsibility? Do you keep repeating the same behaviour over and over again? Are you dissatisfied with this behaviour? Does your behaviour prevent others from being inspired to develop their own sense of responsibility? Are you an effective role model?

The role of emotions in developing positive relationships

It is through successful positive relationships that you will be able to practise your leadership and help others to realise their leadership potential. Being positive is not to be confused with being nice or being soft; it can be an effective way of challenging and motivating others to think, act and take responsibility. Being aware of the emotional strands in difficult situations, the ones that continually recur without resolution, is the key to making progress in improving communications and motivation. Understanding emotions behind behaviours is crucial to dealing effectively with difficult people in these situations. You will be able to influence an effective outcome whereby those involved feel motivated to change and develop their responsibility.

Consider the following scenario:

Example   One of your middle managers not only continually tries to sabotage change initiatives but also lacks any initiative to make or suggest improvements. In meetings and discussions with you and other colleagues he is loud, domineering, pessimistic, negative and refuses to listen.

You recognise his intelligence and he is technically competent in his job. However, he is such a pain in the neck that you have a great dislike of him and this clouds all your meetings. What you have failed to understand is that he lacks confidence and as a result his objections to change arise from his fear of failure. His loud, domineering attitude is a cover-up for his underlying inadequacies. This situation is made worse by your constantly negative attitude towards him. Changing your attitude to him will not be quick or easy, in fact if this clash has been happening for a considerable time then to part company would be the quick and easy option. But if he is not the only person you are failing to inspire and motivate then a serious look at your behaviour and attitude is required.

At this point it is worth turning to our leadership mentor, Shackleton. What did he do to inspire and guide difficult people? Shackleton was always positive, optimistic and fair and as tough with himself as he was with his men. His behaviour stemmed predominantly from two experiences:

- his family had been positive and supportive of each other
- cruel sea captains had left a lasting impression

The contrast in these experiences reinforced his belief that positive behaviour has a motivating effect.

Reflective Suitcase

Now take a moment to consider yourself. Think about your behaviour in the last couple of weeks and note the following:

Think of three times when your attitude has been positive.

How did this affect your behaviour and what reaction did it provoke?

How did you feel?

What drove you to be positive?

Repeat the exercise, only this time think of three times when your attitude was negative.

Understanding when and why you have changed from being positive or negative will not only help you to understand how you inspire people (or otherwise) but will also help you to know how you are feeling in either situation. Knowing why you behave in either a predominantly positive or negative way to life in general will help you to understand how you have learned behaviour that has either enabled you to develop your leadership or detracted from it.

If you are an effective leader who can inspire and motivate, has vision, and pushes boundaries while treating people firmly but fairly, then chances are that you are in tune with your emotions and feelings. Your behaviour is likely to build trusting relationships where others are encouraged to take responsibility.

Know your EI

Understanding your own levels of EI is not always easy. Self-awareness is the foundation for EI development but if this is your weakness it will be difficult for you to make accurate assessments based on your own judgements.

Being aware of how your emotions and feelings affect your behaviour is the basis for developing emotional literacy, that is, being able to read and adapt your own behaviour and being in tune to the emotions and behaviour of others, and using this knowledge to facilitate successful relationships.

Take a look at the questionnaire below and answer it as honestly as you can. Tackle the questions quickly – your first thoughts will probably be the most accurate. In each case try to provide yourself with evidence.

Mark yourself on a scale of 1–4:

1. If you strongly agree with the question
2. If you agree with the question
3. If you disagree with the question
4. If you don't know

1.	Do you respect the feelings of others?	[1] [2] [3] [4]
2.	Do you listen carefully to others?	[1] [2] [3] [4]
3.	Do you speak out for what you feel is right?	[1] [2] [3] [4]
4.	Do you apologise when you have made a mistake?	[1] [2] [3] [4]
5.	Do you praise others and help them to move forwards?	[1] [2] [3] [4]
6.	Do you look for good ideas in others?	[1] [2] [3] [4]
7.	Do you believe what you say?	[1] [2] [3] [4]
8.	Do you understand how your feelings affect your performance?	[1] [2] [3] [4]
9.	Do you recognise your mistakes and learn from them?	[1] [2] [3] [4]
10.	Do you laugh at yourself?	[1] [2] [3] [4]
11.	Do you always have to be right?	[1] [2] [3] [4]
12.	Do you recognise your strengths and weaknesses?	[1] [2] [3] [4]
13.	Do you adapt your plans if needed?	[1] [2] [3] [4]
14.	Do you show that you are optimistic?	[1] [2] [3] [4]
15.	Do you trust yourself to act with integrity?	[1] [2] [3] [4]
16.	Do you have fun and humourous moments with others?	[1] [2] [3] [4]

If you have scored mainly 1s and 2s then you probably have a good understanding of how emotions and feelings affect your behaviour. You may also be able to modify and change your behaviour when appropriate. You have a good understanding of why other people behave in the way they do and how to help them to change their behaviour if needed. However, you will always have something to learn and EI, like leadership, can be developed by continual reappraisal and practice of your thoughts and behaviour. Before you feel pleased with your result, check the accuracy of your score by asking at least three other people to complete it on your behalf and then compare the results.

Tackling such a questionnaire is only one way of getting to know and understanding how EI is contributing to your leadership. Other factors can also help you, such as knowledge of how:

- the emotional and cognitive brain work together – knowing how your past is still influencing your behaviour;

- emotions are triggered and the feelings and behaviour they arouse;

- what is likely to trigger your 'amygdala hijacks' and make you angry or withdraw into yourself.

Reflecting on your behaviour, look out for situations that cause you to:

- repeat unwanted behaviour;

- have negative thoughts;

- be angry in an unhelpful way.

Being aware of how you behave is only the start of developing your EI and enhancing your leadership. Knowing how to work on changing and adapting inappropriate behaviour is far more challenging.

Managing yourself and your relationships

Every day you will encounter situations that cause you anything from mild irritation to outright anger. The final part of this chapter will help you to understand how you can deal effectively with these extremes, enabling you to take responsibility for scenarios that pose a threat to productive relationships. Managing your behaviour under these conditions will allow you to deal effectively with people and problems, be an effective leadership role model and inspire and motivate others through difficult situations.

You will be better equipped to deal with any difficulty, regardless of its intensity, if you regard *all people as equals*. This may not be as simple as it first seems. You will at some time in your life have been exposed to prejudice from either home, school, university, work or peers. The more subtle the prejudice, the more likely it is that you will be unaware of it. Even if you acknowledge the presence of deep-rooted prejudice, it can still be difficult to overcome.

Reflective Suitcase

Take a moment to think. What is your honest, initial reaction to any of the following types of people:

Introverts/extroverts

Young women/middle-aged women/men in suits/people at the top of organisations

Ethnic minorities/working class/middle class/the aristocracy/students

People in a variety of professions – doctors/nurses/solicitors/teachers/engineers/estate agents

In your own organisation – cleaners/shop floor workers/call centre workers/accountants/sales personnel/HR department/the MD

Can any of your reactions be classed as being prejudicial?

If you have highlighted that you are prone to prejudice, how can you deal with thoughts and behaviour triggered by prejudice, no matter how mild it may be? It is crucial to be aware of even the slightest prejudice or mistrust you may be harbouring. Work through the following:

- make a note of your initial thoughts when you either meet any of the above or see news stories in which they may be cited;

- beware of how your prejudicial thoughts may be marking all people in a certain group with the same deficiencies. For example, thinking 'Students are always a rowdy, drunken lot out to cause trouble' is very different to thinking 'Some students are rowdy and drunk but many are hard working and peaceful';

- ask yourself if your negative thoughts are correct, for instance, you know that an estate agent lacked integrity when you tried to buy a house. What can you do to take responsibility to try and rectify the situation?

- notice how you treat people even when you are not angry or irritated by them. Do you make jokes of any weaknesses you perceive in them or continually laugh at their clothes sense or irritating habits?

- do you class all people within a group as being the same or do you see them as individuals?

It is important to understand *when* you may be being judgemental. Dealing effectively with situations that cause you irritation depends upon being assertive and fair in your interactions with others. Following these steps will help you to change your behaviour:

Step 1 – recognise that you are irritated or angry

Step 2 – deal with your prejudices

Step 3 – be assertive and tell the person that their behaviour or attitude is making you feel angry

Step 4 – be positive and tell them how they could change their behaviour or attitude

It will take time to change your behaviour, so be prepared for setbacks. To change you must have the will to persevere. You may have to practise these steps at least 20 times before you see any significant change. They will also be useful in situations that threaten to make you really angry. In such situations you also need to be aware that you may experience a severe 'amygdala surge'. (To deal with this, refer to ← pp. 91–3.)

Message 1. **Developing your emotional intelligence will help you to become an authentic, caring and effective leader.**

Action   Understand the four areas of emotional intelligence;

Be aware of how your emotions affect your feelings and your behaviour – keep a log of your emotional triggers.

Message 2. **Emotional intelligence can be learned and developed but it takes determination and time.**

Action   Accept that you need to make changes;

Ask for, accept and act on feedback;

Keep positive and optimistic.

Message 3. **Any emotional journey will be painful at times. Persevere: the result will enable you to seek a more fulfilling life and successful career.**

Action   Build a support network around you – be available to support others and know you can ask for support from them;

Find out who can effectively coach or mentor you should you require it.

Message 4. **Developing your emotional intelligence will also be the key to enabling many other people to learn and develop their sense of responsibility and leadership.**

Action   Look out for ways in which you can help others to develop;

Develop your social and collaborative skills and improve your relation-ships with others.

Message 5. **Emotional intelligence provides you with the building blocks of taking responsibility and leadership.**

Action   Read widely on emotional intelligence;

Help others to understand that it is not a soft option;

Volunteer to take responsibility, particularly in difficult situations.

7

First Thing in the Morning, Last Thing at Night

Chapter guide:

- understanding how feelings influence your management performance and leadership;

- sustaining your motivation and sense of responsibility and helping others to sustain theirs;

- aligning your natural clock with your work clock.

Contents:

Introduction

This chapter will give you the opportunity to reflect upon your leadership behaviour, provide you with clues as to the origins of such behaviour and suggest ways in which you can make appropriate changes. It is a follow-on from emotional intelligence and illustrates how emotions and feelings affect behaviour and leadership.

The following is an example of feelings affecting behaviour.

Example   Sally lives with her partner, has two young children and works in a senior position for a large corporate organisation in the City. Getting out of bed feeling bright and breezy, looking forward to the challenges ahead is how she would like to start every working day. However the reality is sometimes very different; she often wakes after a poor night's sleep, a night out on the town, or is woken too early by her energetic, boisterous children. Sometimes she leaves home after a row with her partner, rushes to drop off her children at nursery and school and battles with endless traffic queues. Worse still, she often dreads going to the job that she used to love but now finds her management workload overwhelming and the office politics unbearable. Often she starts the day feeling tense, rushed and irritable. When she arrives at her office she ignores those around her and plunges straight into her mountainous workload. She knows that her attitude is not helping her to get the best out of her work and that it minimises her sense of responsibility. She would love to take responsibility for herself, change her behaviour and be motivated to help and collaborate with colleagues but has no idea how to turn herself around.

Whether or not you can identify with Sally's plight, you may realise that there is room for improvement in your behaviour and leadership at work and a need to increase your motivation and sense of responsibility. This chapter will help you to:

- get off to the best possible start with fellow workers;
- sustain enthusiasm for even the most mundane tasks;

- motivate yourself to take responsibility in trying situations;
- pave the way for a smooth transfer to tomorrow.

If, on the other hand, you are one of those fortunate people who is at their best in the morning and finds it difficult not to be cheerful and optimistic, how do you deal with people who are at their best burning the midnight oil and feel at their lowest on rising and coming into work? This chapter will help not only in understanding yourself, but also modifying your behaviour towards those around you.

Work is a major part of most people's lives so it is obviously an important platform from which to understand and practise leadership: it can become the driving force for your journey of leadership discovery. As poet and writer David Whyte points out in *Crossing the Unknown Sea*, 'Maturity and energy in our work is not granted freely to human beings but must be adventured and discovered, cultivated and earned. It is the result of application, dedication, an indispensable sense of humour, and above all a never ending courageous conversation with ourselves, those with whom we work, and those whom we serve' (2001).

Starting on such a journey begins with addressing your feelings at the start of each day in order to maximise opportunities for taking responsibility, motivating others, enjoying your work and being a pleasant, positive person to spend the day with! Your early morning thoughts, feelings, attitude, behaviour and routines affect your leadership capabilities throughout the day. You need to understand:

- what factors influence your behaviour;
- the effect your resulting behaviour has on others;
- how to make important changes;
- the importance of enhancing your sense of responsibility and leadership capabilities;
- how your sense of leadership can help others to develop theirs.

Look to the past – identify your behaviour

Your present behaviour will be influenced by a variety of circumstances and situations, a major factor being memories and learned behaviour from childhood. Together with your personality, drive and intellectual capabilities, these influences will have determined the sort of life that you have been unconsciously carving out for yourself for as long as you can remember. Your learned behaviour will keep you afloat in life, but may not enhance your leadership. Schooldays are a major influence on how you behave today.

Reflective Suitcase

Think back to your schooldays: what did you think and feel on waking, on the journey to school and on your arrival. Were you:

A keen and early riser?

Looking forward to the day ahead?

Ready in plenty of time?

Organised, with all your homework finished?

Friendly and pleasant to all those you met?

Keen to cooperate and engage with people?

Optimistic about the day ahead?

Compliant with the expected behaviour of the school?

Well turned out in a smart uniform?

Always willing to take responsibility?

If you answered yes to these questions then chances are that school made you feel pretty good about yourself and gave you numerous opportunities to take responsibility, and practise and succeed in your leadership capabilities. If you answered no, then your schooldays probably did little to enhance your self-esteem and confidence. The feelings and behaviours from that time may well be exerting severe restraints on your leadership potential.

Start the day as you mean to go on!

Early morning moods are complex and also influenced by circumstances from personal or working lives. Events such as divorce or bereavement have major traumatic effects and a resented lack of balance between work and life will also have an effect, especially if a job is boring and lacking challenges.

Take responsibility for your behaviour each day when you wake, when your behaviour pattern is established. Start in a negative and unfriendly way and your effect on others will be devastating. Leadership development depends upon adopting a positive, optimistic, cheerful, caring start to the day. Progress can be made by learning how to:

- recognise what influences your behaviour – knowing what takes you out of yourself;
- identify behaviour that needs to change and overcoming obstacles to change;
- practise changed behaviour.

Reflective Suitcase

Take a moment to consider how others may view you as you arrive at work.

Make a note of how you think you are perceived.

How well do you communicate with and acknowledge others?

What does your body language and facial expression say about you?

What messages are you giving out?

Are you happy with your initial encounters?

What do they say about you as a manager and a leader?

Do you see a need for change?

There are many factors that influence our early morning behaviour including:

- *personality/drive* – being at your best in the morning as opposed to being a 'night owl' – being extrovert or introvert, loud or quiet;

- *self-esteem/self-efficacy* – your self-confidence and how you feel about your capabilities and yourself as a person;

- *the past* – memories from childhood, especially how you felt when you arrived at the school gate;

- *personal/family life* – emotional problems and baggage that follows you to work;

- *working life* – how you feel about your job and the people you work with, how you feel you are treated by others;

- *work/life balance* – is it a balance or does work dominate? If so, does it matter?;

- *drink or drugs* – heavy drinking in the evening can influence your behaviour, as can drugs, prescribed or otherwise.

Your mood will vary from day to day but there will be a pattern and your colleagues will know what to expect as the norm. If your norm includes a reaction from them that says 'We are pleased to see you' or 'We are looking forward to working with you', then your leadership capacity shines through from the moment you walk through the door. If this is not the reaction you experience, how can you change your behaviour and adopt a positive mood that will have a ripple affect on energising others? Adopting a positive, cheerful and calm approach at the start of the day sets the scene for dealing with the most trying and difficult situations when they arise.

How appropriate is your behaviour? Is there a need for change?

To improve awareness of your feelings on arrival at work follow these suggestions for reflection and learning, make time:

1. Before you leave for work.

2. On the journey.

3. When you arrive.

Reflecting at these moments will allow you to develop an understanding of the interactions of your thoughts and behaviour. You will realise why and how you need to make changes.

On waking, spend time getting to know your internal state. Try to make time for 5–10 minutes of thinking and reflection. Find a place where you can be alone and quiet with no interruptions. (This may require rising 10 minutes earlier than usual.) During this time, listen to your inner self. Take notice of:

- how awake or tired you are;

- how relaxed or tense you feel;

- physical feelings that may indicate anxiety or worry (such as a wobbly tummy or tension in shoulders, arms or legs);

- what is going on inside your head;

- note if your thoughts are negative or positive;

- messages about your work (are you keen and enthusiastic or is there a major problem that is concerning you);

- events from yesterday that may be influencing your feelings and thoughts (either work or personal life), then;

- sum up how you are feeling. Are you feeling happy/relaxed/angry/confused/bored/lethargic?

Reflective Suitcase

Having completed the exercise above, take time to reflect. You are aiming to arrive at work in a positive frame of mind: jot down two things you are happy with and two things you need to work on or change.

On the way to work

This is a time to leave behind any baggage or problems and to think positively. Adopt a positive attitude to the challenges that lie ahead. If you find this difficult or you feel that there will be no challenges, ask yourself, 'Is this the right work for me?', 'Is this really what I want to do?' Even if you find yourself in a difficult working situation, developing a positive frame of mind, acknowledging that you are the only person responsible for your actions, and that you are responsible for helping others, will help to improve even the most difficult situations.

On arrival at work

1. Notice how others react to you – are they positive or negative?
2. Ask for feedback in informal ways.
3. Assess the early morning atmosphere/climate.
4. Understand the influences that prompt your behaviour.

Practising Suitcase

Take time to answer the three questions below to find out what you value and to reflect upon how you are treated.

1. How do I like to be treated?

2. What do I like people to say and do? Think of six people and jot down how they treat you.

3. Do I treat other people the way they like to be treated? If the answer is yes, pick out some of the things that you do. If the answer is no, make a note of things that you need to change.

Understanding yourself cannot be divorced from understanding how you react with other people. Developing your leadership is a combination of reflecting on your inner thoughts and feelings and understanding how important it is to notice the effect your behaviour has on others. Be reflective and critical at various times during the day and you will develop this understanding.

Develop a working lifestyle

If you are fortunate to work for an organisation that encourages flexible working hours then you have the opportunity to develop a working pattern that suits you. To make the most of this you need to consider:

- What period of the day do you work best?
- When do you need breaks?
- Is the balance between your working time and your personal life correct?

Find a way to address any of these issues if they are detrimental to your frame of mind and behaviour at work.

Remember, it is essential to:

Make time for early morning assessment of your feelings.

Try to arrive at work in a positive frame of mind.

Develop an early morning routine, acknowledge others.

Make sure you treat others as you would like to be treated.

Staying positive – taking responsibility

Starting the day in a positive frame of mind will put you in a strong position to respond to the pressures of the day. Maintaining a positive state of mind is easier for some people than others. Dwelling on positive or negative behaviour is a pattern that is established early in childhood and depends upon the environment in which you were nurtured. Staying positive is easier if you are less likely to experience damaging 'amygdala surges' or have difficulties modifying unsuitable reactions to emotional memories (← pp. 91–2). To help you develop a positive approach in dealing with yourself and others, you need to consider:

- developing a positive mind;

- establishing positive relationships – identify your sense of humour!;

- the positive approach – a motivating tool – is not about being soft!

Developing a positive mind

How we view ourselves is reflected in how we view and deal with other people.

> Developing a positive mind is the number one ingredient for taking responsibility and developing our leadership.

Imagine for a moment that you are near completion of an extensive document that you will be presenting at an important meeting tomorrow, where you will be leading a team who have to make important decisions. Your input will be vital! Before you have time to print out the information you experience a power cut. You learn from your local electricity company that it is a major fault and that power is unlikely to be resumed before you need to leave for your meeting. Understanding your first thoughts is key in taking responsibility for the situation. Do you think:

- this is my career ruined – I will look incompetent;

- what other ways can I find to get across crucial information that will help my team to make informed decisions?;

- how can I ask other team members to help out in this crisis?;
- I will see the funny side of this in a week's time but right now it is no joke.

If your thoughts were aligned to the last three points you are well along the road to thinking in a positive way. However, if your thoughts veered more towards the first point, then you need to consider:

- how you view difficulties;
- how often you take a negative view;
- how effective it can be to change negative thoughts into positive ones. (The next section will help you to work on this.)

Reacting with positive thoughts and actions is a key leadership attribute, and essential not only to taking a leading role but also to cooperating, collaborating and learning. It can be the first step in letting go of your own ego, status and power and allowing others to develop, contribute and take responsibility.

How do you react to difficult or threatening situations?

Over the next week listen to any negative thoughts that prevent you from taking responsibility. Do you find yourself thinking any of the following?

- how could I be so stupid?;
- I will never be any good no matter how hard I try;
- that was a stupid mistake to make;
- other people never agree with me/never do what I want them to do;
- I am surrounded by useless people.

If so, focus on developing an understanding of how you respond to each of the following situations:

Situation 1: responding to mistakes

People sometimes do stupid things but they are not necessarily stupid people; mistakes are key to learning and identifying learning needs. Within a well-run organisation the attitude should prevail that if mistakes are made then there is the opportunity to learn from them.

Ask yourself, 'How do I feel when I know that a mistake has been made?' Do I:

- feel resentful and angry?;
- immediately blame the person concerned?;
- want to punish, name or shame the person?;
- take responsibility for some of the blame myself?;
- reflect upon how we can work together to prevent this happening again?

Being positive, firm and open will improve motivation and taking of responsibility. To practise your leadership at such times take a moment to *reflect, keep calm, take control of anger and learn.*

Situation 2: working with challenging people in difficult situations

We are often required to work in a team situation in an open and responsible way towards a common goal. How you behave and take the lead in these situations will help you and others learn and develop. Remaining positive is a crucial element in developing trusting relationships. Leadership in this situation requires:

- acknowledging your own feelings – tell others how you feel;
- developing a positive, constructive approach;
- understanding how others are feeling;
- supporting others;
- asking for support for yourself if it is not forthcoming;
- making time to discuss difficult issues, understanding the feelings surrounding them;

- volunteering to help others;

- taking time for detailed discussion of issues;

- listening to the concerns of others;

- being prepared to change and adapt;

- asking challenging questions.

If you find this difficult, how do you go about changing your negative behaviour into a way that allows you to be positive, constructive and valuable to others? The answer is to:

- change negative thoughts into positive thoughts;

- take notice of the action rather than the person;

- communicate effectively.

Reflective Suitcase

Take a moment to think of a situation in which your negative thoughts dominated. Fold a piece of paper in half, on one half write down your negative thoughts, on the other side of the paper change these thoughts for positive ones. Next time your negative thoughts take over think positive instead and notice the change in your behaviour.

Riding the wave of emotional wear and tear

During your day you will experience peaks and troughs in your levels of energy and motivation according to your areas of interest, depth of challenges, sense of responsibility and physical well-being. How well you balance these highs and lows depends on your self-knowledge and, in particular, an understanding of your natural clock. Dealing effectively with these cycles will help you respond efficiently to daily events.

We all possess a unique natural rhythm to our days, nights and weeks. Take time to consider *your* natural rhythm.

Practising Suitcase

 Over a minimum period of a week notice how your body responds to the 24-hour clock. At the times indicated below record your physical feelings and behaviour. Note in particular when you feel tired, energetic, thoughtful or stressed and how you behave at these times:

- when you wake;

- arriving at work;

- mid-morning;

- after lunch;

- leaving work;

- 10.00 pm.

You should notice patterns emerging and you will be able to plot your high- and low-energy spots and the behaviour traits most common to each. Use this information to motivate yourself at your low spots or use this 'dip' time for rest, quiet reflection or exercise to boost your energy later in the day. By following this exercise you will come to know your peaks and troughs.

Coping with difficult situations in your low spots

Have you wondered why some days you find it more difficult to deal with people and situations than on other days? There may be several reasons for this:

- you are tired or lethargic – this may be due to lack of sleep, overwork or lack of exercise;

- the times you are dealing with these difficult situations or people is coinciding with your dip in energy levels;

- being tired or 'down' is causing you to be in a negative frame of mind;

- as you arrived at work you were irritated by something and this has stayed with you, surfacing in other situations.

How you react to difficult situations depends on developing an understanding of what and who you care about, how well you listen, and how you internalise criticism. Imagine that you are the sort of person who is not at their best first thing in the morning. On this particular day you arrive at work tired and rushed, to be greeted by an angry (more senior) manager who demands to know why the information they required from you for a meeting at 9.00 am is not on their desk now! They are making their disquiet known in a very aggressive manner, accusing you of being incompetent and useless. There is a very good reason why you have failed to provide them with the information but unfortunately you forgot to tell them about this in good time.

This type of situation understandably makes you feel angry and hurt but *the reaction* you have to your feelings can affect your behaviour for the rest of the day. Consider the following reactions:

Scenario A

'How dare they speak to me like that, if only they had enquired in a polite, calm way where the documents are then we could have resolved the situation. Now I feel very angry and unwilling to work hard for them again.'

Scenario B

'I have been negligent; they're quite right, now I am holding up work with an important client. I feel hurt inside that I have been called incompetent but I must learn from this and make sure that it does not happen again. I was feeling more angry and hurt because I had arrived at work tired and stressed. I will now go and apologise and explain why I did not inform them sooner that the work would be delayed.'

Now take time to consider how you think and behave in similar situations. Are you more inclined to think like Scenario A or Scenario B? If Scenario A, then think back to a similar situation. How did you behave for the rest of the day? Did you:

- sulk;
- snap at other colleagues and reports;
- take an extra long lunch break;
- become less diligent with your work;
- constantly allow your angry thoughts to resurface;
- spend a great deal of the day feeling depressed or sorry for yourself?

If you behaved in any of the above ways, then your overwhelming feelings of anger and despair prevented you from taking responsibility for your own motivation and for the situation.

On the other hand, if you reacted more in line with Scenario B then you probably felt and behaved in the following way:

- recognised that you felt hurt;
- reflected quietly and brought yourself round to a more positive frame of mind;
- apologised for your mistake;
- noted why it happened and learnt from it;
- made an effort to be happy and jolly with colleagues – found an opportunity to crack a joke.

If your behaviour followed this pattern, it is likely that you were able to lead yourself out of this difficult situation without losing face with your colleagues. As a leadership role model you will hopefully have inspired others to follow your example. You will also have sustained your motivation for the day's work ahead and used this episode of friction as a motivator. Next time you are faced with a trying situation, compare your feelings for the difficulty faced with the timing of the incident. Has it hit a high or low spot in your day?

Winding down

Knowledge Bank

A leadership-learning journey requires a 24-hour commitment: there is no switching off. It is important that you allow sufficient time for a quality night's sleep, although we all experience times in our lives when this is not possible. If you do have control over your sleeping pattern then it is important that it forms an integral part of your work/life balance. You will know how much sleep is optimum for you. The frame of mind in which you leave work, the amount of work you take home and how optimistic you feel about the next day all contribute to your overall state of mind, feelings and behaviour.

There are many facets of your working day that contribute to overall attitude to leadership and values. In addition to those already covered it is important to look at the frame of mind in which you generally leave work? In addition to knowing your swings of energy and motivation it is important, if possible, to pace the last hour or so of your working day to put yourself in the a frame of mind that will allow you to derive greatest benefit from your home life or leisure time. The best way for you to achieve this will depend on your personality, how you perceive this time of day in terms of your energy and motivation levels, and your working environment. There are many options available. You may choose when possible to:

- use this time to quietly finish your work;

- catch up on phone calls or emails;

- arrange meetings for the following day or week;

- think about tomorrow – what have you learnt from today that you would like to do differently tomorrow?;

- what do you need to do now that will help tomorrow run smoothly?

If you have flexible working hours, it is essential that you consider whether you are *still* making best use of this time. Think for a moment, are you adjusting this time to reflect your high and low energy spots? If not, can you make changes? Or you may consider that your flexitime is not flexible enough to make changes; working to avoid traffic jams may be more important!

Finally, you may also need to make a decision – do you stay and finish work or take it home with you? In making this decision you need to consider how you will motivate yourself to get the best out of your leisure time. You may also think that a slot between work and leisure is an important time for you to reflect on your working day. Balancing energy and motivation after work makes an important contribution to how you deal with every working day. Examine your leisure time, do you have a hobby that helps to recharge your batteries or do you participate in sport or exercise?

Message 1. **Enhance your leadership behaviour by understanding your past.**

Action Recognise which patterns of behaviour have followed you through life;

Be brave enough to make changes.

Message 2. **Being positive is the best way to motivate others and yourself.**

Action Give feedback by focusing first on positive aspects and then bring in any point for improvement;

See negative feedback as learning points which need to be worked on.

Message 3. **Changing a negative mind to a positive one requires practice.**

Action Recognise when you are negative and the effect it has on your behaviour and the behaviour of others;

Change negative thoughts and conversations for positive ones.

Message 4. **It is important to take time throughout the day to assess your behaviour.**

Action Reflect on your feelings and mood before you arrive at work;

Recognise how patterns in your feelings and behaviour change throughout the day.

Message 5. **It is just as important to wind down as it is to wind up.**

Action Lead a balanced life;

Look for leadership opportunities in your personal life and leisure time.

8 Empathy

Chapter guide:

- understanding the importance of self-awareness in developing empathy and how to put yourself in somebody else's shoes;

- learning how the many aspects of 'people reading' contribute to developing effective empathy;

- becoming aware that empathy can contribute to leadership at many different levels.

Contents:

Introduction

Read Chapter 6: Emotional Intelligence before starting this chapter.

Empathy is a strong component of emotional intelligence and is an essential ingredient of successful leadership. It encourages self-responsibility and self-management. It goes hand-in-hand with leadership that refuses to be ego driven, but instead cares about the feelings and needs of others. Developing empathy also means drawing a fine line between over-involvement and encouraging people to take responsibility for themselves.

Successfully developing empathy (being aware of the emotions, feelings and needs of others) and using this knowledge to best effect is a complex process. True empathy grows out of deep self-awareness. You can only start to understand others if you understand the influences that have shaped your own behaviour and performance. Empathy often develops out of experiences where you either acknowledge that you have been treated unjustly or understand that beneficial intervention has aided your progress, learning and sense of responsibility.

To explain this more fully lets look at the awareness and empathy that shaped the leadership of Gandhi, 'One of the most influential and powerful figures of the 20th century, never serv[ing] as a prime minister or president, or even as a member of government' (Arnold, 2001). (Arnold is an expert on South Asian history.) One of the many reasons why he emerged as a leader regardless of his position was his enormous ability to exercise empathy. This ability fuelled his passion and inspired his courage. His empathy developed through many things – his understanding of his inner vulnerability and insecurity coupled with his ability and adaptability to continually reflect, learn and experiment. Ghandi's empathy for the people of India grew out of his own mistreatment and imprisonment in South Africa. His indignation that he, as an Indian, like other 'blacks' in the country, was treated as a second class citizen became one of the roots of his passion for the return of India to Indians and their right to have the freedom to live and work in 'self-governing', sustainable villages. His time spent in prison for his refusal to be treated as a 'black' gave him time to reflect and to learn. He was able to balance views in his empathic dealing of a situation and was aware of how his behaviour influenced the behaviour of others. For instance, in re-establishing India's cotton industry he was concerned about the plight of the cotton workers in Lancashire but understood where his priorities lay. During his campaign for self-government for India he was aware of when his behaviour caused mass hysteria or violence and used fasting to bring order and control. Ghandi's an example of how a shy, introverted individual affected the course of history through self-reflection, courage, empathy and passion, enabling others to take responsibility.

Gandhi's empathy aroused enormous courage and conviction that resulted in large-scale changes, but empathy is just as important in one-to-one relationships and in all aspects of working lives. This chapter will help you to understand:

- how empathy operates at different levels;
- the difference between empathy and sympathy;
- the learning involved in developing empathy;
- how empathy applies to teams and organisations.

What is empathy?

Empathy is essentially being able to 'emotionally exchange places with others', 'take their point of view', 'care for them' and 'consider them to be at least equal and at times more important than you'. Ego-driven arrogance or selfishness can play no part in exercising empathy. Empathy is part of EI (← p. 88) and is a tool that combines with emotional self-awareness to allow you to understand the needs of others and to effectively interact with them.

Empathy is about caring in a tough way – it is not a soft or easy option as often difficult decisions have to be taken. Developing and practising empathy requires skill, intelligence, determination, humility and an immense understanding of your own and other people's emotions and feelings. According to clinical psychologist Claude

Steiner, 'empathy is a form of intuition about emotions … when being empathic we don't figure out or think about, see, or hear other people's emotions. It has been suggested that empathy is actually a sixth sense with which we perceive emotional energies in the same manner in which the eye perceives light.' However, being blind to these energies is common and it is never too late to learn how to empathise. The initial learning process does demand that it starts at a more conscious level.

On a personal level the benefits of developing and exercising empathy are numerous:

- relationships become strong – debating a difference of opinion while being empathic is more likely to involve learning and to lead to win–win outcomes;

- communication becomes more effective – there is less likelihood that misunderstanding will occur;

- you are less likely to become angry with others and you will be able to understand their point of view and anticipate their behaviour and reactions;

- trust and collaboration will also be improved.

Empathy can and should be exercised at a variety of different levels. In organisations this can vary from being empathic in your dealings with individuals to understanding how empathy can play a part in motivating teams or whole organisations to work together effectively. Empathy is an important part of helping others to learn and therefore an essential component of coaching and mentoring. Additionally, it is a crucial consideration in rallying employees in difficult circumstances and retaining your best talent. Lack of empathy is one of the most common causes of stress and underperformance, as illustrated in the following example:

Example   Julian was off sick for several weeks because his doctor identified that he was suffering from mental stress. His manager's reaction to this was, 'I can't understand why he is stressed, he doesn't work that hard'. What he had failed to realise was that Julian didn't have the right levels of skill and competency to carry out his job effectively. Julian was almost ignored by his manager because he was always perceived as having his head down and working hard. But

Julian spent his days making himself look busy on trifling work and his incompetence was only highlighted in team meetings. After these meetings his boss complained to others about Julian's behaviour but never tackled him about it.'

Julian's boss showed no empathy towards him or the situation because:

- he failed to consider Julian to be important, let alone more important than him;
- his lack of contact denied him the opportunity to develop a personal, caring relationship in which communicating effectively, listening to concerns and considering feelings could be taken into consideration.

Empathy and emotions

Empathy is essential to developing EI. ← p. 88 shows that it is the third critical component of EI, following on from being aware of who you are and what you care about, and being able to manage your emotions and behaviour. Empathy works through the emotional brain (← p. 90) and the amygdala in particular plays a significant role in helping you to be emphatic. Paul Ekman (2003) has identified that empathy is not an emotion – it relates to 'our reactions to another person's emotions'. It is the interaction of the emotional brain (the limbic system) and the cognitive brain (cortex) that aids empathy. This is further illustrated by considering the three components of empathy that Paul Ekman, world reknowned expert on human expression, has identified (2003):

'*cognitive empathy* – where you recognise what another person is feeling.'

'*emotional empathy* – where you actually feel what that person is feeling.'

'*compassionate empathy* – where you want to help a person deal with their situation and their emotions.'

Cognitive empathy is essential for achieving emotional and compassionate empathy but compassionate empathy can be felt without experiencing emotional empathy.

Experiencing all three forms of empathy simultaneously is required in developing your leadership. Only this deep understanding of empathy will enable you to emotionally put yourself in somebody else's shoes and be able to consider them to be more important than you. The following story will help you with your understanding of this:

Example Barbara and Alan (unknown to each other) holidayed on separate occasions in a central African country. During their stay they were both shocked at the contrast between the luxury of their hotel complex and the poverty of the indigenous population (cognitive empathy). How they both dealt with this shock and dismay was very different.

On returning home they both started two very different fund-raising campaigns. Alan's campaign focused on raising money for a school and providing English-style uniforms. Barbara's campaign focused on raising money to help improve the agricultural system and to help the population to help themselves.

Alan's campaign was ego driven and based on cognitive and compassionate empathy; he wanted to be seen to be doing something for the plight of these people but he wanted the glory from it. He was frequently pictured in his local paper reporting his achievement.

Barbara, on the other hand, was able to use all three aspects of empathy and through this the citizens of the African state became more important than herself. Her campaign focused on helping them to identify their needs and raising money to buy the expertise to help them. Being recognised for doing this was not important to her. Eventually Barbara sold her house and moved to the state. She extended her campaign to help large numbers of people to improve their basic agricultural existence. Having contacts in Britain helped her to secure international aid. Barbara's outcome is not surprising as research has show that women are more likely to be more empathic than men.

Understanding the three different aspects of empathy also helps to explain the difference between sympathy and empathy (which are frequently confused). Sympathy can often arise out of experiencing only cognitive empathy. Sympathy is purely a reasoned mental process that does not involve being in tune with another's emotions. In experiencing sympathy you are more likely to feel too sorry for the person, your goal will be to help them and you may fail to balance their needs with other criteria such as the need for them to be able to help themselves. In the work situation, being sympathetic could mean that you fail to consider the needs of the organisation as opposed to the needs of the person. In sympathy, your cognitive brain will work with an absence of emotions and your judgement will be limited, as you are unable to connect emotionally with the other person.

Developing and using empathy

Before you can successfully exercise empathy, you need to be well along the road of developing your EI. Using empathy relies on being in tune with your emotions, being able to look for your emotions in physical feelings, and using this knowledge to manage your behaviour.

It is often difficult to be empathic towards people who 'rub you up the wrong way' or display their arrogance by always insisting that they are right. Often these people are covering up insecurities and in doing so fail to ask for help – as a result their learning may be inhibited. Such people can appear superior or try to dominate, and they may make you feel jealous and inferior. It is this jealousy that can inhibit empathy and prevent you from being able to equate yourself with this person, let alone consider them to be more important than you.

Practising Suitcase

Now test your empathy.

Try to think of a person to whom you find it difficult to offer help – it may be someone you find it difficult to discuss work-related issues with. This person may be a colleague who lacks enthusiasm and motivation but through their arrogance they fail to recognise this.

Think back to two or three occasions when you realised that the way you tried to enthuse and motivate this person has failed.

Now focus on yourself during these interactions:

What emotions did you experience?

Where did you feel them physically?

How did you behave?

Where you able to treat this person as being more important than you?

Could you put yourself in their shoes?

Was the outcome successful for all involved?

Compare how you felt and behaved to this person, and the outcome, with a situation in which you were required to be empathic with somebody who you care about a great deal.

Again focus on yourself and consider the above questions. How do your answers differ?

To develop empathy you must first focus on your own emotions, feelings and behaviour and understand how they influence the empathy you can feel and show for others.

Taking time to reflect may have highlighted that there is a need for you to work on various aspects of self-awareness. Now that you have some knowledge of how important your emotional role is in applying empathy, the next step is being able to read people.

Reading people

Research shows that on average when you communicate with other people the signals and meaning that you pick up will come 7 per cent from the words spoken, 38 per cent from their tone of voice and 55 per cent from their body language. Remember, they will be picking up clues from you in the same proportions. There are many ways in which you can pick up these verbal and non-verbal clues which are indicators of otherwise hidden signals of feelings. Failing to retrieve these clues can affect your behaviour and empathy towards other people. Most of these clues will be subtle, therefore you will need to be in a calm, receptive frame of mind to absorb them and appreciate the other person's perspective.

Reading people depends upon being skilled in decoding verbal and non-verbal clues. Homing in on verbal clues depends initially upon developing effective and non-judgemental listening skills. This involves not only listening to words and phrases but also looking for hidden meanings that may indicate how the person is feeling. Tone of voice is an important indicator of the meanings behind the words. How well do you do this? Make a start in assessing yourself. Think about the last meeting you attended; was your listening impaired by any of the following thoughts and behaviour?

- thinking about something else;
- worrying;
- wishing/imagining you were somewhere else;
- anticipating that certain people will say things that will make you angry;
- trying to shout people down;
- failing to make eye contact, tapping fingers and being impatient;

- jumping to conclusions or finishing sentences for other people;
- talking too much and not allowing others to have their say.

Failing to listen, being ready to put others down or not allowing the space for everyone to have their say impairs leadership capabilities and is the trap into which many bad leaders fall. On the other hand, the following thoughts and behaviour may be more applicable to you, and you will have been able to:

- clear your mind of distracting thoughts;
- focus on the person speaking – make eye contact;
- listen to the important facts;
- only speak or reply in obvious gaps;
- avoid rushing the other person to finish;
- think about how you could add to or help the conversation.

If you identify more with this second list then chances are that your listening skills are fairly effective.

To put these skills to good use and combine them with exercising empathy must include recognising non-verbal clues such as tone of voice, expression, gestures and eye movements to help you to discover feelings otherwise hidden. Now go back to your meeting and, if you can remember, make a note of any of the following non-verbal behaviour:

- facial expressions;
- arm movements and positions;
- finger tapping;
- eye contact or lack of it;
- sitting positions in chairs – did you notice any slouching?

Does reviewing this list alter your perception of how people may have been feeling in that meeting?

To practise observing non-verbal clues and searching for hidden meanings in conversation, look for an opportunity to listen to a conversation where remembering the facts is less important than responding to how the person is feeling.

What feelings are you picking up?

Which clues are giving you the information?

If you practise this as often as possible, picking up on non-verbal clues will almost certainly become second nature. You will then have more tools to help you to develop the empathic side of leadership.

When trying to perceive or interpret non-verbal clues it is often more helpful to take a holistic view of the person and to look for clues in as many different places as possible. Non-verbal clues that give away feelings are to be found in facial expressions, body language, eye movement/eye contact, gestures and personal space. The more intimately you know a person the easier this will be.

The best place to start your understanding of non-verbal clues is with yourself. Here are some activities to try:

1. Experiment with making yourself feel different emotions by remembering events, places and people. Watch yourself in a mirror or on video and see if you can observe changes in your own face and body as your emotions change (from *Six Seconds – Handle With Care*, 1997).

2. Notice your body language in different situations: look out for when you adopt any of the following – folded arms, pointing a finger at a person, banging the table. Compare your body language with how you are feeling. Do the same feelings always coincide with the same body language? For instance, when you sit with arms folded do you experience the same emotion, for example, feeling

defensive towards the person you are talking to, or is it sometimes because that is the only comfortable way to sit on some chairs?

Practising Suitcase

Try this initially with people you know very well and secondly people with whom you may have a lot of contact but are not close to on a personal level. For each activity take one aspect of non-verbal communication at a time.

Choose your focus of non-verbal communication, such as facial expression, use of hands, eye contact/eye movement, gestures or personal space. For each one, spend sometime observing these in your chosen person. Make mental notes and later make written notes if you feel that it is necessary. Completing this exercise will help you to analyse non-verbal clues quickly and almost subconsciously. Taking a holistic view of how people are feeling will then start to come naturally to you.

Now that you understand the importance of developing your personal expertise in empathy, and of taking a holistic view when exercising empathy with others, we will move on to the role of empathy in teams and organisations.

Empathy and teams

Developing empathy in teams is crucial if every team member is to have the opportunity to develop and use their leadership potential. Empathy helps teams to build trust and collaboration and to work together effectively. Understanding empathy in teams relies upon an initial grasp of the role of emotions in successful interpersonal communication. A starting point for developing team empathy is having a significant number of team members who are competent at recognising and managing emotions and exercising empathy at interpersonal level. However, this alone does not ensure that empathy will surface at team level. Developing empathic understanding depends upon these individuals and the team leaders working together to achieve a team ethos that encourages:

- a constructive and positive approach to communicating at interpersonal level, especially in uncomfortable situations;

- support for learning and other difficulties as soon as they arise;

- everyone having equal opportunity to voice opinions and concerns;

- justice for all;

- valuing all team members equally;

- understanding emotional clues in interactions;

- being able to regulate emotions in interpersonal interactions;

- caring for each other and acknowledging feelings.

These are all essential components for team members being able to 'take somebody else's point of view'. There are times when it is beneficial for teams to work together, for instance in a manufacturing process where two teams may be working towards the same goal but on different aspects of the project. Empathy *between* teams is essential. Each team must exercise empathy within its own members before it can be transferred. Look at this example taken from an exercise at a leadership workshop:

Example   Thirty participants were divided into six teams and each team was given an identical number of Lego™ pieces. They were asked to 'Build the tallest tower that you can'. Immediately, each team set out to compete with each other. The more creative teams were able to work on alternative ways to make their tower taller, for instance, to hold up the completed tower while standing on the table. There was one prize for the winning team. Had all the teams cooperated and worked together to build one tower then all could have shared the prize. After all, the instruction was to 'Build the tallest tower that you can': there were no other instructions or rules.

This story indicates not only how difficult it is for teams to 'put themselves in somebody else's shoes' but also that empathy between teams is probably harder to achieve than developing empathy within each team. Competition is the killer of team empathy, competing to be the best team can be more important. You may well ask, 'What has this got to do with developing leadership capabilities?' Knowing that everyone has some leadership potential, then developing leadership for all and allowing teams to take the lead in working together, will ensure that more individuals have the opportunity to learn and practise leadership.

Wholescale empathy and leadership

Let's return to our leadership mentor for this chapter, Gandhi. What was most remarkable was the way in which he used empathy and self-management to regulate the behaviour of the Indian population, encouraging them to take responsibility for their future. The underlying message was non-violence and he used fasting as a means of returning to this after the many occasions when violence broke out.

Leading with empathy from the top of an organisation can have a remarkable effect on the empathy of teams and individuals. Empathy at this level involves recognising the emotions behind the motivation and behaviour of the workforce and balancing this with the need to be profitable and stay in business. It can result in a change of culture and structure within the organisation and these changes are frequently the catalyst for individuals to start to develop empathy.

Emphatic leadership almost always produces a successful organisation that cannot be copied by anyone else. Remember (← p. 97) that you cannot become like our leadership mentors but you can learn from the processes they have gone through to develop their leadership qualities. Likewise, you cannot copy the leader of an organisation but you can develop and apply empathy to improve your leadership.

The role of empathic leadership is best explained by considering a successful organisation that has emerged from the emotional awareness and empathy of its top leader.

The company is SEMCO in Brazil and the leader, who developed his responsibility from recognising that his own health problems were stress related, is Ricardo Semler.

Semler describes his factory as the world's most unusual workplace; his empathic leadership has grown out of values and purpose that balance the needs of satisfied customers, making a profit and employees' job satisfaction. Employees work in small units where the emphathis is on trust and empowering workers to make their own decisions, targets and schedules. They share information, are open, encourage creative thought, personal freedom and empathy. The following quote from Semler's book, *Maverick*, shows how empathy has developed among employees without any enforcement, training courses, or words such as 'you must care about each other'. Semler's favourite innovation by employees was '[a] board at the plant entrance with the name of each employee and next to it a wooden peg. As each person arrived in the morning he would hang one of three metal tags on the peg: a green tag stood for "Good Mood", a yellow tag for "Be Careful" and a red tag for "Not today please". Maybe it was cute, but the kids took it seriously, selecting their tags carefully and paying heed to those of others' (1994).

Message 1. **Empathy is a crucial component in developing self-responsibility and encouraging responsibility in others.**

Action   Notice how many times a day you volunteer to take responsibility;

Review how effectively you encourage others to take responsibility;

Understand how empathy helps you to carry out both of these actions.

Message 2. **To develop empathy you must consider others to be more important than yourself.**

Action   Be helpful and open when asked for advice;

Avoid feeling threatened that others may outdo you and avoid covering your own back;

Help others to work effectively towards goals and targets;

Speak out or even blow the whistle to support others.

Message 3. **Developing leadership capabilities requires that cognitive, emotional and compassionate empathy all combine in the empathic process.**

Action Be aware of your own emotions in the empathic process;

Understand the difference between recognising what another person is feeling and actually feeling what they are feeling;

Be aware that you need to balance the emotions you feel in empathy with the needs of the person or the group.

Message 4. **Empathy involves reading non-verbal clues.**

Action Be aware of your own body language and notice how it reflects your feelings;

Look out for changes in other people's body language and facial expression; try to understand what these changes may be telling you.

Message 5. **Listening effectively is essential to developing empathy and exercising leadership.**

Action Take time to understand how effective you are at listening;

Give people time and space to talk;

Listen to the facts and look out for the emotions;

Make eye contact;

Reply constructively.

Message 6. **Exercising empathy can apply to individuals, teams and organisations.**

Action Understand the effect your behaviour and leadership has on others either individually or collectively;

Exercise empathy across teams and organisations and raise morale.

Trust

Chapter guide:

- understanding the importance of developing trusting relationships and being trustworthy;
- developing a strategy for building individual and organisational trust;
- becoming aware of how trust is linked to leadership.

Contents:

Introduction

Trust is a major issue affecting every aspect of our lives. We need to be able to trust those around us, from politicians to family and colleagues, to be truthful, conscientious and loyal. In addition to placing our trust in people, we also need to be able to trust the technology, medicines, procedures and systems that are all part of our modern world. This need for trust is far-reaching, extending from the belief that the care we receive in hospital will be of the highest standard to having faith that financial organisations will show integrity when dealing with investments, mortgages and pensions.

No matter in what material or technological form, trust is paramount. The assurance of quality and integrity it demands can only be achieved through people, who are themselves trustworthy and trust those around them. Trust is therefore a critical component of leadership at any level.

Our concept of trust is often clouded however, as we live in a world where media reports are often ill balanced, with an emphasis on reporting more incidents of mistrust and suspicion than news articles where trust has prevailed. Take for instance the following report on the *Columbia* shuttle disaster in early 2003, where seven astronauts died. It stated that:

Example   The technical faults that caused the disaster could have been averted with improved human practices on the ground. Highlighted in this report was the issue of 'ineffective leadership' which, it is stated, 'failed to ensure the safety of the crew'. The report went on to cite the structure and a 'self protective' culture of NASA as being a primary cause for 'flawed safety procedures', 'increased levels of risk', and accepting 'some flaws as normal'. Overall a culture of lack of concern prevailed, with top officials showing little interest in technical problems engineers brought to their notice. Painting a picture of an organisation 'that sends human beings on the most perilous journeys known' (*Independent*, 27th August 2003) but, despite its advanced technical expertise, could not be trusted to ensure the safety of the crew. The report concluded that unless these issues were addressed another catastrophe couldn't be ruled out.

Quite clearly this report lays the blame on management and their lack of leadership. However, this lack of leadership and trust may be as much about our increasing demand for accountability, which can overwhelm many unprepared managers and leaders. Today we quite rightly demand that leaders and managers are ethical and beyond reproach but they constantly fail to live up to this expectation, often because of a lack of access to education and environments which could help them to reflect, learn, develop and exercise the necessary skills.

This chapter will:

- allow you the opportunity to reflect upon who you trust and why you can trust them;

- help you to understand the importance of giving and taking trust at an individual level;

- demonstrate how organisational structure and culture can either influence an ethos of trust or cause ungrounded suspicion.

Developing trust

First we look at developing trust at an individual level – how you trust yourself, how you build trusting relationships, how you help others to trust themselves and how you are viewed as being trustworthy. Trust is developed and radiated out by you, your thoughts, your actions and your decisions. Developing trust equates with developing a core emotional strength; according to author and expert on trust Robert Cooper (1997), this emotional strength 'begins with a feeling of self worth and purpose that we're called to extend outwards to others… This warm, solid gut feeling you get from trust – from counting on yourself and trusting and being trusted by others – is one of the great enablers of life.'

Trusting yourself

Trusting yourself comes from knowing and understanding your emotions, behaviour and capabilities. From being certain that you can manage your behaviour and knowing the limits of your understanding, knowledge and expertise and swallowing 'humble pie' by asking for help and advice when appropriate. Trusting yourself also comes from your inner belief that you are a good and honest person and that you value integrity and treat others as they like to be treated. Behaving in a consistent manner but being adaptable when appropriate is crucial to trusting yourself.

Reflective Suitcase

Make a start – how much do you trust yourself?

Do you feel confident that you always act with integrity?

If so, make a note of why you think this, what evidence do you have?

How do you feel when you act with integrity?

Who has been your role model for developing this behaviour?

If you don't think that you act with integrity, make a note of the occasions where lack of integrity has let you down.

How did you feel when you acted without integrity?

Were you treating people the way that you like to be treated?

What were the consequences of your actions on these occasions?

Do you have a role model for behaviour? If so, do you trust this person?

If, from this reflection, you feel that your trust in yourself is lacking, then it may be worth revisiting the chapter on emotional intelligence (← p. 87) and in particular the sections on emotional self-awareness and self-management.

Developing trusting relationships

Trusting yourself even in the most difficult of situations is the foundation for building bridges and forming trusting relationships. It depends not only upon treating others the way that you would like to be treated but also finding out what really matters to other people – what motivates them, annoys them or stimulates their thinking.

Example To find out whom you consider to be trustworthy, consider the following exercise. (*This exercise or a variation of it often turns up in books or training courses, so you may have come across it before. Even so, it is always worth revisiting from time to time. This exercise should always be treated in a confidential way; don't show it to anyone and destroy it when you have finished.*)

- on a blank piece of paper draw three circles, one inside each other;
- in the innermost circle put the names of all the people that you trust – you shouldn't have to think about this for long;
- in the next circle put the names of people that you are unsure about – sometimes you trust them, at other times you don't;
- in the outer circle put people you definitely don't trust at all, at any time.

Look at your circles of trust and make a note of why you:

- trust people in your inner circle;
- are unsure about some in the middle circle;
- don't trust other people at all in the outer circle.

First, look out for trusting behaviour, body language that shows sincerity, actions that show concern for you and the environment, and prized values. You may come to the conclusion that you don't trust some people because you don't know them well enough. If this is the case, think how you can find out more about them. Some people appear more naturally guarded than others. Does this prevent you from developing a trusting relationship with them? Do you naturally trust people who appear to be warm and friendly as opposed to people who are quiet or withdrawn? If so, are you always right in your judgements or assumptions? Asking these questions will help you to understand why trusting some people is more difficult than trusting others. First appearances are sometimes, but not always, an indication of how trustworthy somebody may be, as shown below:

Manager A   is naturally gregarious and finds it easy to talk to people. On first meeting she appears warm and friendly, makes good eye contact and is happy to talk about work and related problems. But this manager is not good at doing what she says she will do and frequently lets people down. As a result she loses the trust of colleagues.

Manager B   is a quiet person who takes some time to get to know. At first he appears to find it difficult to form relationships. However, not only is he a very good listener when people come to him with queries or problems but he is also very quick to deal with problems and to find solutions. Trust in him grows as people get to know him.

Knowing who to trust and who to be wary of was a major issue during the Second World War. This was demonstrated by a group of Russian Jews, known as the Bielski Partisans, who collaborated to avoid capture by the Nazis and provide a safe haven for those who escaped the Holocaust. Trust bound them together and increased their chances of success, and collaboration encouraged everyone to endorse the risks necessary for survival. This trust was built upon knowing that Jews needed to help and trust each other, as this extract from Kagan and Cohen's *Surviving the Holocaust with the Russian Jewish Partisans* (1998) illustrates.

> 'They …won the respect of many villagers who were opposed to the Germans … any Jew who found his way to the group would be welcomed, regardless of age, sex, or position, so that those escaping from the ghettos would have a place to go. No Jew would ever be sent back to the hell he or she had fled from; mutual aid, responsibility and unity would be the guiding principles.'

This trust was built on the fact that 'We know you are a Jew and that you want to be saved from the Holocaust – for that reason we know we can trust you to be loyal.' Trust also arose from having a trustworthy leader and openly debating the nature and purpose of the group.

Although this is an extreme example of how trusting relationships can develop, it does show that criteria and goals as well as being interested in individuals are necessary to develop trust. Of course being trustworthy yourself and knowing how to develop trust in others are also important.

Reaching out to others – displaying your trust and removing barriers

If to developing trust exists a barrier, then taking the lead in removing it needs to come from you! First, you need to demonstrate that you are without reproach and totally trustworthy before you can expect trust to be returned and sustained. Being empathic towards others is the foundation of forming trusting relationships. (*If you haven't already done so, read Chapter 8: Empathy,* ← p. 132.) Treating other people as more important than yourself is an important connection between empathy and trust. Empathy, like trust, starts with understanding yourself. Now that you understand how and why you trust, you can reach out and not only encourage others to trust in you but also help them to develop their trust. Open the next suitcase and take a look at behaviour that demonstrates trust and the feelings that are likely to fuel it.

Reflective Suitcase

How do you show that you are confident that people can do a good job? Your behaviour will be different when you know that you are dealing with somebody who is competent at their job, as opposed to someone you feel is useless.

Take time now to appraise your feelings and behaviour to both of these types of people. Consider these questions:

Do you treat both people fairly?

Do you treat them as being more important than you?

Do you listen to their concerns with equal empathy and understanding?

Do you treat them both as human beings?

Do you give them equal time to air their views, comments or concerns?

Do you sit down when listening to them and avoid looking at your watch or the clock?

Do you help both to learn and develop?

If your answers indicate that you treat people you trust to be competent in a different manner to those who you don't trust, then it is unlikely that others view *you* as being trustworthy. This view of you is likely to be held by everyone in everything you do, including your family and friends.

If you have identified that you may be perceived as being untrustworthy, rectify this perception and remove barriers to others trusting you. Here are some suggestions:

1. Become reliable – as solid as a rock – walk the talk. Endeavour to do what you say you are going to do. If problems occur that prevent you from achieving this, make it known straight away. Do not cover up.

2. Be open and honest, share information and concerns with others. Speak out – offer your opinion.

3. Examine your attitudes and beliefs – make sure you treat people fairly regardless of your opinion of them.

4. Be loyal – give criticism that is always constructive – face-to-face and where appropriate one-to-one. Always respect confidentiality.

5. Be positive and optimistic.

6. Give your time, be there for people, be ready to listen and to offer advice.

7. Give other people space and time, relax control, indicate that you trust them to be competent.

8. Believe in yourself and work to overcome fears.

9. Be flexible and be able to make tough decisions.

10. Understand that trust does not always involve being liked – it is about being ethical and authentic.

Consider this scenario of how a senior manager displays his trust and leadership:

Example   Despite his senior position in a food manufacturing company, William had a good rapport with people, always treating then consistently and as equals. When a crisis occurred in his department he immediately called together the people involved to discuss the situation. He discovered that the problem was being caused by shortage of staff and lack of knowledge of procedures. William's immediate action was to 'muck in' and work alongside the group until further people could be employed and trained. Through this flexible action he gave the group direction, raised moral and showed his trustworthiness.

Leadership and trust call for 'personal advertising'; making people aware of your capacity for trust is essential if you are to be taken seriously. Make sure that you don't hold back and use every available opportunity to promote your truthful, trustworthy image. The latter can only emerge if you engage in the process of self-awareness and feel emotionally comfortable with yourself and other people. Sustaining such an image depends upon exercising human compassion, open communication that always seeks out the truth, and an equal relationship with others which is free from 'put downs'.

Conversely, if you find it difficult to know whether or not to trust people then spend time finding out. Make sure that you see beyond the image to check fully for trustworthiness and integrity. This requires knowing people well, listening and watching their behaviour in a variety of situations and using this information to judge their thoughts and intentions. When you know people well you will understand where their loyalties lie.

Practising Suitcase

 Keep these suggestions in mind: always be on the lookout for barriers to developing and keeping trust. Think, 'The barrier may have been put up by me.' What can I do to bring it down?

Leadership that builds trust in organisations

Trust in organisations 'oozes out of the brickwork', embodying all that an organisation stands for: its integrity, authenticity and empathy. True trust is embedded in and influences both the structure and culture of an organisation. Employees, customers and profit all share equal importance. To understand this in action, take a look at the two contrasting organisations below and the effect of differing levels of trust on employee motivation.

Example 1   *A high-trust organisation*

Trust in SEMCO is based on openness: internal walls are kept to a minimum and individuals do not have their own desk and instead work wherever they can find space. Managerial staff are trusted to set their own salaries and shop floor workers set their own productivity targets. The company books are open to everyone and training to understand and interpret them is given if needed. Because an ethos of trust exists, formalities can be kept to a minimum – the need for meetings and approval at different levels is deemed unnecessary. The owner and sometime CEO Ricardo Semler initiated this ethos of trust. His integrity and leadership allowed him to develop this by initially rearranging the organisational structure into groups of manageable sizes and encouraging responsibility through dialogue and knowledge.

Example 2   *A low-trust organisation*

In this example trust is continually in a downward spiral that began 10–12 years ago. In this time the organisational culture has changed from being empathic and caring and supportive, 'a good company to work for', to a culture of blame fear and suspicion. Continual downsizing, on average at least once a year, which has been handled badly, has been the prime cause of this cultural change and loss of trust. Coupled with this senior management within a primarily top down structure have remained aloof and detached blaming employees for the slightest mistake. There is also a closed system of communication and consultation is almost non-existent. What now remains is a defensive, shattered workforce keeping their heads down, failing to trust, loath to change and fearful for their jobs. The downsizing is still continuing together with a distrust of management and a very demoralised workforce.

One of the most striking differences between these two organisations is that in the high-trust organisation employees are motivated to take responsibility. Their access and knowledge of the company books engages them in a concern for the company's profits. This openness, knowledge and involvement ensure effective communication, a sense of being in control in your own part of the organisation's operations. It also ensures that employees can be certain whether or not they are being treated fairly. Here everyone is encouraged to develop their leadership potential and to take responsibility. In the low-trust organisation employees are kept in the dark and the blame culture ensures that they become fearful for their future. Building trust in organisations has to start with a leader who trusts themselves and has the vision to set the scene for wholescale trust to develop.

Reflective Suitcase

 If you are the leader of an organisation or a department, consider for a moment the levels of trust that exist among your workforce. (You have already had the opportunity to examine to what degree you trust yourself and how you reach out to form trusting relationships.) Consider first the behaviour of individuals. Answer the following questions.

- what proportion of your workforce do you feel you can trust?;
- do you trust people equally at all levels of the organisation?;
- what behaviour do you look for when deciding whether or not to trust?

Now consider yourself and the ethos of the organisation. Provide evidence to support your answers to the following questions. Use these questions as a starting point when discussing trust with your board or senior managers.

- do you consider that trust in your organisation is important? If so, why?;
- is your organisation a high-trust organisation or a low-trust one? How do you know?;
- do you think that all employees are treated fairly? If you don't know, then maybe this is the time to ask them;
- is communication throughout the organisation open? Are two-way discussions and debates encouraged? Is feedback asked for and acted upon at all levels?

Just as with developing your individual field of trust it is important to be self-aware; developing trust throughout an organisation can only begin with knowledge of the status quo.

The benefits of increasing trust

According to the author of *The 7 Habits of Highly Effective People*, Stephen Covey, trust is ' the highest form of human motivation. It brings out the very best in people. But it takes it takes time and patience, and it doesn't preclude the necessity to train and develop people so that their competency can rise to the level of that trust' (1989). With trust, motivation and development working together the spin-offs are numerous, providing for the possibility of increased learning, risk taking, creativity, collaboration, communication and morale. All of this opens up the gates and encourages leadership to flourish.

Message 1. Trust begins with you.

Action   Be open, honest, flexible and approachable;

Mean what you say and do what you promise to do.

Message 2. It is important to know who you can trust.

Action   Get to know people really well;

Interact with people in as many different ways and situations as possible.

Message 3. Take the initative to overcome obstacles to trust.

Action   Take the lead and show that you are responsible and trustworthy;

Be visibly ethical and conscientious;

Treat and talk to all people as equals.

Message 4. A high-trust organisation is based on openness and integrity.

Action   Carry out a trust audit;

Find out in what areas the organisation is trusted and how trust needs to be strengthened.

10

Being a Leader

Chapter guide:

- knowing what drives you to be a leader;
- understanding how you can express yourself fully and freely;
- learning from others who express leadership.

Contents:

Introduction

Think of the leaders you have known and pick out the ones you regarded highly: consider for a moment why they were such good leaders. You may come up with a list that includes: being passionate, positive, confident, optimistic, cheerful, caring, good communicators who were always fair in their dealings with people. Or maybe it was their integrity, keenness, enthusiasm, interest, honesty or some indefinable quality that they possessed that you admired? Still there may be something that you can't quite put your finger on, but you feel that it may have something to do with how they were as a person, how they made you feel about yourself or how you noticed they dealt with other people. If you can identify any of the above in your leaders, chances are that at some point in their lives they crossed an important threshold that signified the start of their personal journey as a leader. It undoubtedly means that being a leader touches every aspect of their lives and these leadership qualities have risen above being something that they express within an occupation.

This chapter shows how you can cross the magical point where you develop a deeper understanding of what being a leader means to you. You have had the opportunity to understand what leadership is and how it can be learned and expressed (Part One), and how to develop your leadership capabilities (← p. 27). Now you can extend your knowledge and find out: Who is the real leader in you? What drives you? What do you care about? And to ask: What does being a leader mean to me? Am I there yet? If not, what am I looking for? Every leadership journey is unique and is a combination of psychology, upbringing, education and experience.

For many people adversity leads to a highly developed understanding of themselves and the meaning of life around them. The extreme suffering of the Jewish people during the Second World War was the catalyst for the writings of two authors whose in-depth contributions are valuable illustrations of self-knowledge and how it contributes to taking responsibility and being a leader.

The first author, Anne Frank, wrote her famous diary between the ages of 13 and 15 while hiding from the Nazis in the Netherlands, displaying a unique understanding of personal authenticity and relationships. Out of the boredom of her self-imposed imprisonment and a wish to communicate, she wrote her diaries. During these two years she watched and listened to the adults who came and went in her world; from this experience she had no wish to emulate any of the role models who shared her existence. Her real self during this period was her understanding of her ability to write and to recall the suffering of the Dutch under the regime of the Nazis and her aim was for her diaries to be valuable evidence after the war had finished. But in doing so she also recorded a remarkable understanding of human beings, asking, 'Can you tell me why people go to such lengths to hide their real selves?' (*The Diary of Anne Frank*). She not only noticed when people trusted or distrusted each other but also that she herself behaved differently with different people. She understood how and when her attitude to people changed and how she made leaps forward in her thinking. Her self-awareness at such a young age was amazing.

The second author, Viktor Frankl, was a prisoner in a Nazi concentration camp. He wrote about the importance of understanding who you are as a person, your reason for living and how these thoughts influence your behaviour. His survival at the hands of the Nazis was due to his determination to find a reason for staying alive amidst the suffering and death he witnessed in his own family and fellow Jews. During his time in captivity he noticed that people who could retain a reason for living no matter how small or how trivial stood a greater chance of survival. A general state of mind appeared to be picked up by the Nazi guards and those indicating more depression or a greater loss of self-respect were more likely to be tortured or condemned to death. Frankl's writing illustrates the importance of knowing your purpose in life, what drives you, and taking responsibility to live out this purpose in a fair and ethical way.

The conscious leader

Who are you as a leader?

Do you really know?

Do you acknowledge that emotions influence your behaviour?

Do you see yourself as others see you?

Does your behaviour reflect an ethical and trustworthy you, capable of thinking, reasoning, learning and taking responsibility?

Do you know what drives you?

If you answer 'yes' to most of these questions then it is likely that you are conscious of your leadership role, but you may learn more about yourself from this section. However, if you have yet to cross the invisible line between holding a leadership position and being a real leader or if you are still searching for that elusive boundary, then understanding the meaning of being a conscious leader will help you on your journey.

To become a conscious leader requires knowledge of your inner self and, in particular, an understanding of your 'leadership' brain. This requires knowledge of how your emotional and cognitive elements interact, and how your brain works to drive you in one direction or another. You now have the opportunity to assess your leadership behaviour and take with you on your journey knowledge that will enable you to grow and change at appropriate moments.

In Chapter 6 we saw how emotions cause feelings that affect behaviour. Becoming a conscious leader demands that you add to this an understanding of the basic drives of human nature. Let's look at the work of professors at Harvard Business School, Paul Lawrence and Nitin Nohria (2002). Their research led them to determine that as humans we have four basic, innate drives that originate in the limbic system, interacting with our conscious brain to affect our decision-making, learning preferences, skill base and concept of life. The four drives are:

1. The drive to acquire.
2. The drive to bond.
3. The drive to learn.
4. The drive to defend.

They argue that we experience each of these drives independently and being driven by one does not influence a need to be driven by any of the others. They understand that although the drives are not definitive, they do encompass the major routes.

It is important to understand the basic characteristics of each drive. Let's look at them in some detail.

1. *The drive to acquire:* urges us to compete with others in a variety of ways, ranging from acquiring possessions that imply status or maybe moving up the organisational hierarchical ladder to enjoying perks and privileges not available to others. The basis of this prehistoric drive was competition for food and survival that was the only way in which Early Man could survive. However, as we realise today, the drive to acquire is never satisfied, it merely fuels our existence.

2. *The drive to bond:* is shared by all humans. This drive enables humans to form social relationships and to cooperate with each other. It is the drive that enables us to develop the capacity for, and to express, empathy, love, trust, compassion and caring. It is through bonding that we develop the capacity for partnerships, friendships and belonging. Exercising bonding encourages fairness, loyalty and respect, but any relationship includes both the need to be competitive and the need to cooperate.

3. *The drive to learn:* is an innate drive that enables humans to satisfy their curiosity about themselves, the world and their place in it. It is through the drive to learn that we come to understand who we are, what we are good at and how much we need to learn. It is a drive that can be satisfied by acquiring knowledge, working with others, reflecting or obtaining qualifications.

4. *The drive to defend:* is a reactive drive that thrives on anger when any of the above drives are threatened. Any threat to possessions, position, friendship or partners will trigger a defensive reaction. As will any threat to our self-image or our tried and trusted beliefs about the world and ourselves. This drive operates from the limbic system of the brain with little input from reasoning and knowledge.

These basic drives appear more prominently in some people than in others. For example, in the field of competitive sport, to be the world's best is an overriding factor in training. In politics, the drive to be in a position of power can often be prominent in general elections. With academics or creative, forward-thinking people, the drive to learn is like a drug. 'Neighbours from hell' are usually driven by the need to defend.

Being driven by our basic instincts is natural for all of us and we usually follow them in conjunction with our partly genetically-programmed cognitive abilities.

Knowing yourself in terms of your instinctive drives and understanding the need, when appropriate, to either balance these drives or accelerate a certain drive is an integral part being a leader. Reasoning and logical thought are influenced not only by basic emotions but also how we are influenced, sometimes without noticing, by the attitudes of other people. Becoming a leader demands that we recognise the multitude of influences that bombard us everyday and that we understand our unique way of dealing with them. Knowing whether or not we allow our sense of responsibility to be compromised or whether we become complacent about some issues is crucial. Do we allow ourselves to be so driven in one particular area that we become blind to our other responsibilities and the needs of other people? For example, workaholics may drive themselves so hard to achieve in their career that they neglect family and friends and adopt a lifestyle that is detrimental to their health. In doing so they take responsibility for only one aspect of their lives.

Take a moment to reflect on your leadership brain; think about how and why you are driven to behave as you do. Referring to each of the four drives above, ask:

- how strong and prominent is each drive in your life?;
- does one drive propel you at the expense of the others?;
- do you experience equality in the drives?;
- how strong is your drive to defend? Does it prevent you from exercising your other drives adequately?

How does your reaction to the four drives fit in with who you would like to be as a leader? Are you still on the right course to becoming the leader you would like to be? If yes, carry on; if no, then what changes do you need to make to get back on course?

Becoming a conscious leader requires that you recognise the part these basic drives play in your life, their interaction, and possible dominance. A conscious leader will be striving to balance (but utilise when appropriate) the drives of acquiring, bonding and learning, while guarding against the overwhelming desire to over-defend.

The adaptable leader

Exercising leadership is about understanding how you behave and the effect your behaviour has on motivating others. An adaptable leader is able to:

- learn from mistakes;
- give and take, work towards win–win situations;
- reflect and change behaviour;
- express leadership in a variety of situations.

As you practise leadership you will come to recognise that there are certain behaviours that you favour and that these form your leadership style. However, it is important that you occasionally evaluate the effectiveness of your style in a variety of situations.

Imagine that you start a new job and it is your brief to turn around a failing department or organisation. You are faced with low morale among the workforce, a low order book and falling profits. The following example illustrates two opposing leadership styles and their effects.

Example   Jim takes over a manufacturing department in a large corporate organisation. The profits of this organisation are falling despite a full order book. Morale within the department is low and communication is almost non-existent. Jim has empathy with the workforce because he knows that their previous manager's leadership style was 'Do as I tell you', 'Do it this way' and 'Do it now'! This has had a negative affect on morale, the willingness to take responsibility and on the improvements necessary for efficiency and hence turnover and profit of the department.

Jim understands that in order to increase motivation it is essential to include everybody in thinking and decision-making at all levels. His attitude is that everybody's opinions matter and that these and relevant information are communicated effectively at all levels. To achieve this he communicates his vision to everyone, organises the workforce into teams and initiates opportunities to communicate with each other. He sets these teams two major tasks, one is to improve their working practice and the other is to help each other to improve their individual skills. The positive effects of his actions are that individual responsibility increases and people are able to act on their ideas. They are able, through discussion, to modify and improve their own and others' ideas and a larger percentage start to see the need to develop their own learning and to encourage others to learn and develop. All these actions, coupled with the fact that communication and debate have increased both at individual and collective level, have helped to bring about a change in how people think.

Your leadership style may be very different to Jim's but just as effective in a similar situation. Being a leader demands that you recognise your leadership style and its effectiveness, but that you are able to adapt your thinking and behaviour when appropriate.

Research carried out by Hay/McBer and reported by Goleman (*Harvard Business Review*, March/April, 2000) suggests that successful leaders are flexible in their approach, know their dominant style but by experiential learning are able to be flexible and employ a variety of approaches. Six different approaches that derive from the emotional and leadership brain have been identified by Goleman, four of which have a positive affect on others:

1. *'Authoritative' leadership style:* this is the style of a self-confident, visionary leader who has a strong sense of empathy with others. This style has the message – change is necessary, jump on board with me and together we will make it happen.

2. *'Affinitive' leadership style:* here the predominantly empathic leader considers people and their needs above all else. How people communicate and get along together is the key to how this style of leader motivates others.

3. *'Democratic' leadership style:* collaboration and communication are important to this style of leader. They regard consensus as being essential for motivation and favour teamwork.

4. *'Coaching' leadership style:* this is the style adopted by a leader who understands the relationship between leadership and learning and therefore developing others is important to improving performance.

Two negative leaderships styles are also identified by Goleman – 'coercive' and 'pacesetting' leadership. Both of these styles are strongly connected with the drive to achieve and the need to control. They are both 'tell' and 'do' styles, often used by leaders who lack empathy or self-confidence and who regard telling people what to do as being the quick and easy way of getting results. However, the opposite is often the result, as the long-term use of both styles is likely to have a negative effect on morale and motivation. Used very sparingly and at the right moment both styles can be effective, especially in a crisis situation.

How do our leadership mentors fit into these styles? Ghandi displayed the empathic 'authoritative' style. He was against a coercive style and instead of telling people not to engage in violence used his own passive hunger strikes to turn their views around. Shackleton, on the other hand, had a predominantly 'affinitive' style, believing in the importance of comradeship and keeping everybody positive during their stressful times surviving in Antarctica. When the going got extremely tough and he needed to take his people with him quickly and safely, he turned to the sometimes negative leadership style of 'pacesetting'. He lead by example, sharing the physical and emotional rigours of his men. For example, he was the first to discard sentimental personal possessions, empathising when he had to tell the men why and to what degree they needed to discard their belongings.

To become an adaptable leader it is important not only to understand your prominent style but also other styles that it may be appropriate for you to utilise from time to time. To do this effectively you must be a self-confident leader.

The self-confident leader

When Sir Edmund Hillary was a boy he was regarded by teachers as being physically weak. He lacked confidence in almost everything he did, believing from the start that he would not succeed. All this now seems unimaginable as the first man to climb to the summit of Everest has gone from strength to strength, not only in his climbing achievements, but also in the leadership he has shown helping the people of Nepal to develop their country. The change Hillary has undergone shows how he has grown in confidence as a leader, being confident not only in his own abilities, but in the way he perceives he is able to help others develop their lives. His life has focused on extending the limits of human ability. How Sir Edmund made that change is not only admirable but also illustrates the impact that a self-confident leader can have on others.

Self-confidence in leadership emerges at different points in people's lives and is often linked to success that is achieved through support and learning or the emergence and recognition of a natural talent.

A self-confident leader can usually be recognised because they:

- speak out when needed;
- follow a passion for which they have a talent;
- are positive in their behaviour and thoughts;
- are willing to help and support others;
- want to make a difference in the world;
- show concern and compassion for other people.

How does a self-confident leader emerge? It is important not to assume that all people who appear loud, articulate or outgoing are confident leaders. These people may well be extroverts whose dominant learning style is linguistic, and their loudness may well be covering up for a lack of confidence. A self-confident leader may appear quietly spoken, a good listener and may take some time to get to know. Underneath you are likely to find someone who recognises their vision and passion in life, something that has often been referred to as 'a calling'. But most importantly they will be someone with a positive *inner voice*.

Your inner voice is talking to you all the time and can appear as negative or positive thoughts. Think for a moment about the thoughts you have before you tackle something which you know is going to be a problem, such as having a meeting where you have to confront somebody about deficiencies in their work. Do your thoughts go something like this, 'I know I'm not going to be able to do this. I'll say all the wrong things?' Or do they go like this, 'This is going to be difficult but I have to be prepared and I need to find out certain things that I can use as evidence', 'I'll be difficult but I can work through it to give us both an agreeable outcome'? The difference is whether you listen to your negative or positive inner voice. Listening to a negative voice will enforce a lack of confidence, a view that there are winners and losers in situations and prevent you from learning from the experience. Before you can make changes to your inner voice you need to recognise the effect it has on your behaviour.

Reflective Suitcase

Think back over the last week or month:

- make a note of when your inner voice was negative – notice how this negativity affected your behaviour and motivation;

- notice when your inner voice was positive and your behaviour was positive as a result;

- were there any times when you were able to change your negative voice into a positive one? If so, how did your behaviour change?

Changing a negative inner voice to a positive one builds self-confidence. Like all changes in behaviour it takes practice and time, and you may require help to a varying degree, ranging from family and friends to experts.

Developing self-confidence in leadership is intertwined with developing a positive inner voice, and understanding how to give, ask for and receive positive 'strokes'. According to Steiner, 'People interact to get strokes. Strokes can be physical or verbal ... Verbal strokes are statements that acknowledge some feature of another person in a positive way' (1997). Strokes are a way of acknowledging your love, friendship or allegiance to another person. Receiving mainly positive strokes, as opposed to negative ones, can influence your inner voice. If you know that people feel positive about you it can boost your confidence, not only to feel positive about yourself, but also to have a positive approach to dealing with difficult situations and challenging learning. It is only through this self-confidence and self-awareness that you can understand who you are as a leader and be capable of adapting your leadership style when circumstances demand.

The rebel leader

Becoming a rebel is synonymous with knowing who you are as a leader, having the courage to let the world know what you can contribute and yet always acting in an ethical and honest way. It does not mean acting without responsibility or being the cause of anarchy!

Rebel leaders are the ones who:

■ press for change, move the boundaries;

■ challenge the status quo and only comply when they are sure that it is the right thing to do;

■ are ethical and follow the law;

■ make informed decisions through effective research;

■ understand the importance of creative and critical thinking;

■ rise to challenges and problem solving.

We can argue that both Pankhurst and Ghandi were rebel leaders who took their behaviour to extremes because they felt that was necessary to fight their cause. We are not suggesting that you chain yourself to railings or go on a hunger strike, but that you use your knowledge of the world in general and your daily environment to understand what important changes you need to influence or instigate. Such changes may vary from knowing why you disagree with the Community Charge and lobbying your MP for changes, to knowing how and why you can influence supermarkets to sell more local produce. In recognising that changes are necessary it is vital you have the relevant knowledge before you act. Getting your facts right is as important as understanding your leadership strengths and knowing the most effective way for you to act. By now you should have an understanding of both positive and negative leadership styles, you will understand the importance of balance in your intuitive drives and you will know what your emotional triggers are likely to be. Using your self-knowledge is just as important as researching your subject. They are both tools of a rebel leader.

Being a rebel leader is also about changing from being passive to being proactive in whatever situation you find yourself. Do you ever sit in a meeting and form opinions but never have the courage to voice them? Instead, you wait until you are out of the meeting and moan and groan to others. Do you often hear yourself saying 'they' should do something about it because you don't think it is your place or that you are in the right position to act? Even in this small way, being a rebel is about having the courage to speak out and voice your opinion about change or your suggestion to a problem. If you find this difficult then perhaps your inner voice is the barrier.

It is one thing having the knowledge, confidence and will to act and speak, but can you be sure that what you have to contribute is founded not only on the right evidence but is also well thought out? To be a rebel leader you have to be sure about what you are saying. Challenging requires patience, determination and the ability to think, solve problems, think laterally, and be constructively critical.

Message 1. **Leadership is about knowing your purpose in life.**

Action Understand how the major drives in your life affect your behaviour;

Address any imbalances in how you are driven.

Message 2. **Taking responsibility requires balancing internal drives with external influences.**

Action Be ethical and behave with integrity;

Avoid behaviour which is influenced by outside criteria which you may not agree with.

Message 3. **Leadership requires the self-confidence to challenge and to question and the ability to be constructively critical, adaptable and pro-active.**

Action Poke your head up above the parapet, be visible, speak out for what you believe is right;

Ask awkward and difficult questions, be persistent until you have the right answer or get to the truth.

Message 4. **Understanding different leadership styles is important in acknowledging the significance of your own leadership behaviour.**

Action Try out appropriate styles in different situations;

Learn from any inappropriate behaviour and change your behaviour.

Part

3

Followers and Leadership

11

Beyond the Rubicon

Chapter guide:

- an introduction to the challenge of working with others;
- understanding power and its relation to leadership;
- the stages of conflict and bringing about resolution.

Contents:

Introduction

So far we have focused on you as a leader, but leadership is not something that occurs in isolation. Leadership involves *others* and is influenced by its *context*. We will now focus on relationships with others and Part Four will explore context in more detail.

In a dynamic relationship with others how does leadership work – or not work? Warren Bennis uses a story that explains this. He tells how Nikita Khrushchev came to the US and met reporters in Washington. The first question asked was: 'Today you talked about the hideous rule of your predecessor, Stalin. You were one of his closest aides and colleagues during those years you now denounce. What were you doing all that time?' Apparently Khrushchev's face grew red and he shouted, 'Who asked that?' No-one answered. So again he roared, even louder, 'Who asked that?' Silence. 'That's what I was doing,' answered Khrushchev.

Tyrants suppress others; leadership transforms followers. Leadership is a relationship with others and therefore you cannot understand leadership without understanding followership. Leadership requires high expectations of followers and belief in their ability to achieve goals. Do you have this expectation and belief in those you work with? If you had to make a very difficult decision would they follow you? Followers are not stupid, they choose who they follow.

Now imagine we stand by the Rubicon, the river that divides us from where we are to where we think we should be; which once crossed means irrevocable commitment. To go forward requires the next two stages of leadership: connecting with and engaging others for action, and challenging and transforming your organisation so all can express leadership. Not everyone will cross, but for those who do we will prepare you for the journey with the ability to understand the relationship between power, influence and leadership. We will show you how conflict develops and how to resolve it. What can we learn from crossing the Rubicon? Can we distinguish powerholders from leaders? How do you connect with others to enable them to be followers and leaders themselves?

Knowledge Bank

On 1st January 49 BC the consuls in Rome put into action the removal of Julius Caesar as head of the Republic. There was a belief that no one man should rule for too long and over his 10-year rule Caesar had made some enemies. Now his opponents had put in place the process to settle the matter after two years of trying. The Senate decided that if Caesar had not laid down his command by a certain date he would be acting against the Republic.

On 10th January Caesar received the news from a courier. He was at Gallia Cisalpina and his response was to send a troop of soldiers towards Rimini that lay beyond the narrow river Rubicon on the boundary of his province. The bulk of his soldiers were still in Gaul. He joined his men at the Rubicon that was swollen after heavy rain. Here Caesar stopped and reviewed his situation. The choice he was about to make would decide not only his fate but that of thousands of others, the Republic itself and even the whole of the known world.

Caesar stood silent. He knew that to go across would mean war and the death of many men. If he didn't cross he would probably be arrested and tried for treason. He reportedly said, 'To refrain from crossing will bring me misfortune; but to cross will bring misfortune to all men.' He stood at the Rubicon and hesitated with his thoughts.

Eventually Caesar moved and said, 'The die must be cast' and crossed the Rubicon, leading his soldiers into the city we know today as Rimini. So began a civil war that was to last nearly five years, with many dying. The outcome was to shake the foundations of the Roman world.

For Caesar, the Rubicon was a pivotal moment. He held power and had to decide how to use it. Was he right and just or selfish and wrong? These are questions leaders often have to address. What we learn from this moment in history is that our actions often set off chains of events that don't just affect us but many others. Leadership requires taking responsibility and we often see this lacking in organisations. Decisions are too often taken without responsibility for their consequences.

Practising Suitcase

1. You are the director of a company and are under pressure to reduce costs even though profits are good. There is an option of replacing employees in the UK and outsourcing the work to a part of the world where salaries are much cheaper. To do so will mean many redundancies but the bottom line will improve short term. Another option is to reduce the number of employees but keep most and focus on improving their performance, service to the customer and teamwork. Long term you know this choice means customers would be more likely to stay and build up trust in the company, resulting in more business. What would you do?

2. You are the head of a primary school in a village that is expanding fast. Most of the children come from poorer homes where issues such as shift work and parents who did not enjoy their schooling influence school activities. Over the years with your staff you have created a school where the pupils enjoy challenges and work hard. The government is more concerned with targets and looking at performance in a narrow way. Do you carry on with what you believe is right and ambitious or do you follow the government's mandate and focus on its priorities?

In the first scenario above the director convinced the rest of the board and shareholders to take the second option for two years and give a strengthening strategy a chance instead of adopting a cost-cutting strategy for short-term goals.

In the second scenario the head and staff agreed to move forward by spending as little time as possible on the government's priorities to show they had done the work focusing more time on their ambitious work in the school that was changing the lives of the pupils.

What have been the Rubicon moments in your life?

Power, influence and leadership

Power

One of the dynamics that affect working with people is personal *power* and its relationship to leadership. We all have power of some form but not everyone has the motive or resources to use it. Power takes many forms, from pure coercion – making people do something they don't want to – to using information or personality. Personal power comes from a variety of sources and individuals may have one or several of these sources at their disposal. They include:

Expert power – the power of knowledge.

Referent power – based on how you relate to others, sometimes known as charismatic power.

Legitimate power – based on formal position or role in a hierarchy.

Reward power – having control of desired resources.

Coercive power – using negative sanctions or fear.

Information power – having access to information not everyone has but is valuable to them.

Connection power – based on who you know and who respects you.

In most interpersonal situations there is a balance of power. This is because everyone has power of one sort or another. What power do you have and how do you use it? (Diagram 4 Power Net.)

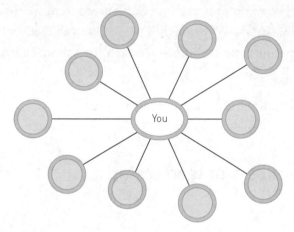

Diagram 4 Power net

Practising Suitcase

 You are in the centre of a group of people who have an important effect on your work – they will come from a variety of roles and positions and are probably both inside and outside the organisation. Identify them. What type of power (from the list of different sources above) does each person have in relation to you. Do they have the right to decide what you do? What information do you need? What is their power based on? What sort of power do *you* have in relation to them? You will see that power is a two-way relationship.

Which of these power sources do you see at work? You may see all of them, but which one is used the most? This will tell you about the culture of the organisation so be aware of this for the next part when we explore culture (p. 270 ➜).

Power, like leadership, is a relationship between people. Like leadership, power has purpose. Leadership, however, differs from this in that it cannot be separated from the needs and goals of the followers. The relationship between leaders and followers is based on trust and mutual respect whereby both work toward a common purpose through collaboration.

Those who wield power often do so to control people or situations. To control things such as money, tools, energy or mineral resources is an act of power, not leadership. This is because *things* do not have motives or needs whereas people do. Those who use power may treat people as things but leadership doesn't. The idea of military leadership that is based on making people do what you want them to do is not always leadership but use of power and position. When people want to follow because they and you both believe in the same outcome then it is leadership. Therefore all leaders are potential or actual holders of power, but not all powerholders are leaders.

There are two key points to remember about power:

- power is not an infinite resource;
- the amount of power one person has in relation to another depends upon the other person's *perception* of that power, how strong they believe it to be, whether the other's particular power base has any value or meaning for them, and whether they believe that the power will actually be used in an attempt to influence them.

Influence

Let's return to the Rubicon. You are faced with an opportunity to run your organisation or department. You want to use leadership to do this. How would you convince the employees that you were the right person and what would be the first thing you would do as an act of leadership? How would you ensure success?

In interacting with others to express your leadership you need to understand *influence* as well as power. Power is a resource but without influence it can be ineffective.

Knowledge Bank

 *Influence* is an active process whereby one person or group modifies the attitudes or behaviour of another or others. Therefore influence is only successful when there is a change in attitudes, beliefs or behaviour. Power is a resource that gives an individual the potential to influence. How someone influences others depends on context, timescale and the individual.

How do you apply this knowledge to the questions above? You have two choices. If you know where you want to go and have already decided on the solution to a problem, the strategy you may use is as follows:

You will set the scene by identifying the problem or opportunity and put forward your proposal. You may invite reactions, at the end of which you will summarise the discussion, deal with the objections either using persuasion or authority, check that everyone understands and agree who is going to do what and by when. This approach may be successful but it can cause resentment and the outcome is compliance.

A different strategy is more effective if you require other people's commitment:

You will state *their* view of the problem and then ask how others see the situation. Together you work on an agreement to resolve the problem or opportunity and look for the solution using as many of the others' ideas as possible. This gains commitment but takes longer. However, the joint agreement will have the commitment of everyone because they are being pulled rather than pushed into something.

There will be occasions for both strategies, for example, new legislation may require the first to ensure it is carried out immediately, whereas improving customer service will require the second. Please do not regard this as manipulative – influence and power are always present when we interact with others. Understanding the complexities of these concepts will help your leadership potential. You make the moral decision of how and when to use this knowledge and that is why integrity and courage are also required in leadership.

Reflective Suitcase

When would you use the first strategy to influence others at work? When would you use the second strategy at work?

Powerlessness

Having explored power and influence we must examine something that also affects leadership – powerlessness.

We feel powerless when we are:

- ignored;
- on unfamiliar ground;
- exhausted;
- told what to do without a choice;
- controlled or manipulated;
- isolated in a group;
- kept in the dark;
- need approval.

We feel powerful when we are:

- energetic;
- receive positive feedback;
- clear about our own goals;
- healthy;

- in a supportive group;

- believe in and trust ourselves;

- knowledgeable;

- telling a good joke.

Organisations are more effective if they emphasise 'power with' rather than 'power over' which just leads to compliance and reduced performance. When everyone can use their power and influence positively it is a healthy environment as long as the focus is on achieving the goal not scoring points. Managers who say they do not have time for this are using an excuse for maintaining control. That control will not result in better outcomes and that is why so many pursue short-term goals such as cost-cutting and targets that will only postpone what is really required.

In a control system knowledge is lost if the person doing the job isn't given the chance to influence; it suppresses the human need to control one's own life, resulting in stress; it demotivates the individual from doing their best, resulting in disassociation from their work; and, it takes away any sense of responsibility from the employee, resulting in their feeling powerless and certainly not being able to develop and use their leadership.

Of course, there will be those who want to have power over others but research shows that individuals and organisations perform best when they work on the basis of shared responsibility rather than command and compliance. The word 'power' comes from a French word 'pouvoir', which means 'to be able' and it is this we must remember about power and its relationship with leadership.

Leaders develop their followers to become leaders themselves.

Conflict and resolution

Most people dislike conflict and many will walk away rather than try to resolve it. Yet to cross your Rubicon and make your leadership a reality it is vital that you understand conflict and have a strategy to resolve it.

One of the key characteristics of conflict is its tendency to escalate until each side tries to destroy the other, with the belief that their action is legitimate. To prevent this happening regression must be halted. Those involved need to see each other as fellow human beings and take responsibility for how they behave and what they do. This is possible when those involved confront the reality of the situation and that includes what has transpired and what is currently happening. To resolve conflict in this way leaders must understand the escalation process, especially being able to identify where the points of no return occur.

The nine levels of conflict are grouped below in three phases and the boundaries to these are the key turning points. As we describe them, relate the phases to situations you have experienced or are aware of. To help, we are going to use three workplace scenarios for each phase.

Phase 1

In this phase the following characteristics are visible:

- the parties are mostly problem orientated;
- they have a different idea of what the problem is;
- together they still might be able to solve it;
- each sees the other's weaknesses as greater than their own;
- in order to resolve the issue they will abide by the existing norms and standards.

The scenario here is of two managers: the marketing manager, Peter, and the production manager, Jim. Peter is fed up with having to spend time apologising to customers because orders are late, while Jim is fed up with receiving orders he sees as unrealistic. The two meet and both raise examples of incidents that are causing the problem. As the conflict unfolds at this point it goes through three stages:

Stage 1: Discussion

Particular incidents stand out.

There is an awareness of tension building.

The parties are cautious and won't take any risks.

There is verbal confrontation.

A rational solution should still be possible.

The basic attitude is one of cooperation with an element of competition creeping in.

The issues are not resolved and so their meetings become more heated. Both regard their contribution to the business as more important than the other's.

Stage 2: Debate

The style becomes one of negotiation where psychological pressure is exerted.

Unfair tactics start to become acceptable.

Contradictions and weak points in the other side's arguments are noted so it becomes a point-scoring contest.

The confrontation is mainly verbal and rational but with some emotions creeping in.

Motives become mixed – there is uncertainty in what is being done.

The parties are now both cooperative and competitive.

The discussion between the two takes a more personal stance and they begin to attack each other rather than try to resolve the problem.

Stage 3: Deeds, not words

The parties begin to show their resistance non-verbally.

Each pushes their own ideas and shows their strong will.

They begin to say one thing but do another.

They insinuate that the other party says one thing and does another.

They are now mostly competitive with just an element of cooperation remaining.

Let's stop here and try to resolve the problem, as it is still resolvable at this stage. Both sides need to begin with how each understands the problem. It is agreed that the marketing manager should begin. Peter explains that he is under pressure to achieve sales targets and that the sales people often find themselves in the situation where a customer wants certain modifications to the product and they want it delivered quickly as hold-ups affect them. Without trying to defend himself he concludes. Meanwhile the production manager has been listening without comment.

Now it's time for Jim the production manager to explain how the modifications and deadlines affect his team and how he feels about it. This time Peter listens without interruption. The key is that each party listens without comment or trying to score points. Understanding how each is affecting other parts of the business, they then try together to work for a solution. They agree that the sales force must take responsibility for the pressure on production and that they need to persuade customers to either modify their requests or accept that they will take longer to achieve. Meanwhile production can explore ways of improving the time scales without reducing the quality of the product. They communicate their solutions and the business begins to run more smoothly.

At the same time another conflict has failed to be resolved. This time the scenario is a public service institution and the issue is about changing the hours of work. The change has come about after new legislation was introduced with the aim of reducing absenteeism. The trade union has become involved and having not resolved the issue in the first phase has progressed to this second phase with senior managers.

Phase 2: Neurosis

The conflict process is now characterised by a different set of features, such as:

- the interaction becomes highly competitive;
- each party looks for opportunities to bend the rules to their advantage and to look for deficiencies in the rules to use them against the other party;

- the major issues at stake become the mechanisms of the conflict itself, not the underlying problem;
- each doubts the integrity of the other;
- resentments and feelings of revenge build up.

The issue of absenteeism is not addressed and the focus is on the effects of the change in work hours. Defensive behaviours cannot be changed and the divide between the two sides becomes wider.

Stage 4: Fixed images

The parties imitate and caricature each other.

They look for supporters and build up coalitions among others whom they regard as being 'like us'.

They make promises to gain support and carry out campaigns to gain sympathy.

Each make stereotypes of each other and fix them in this image.

They then confirm the expectations of others by acting as expected.

Threats and angry exchanges fill the room and both sides begin to wonder where it will end. It is getting difficult to manoeuvre.

Stage 5: Loss of face

Attacks or threats are used, as one must not be seen to have lost.

Doubt is purged, behaviour ritualised and dissenters thrown out.

The double in the other side is recognised and fixed.

Each party degrades the other as much as they possibly can.

'At last we see them for what they really are' is heard.

There is now no room for compromise.

Finally, serious threats and words such as 'betrayal' abound. The issue of working hours is no longer raised, just insults.

Stage 6: Strategies of threat

> One side presents itself to the other in terms of the negative things they can do to them.
>
> The disadvantages of the current circumstances for the other side are emphasised.
>
> There is absolute commitment to the side so bridges have been burnt.
>
> One side will react to whatever the other does, only worse.
>
> Each lays down trip-wires for the other side.

To try and resolve this now is almost impossible but can be achieved with a third party who doesn't have an interest in taking either side. The first thing that needs to happen is to calm people down and this can be done by placing the two sides in different rooms. Each side is listened to and asked to say how they are feeling. These feelings must be brought out. Then both sides are encouraged to accept that absenteeism is a problem that must be resolved. The union believes that the solution isn't only changing working hours and puts forward other suggestions as each side explains their perception of the issue. The ideas from the union are discussed with the senior managers. Some are agreed to but not all. When both sides agree on what can be changed to improve absenteeism they are brought together to work out the best way forward for all.

For those who *do not* address the feelings and perceptions on both sides the conflict can continue to spiral. We may not see this in the workplace but we do see it in society. To show how this spiral of conflict continues we will use an example outside work, the political conflict in Northern Ireland during the 1990s. The parties refused to sit in the same room and would not speak to each other, making it really difficult to make any progress.

Phase 3: Self-destruction

At this phase of a conflict there is only self-interest at any price. The conflict is only concerned with its own process. This means:

■ destruction of the other party is more important than gaining anything for oneself;

■ norms and standards can be violated and broken legitimately;

- a compulsion to push on at any cost.

Children were intimidated on their way to school.

Stage 7: Inhuman

Preventative actions are paramount, so parties prepare to defend themselves.

Concentration is on destroying the other side.

Radical means are acceptable to get rid of the other party.

Goals are mainly preventative and defensive.

People were singled out and killed in their homes and public houses.

Stage 8: Attack on nerves

The aim is to attack the nerves of the other party to cut off their power supply.

This includes cutting off their means of retreat so there is no going back.

Finally to cut them off from their base and supporters.

Withdrawal is now impossible.

The final stage results in talks collapsing as parties refuse to believe others. When politicians try to make moves forward others in the party try to replace them.

Stage 9: No way back

Destructive goals dominate.

Calculations become irrational.

Withdrawal now becomes a worse fate than self-destruction.

The other side must be made to follow to disaster.

Conflict escalating in this way is totally destructive and it is imperative to keep parties talking so as not to allow things to reach this point. In Northern Ireland it was the Women's Coalition and MP Mo Molam who took the view that they should talk to anyone and everyone, because if they were talking they were not fighting. However, much of the talks had to go on in different rooms as the men wouldn't sit in the same room with each other. What can we learn from this destruction?

In the business world mergers work better when both sides keep talking and this can extend to government departments. These talks need not be only formal meetings, where each side defends themselves, but also informal meetings.

The leader's guide to resolving conflict

What are the key lessons from an understanding of conflict?

1. The earlier conflict is resolved the better, as the process shows. In leadership this means that not doing anything is not the best solution.

2. You need to establish:

   (a) issues – what issues emerge as key? What purpose does the conflict have in regard to the issues?

   (b) commitment – who is committed? In what way are they committed?

   (c) history – what have been the crucial events, turning points, attempts at resolution during the history of the conflict process? How much escalation has occurred?

   (d) parties – who are they in terms of groups and individuals? What is the interdependence of parties?

   (e) mechanisms – are positions fixed? What are the attitudes? What patterns of behaviour have emerged? What level of escalation has been reached?

3. When you have the information above it is time to act. If the conflict is beyond Phase 1 then rational discussions of the issue may result in further escalation.

4. Further on in the escalation it is better to begin with how each side feels. Get the feelings and emotions out. Then get each to explain how their feelings are making them behave. At this stage the issue has disappeared and you are focusing on each party understanding their feelings and behaviours so they can see what they are doing to each other. When awareness is made you can then deal with the issue from both sides.

Resolving conflict may be required of you as you move from self-leadership to leadership in groups. You will then be taking responsibility for yourself and others. But there is one more hazard to learn about before crossing your Rubicon.

The drama triangle

When leading others you need to understand a dangerous dynamic that sometimes occurs. What you see are 'games' that are played out that even the person playing the game is often unaware of. The three main destructive games that some people play are known as the 'drama triangle' (comes from Transactional Analysis).

Knowledge Bank

At each side of a drama triangle is a role: The first is the role of *rescuer*. This is someone who has learned to appear to offer help but they do so because it feeds a need in themselves. They may not really want to help or they end up doing more than is necessary, keeping the individual in a helpless state. The problem is that this person can end up resenting their role and feel angry and bitter but they don't know how to stop playing the rescuer. The person being rescued can also end up feeling angry because the rescuer is taking away their personal power.

At work the role of rescuer is often assumed by someone who is very poor at delegating, and yet at the same time they complain about the work they have to do because others are not perceived as being capable of that work. Working for someone like this results in employees feeling less and less confident about their own abilities.

The second role is the *victim*. This is someone who perhaps had something happen to them in childhood that led them to feel the world is a nasty place and everyone is out to get them. They learn to play helpless and can't make decisions. The victim will keep putting themselves into situations where they will again feel a victim and so justify their role. In relationships they will seek either a rescuer to save them or a persecutor who will put them down, so they can keep playing a victim. At work, they may play games such as 'kick me'. Their work will slide until they are 'kicked' by the manager, resulting in improvement, but will slide again until they are kicked again, and so it goes on.

The third role is the *persecutor*. They criticise and punish unfairly because it may make them feel better about themselves or they learned this behaviour from parents.

We see each of these roles in the workplace. You need to be aware of them so as not to be drawn into the triangle yourself because then you will not be able to express leadership.

Once drawn into the triangle playing any role you will at sometime end up playing one of the other or all three roles. Why do people get caught in this triangle and keep playing the roles? There is no easy answer, but it seems that we often learn these roles and games when young and get stuck with these outdated strategies, because they certainly do not make us happy. However, they confirm our beliefs about self, other people and the world around us. People play the games to reinforce their beliefs and get caught in the triangle. The first step toward getting out is awareness of what is happening.

You may come across these situations and if you understand them you can be prepared. We have given you the tools to deal with power and conflict but this final issue requires expert help from someone such as a professional psychotherapist.

Steps in dealing with the drama triangle

1. Be careful that you don't get dragged into the triangle. Use your leadership to try to help the individual recognise and accept their behaviour.

2. When they do this, other options and choices can to be offered in how they respond to things and people. This is where you can encourage them to change their responses.

Leadership has many challenges and collaborating with others is one that requires constant learning. Now you have stood by the Rubicon and thought everything through. Are you ready to develop your leadership with others? If so, cross, and remember, 'The die must be cast'.

Message 1. **There are different forms of power but we all have power.**

Action Identify what power you use and how you use it;

Practise using other forms of power.

Message 2. **Power itself is not an absolute resource.**

Action Know when to influence;

Use the pull strategy when you need commitment from others.

Message 3. **Conflict tends to escalate and therefore needs to be resolved.**

Action Ensure conflict is resolved before it escalates;

Use the 'leader's guide' to deal with conflict.

Message 4. **Some people are stuck in a triangle and this results in different games that makes it hard for them to find their authentic leadership.**

Action Recognise games at work and realise the cause;

Ensure you don't get pulled in;

Make individuals aware of their behaviour if you need their performance.

12

Engaging People

Chapter guide:

- understanding that leadership begins with you but ends with others;
- differrent models of leadership and what they really mean;
- why communication is so important and developing these skills.

Contents:

Introduction

Leadership begins with you but ends with the achievement of others. This chapter focuses on how you can use your leadership potential to enable others to use theirs. We call this 'engaging people' because to engage means to participate, be involved and take part. As an individual, no matter how good your skills, to achieve what you need to in any organisation the outcome is never down to just one person. It is also reliant on the skills, attitude, behaviour and leadership of others. So *how* do you engage others?

When exploring the black civil rights movement in the US most people will mention Dr Martin Luther King and the large gatherings. However, the movement was a very long, arduous campaign that involved millions of people over many decades engaged in one purpose – to free themselves of discrimination. Ordinary men and women contributed, participated and took part in expressing their contribution to the end result. People like Rosa Parks, who in 1955 decided not to give up her seat to a white passenger, and people like Bette Wimbish who in 1960 took a seat at a 'white only' counter for lunch in a Florida department store.

So how did King and other leaders of the black rights movement engage people so effectively?

- at 26 he reluctantly agreed to accept the leadership of a bus boycott, showing his commitment to the cause;
- he listened to what people said and was constantly learning;
- his skills of oratory were mesmerising;
- he united people in a shared vision;
- he was authentic about the cause;
- he was human, with human frailties.

Reflective Suitcase

This is an extract of what King said in 1963. Imagine you are there with thousands of others, listening, and reflect on how you feel. Then ask: would this make me want to act? Would this person engage me in helping by expressing my leadership too?

'I have a dream that one day this nation will rise up and live out the true meaning of its creed: "We hold these truths to be self-evident; that all men are created equal."

I have a dream that one day on the red hills of Georgia the sons of former slaves and the sons of former slave owners will be able to sit down together at the table of brotherhood ...

I have a dream that my four little children will one day live in a nation where they will not be judged by the colour of their skin but by the content of their character.

I have a dream today.

I have a dream that one day the state of Alabama, whose governor's lips are presently dripping with the words of interposition and nullification, will be transformed into a situation where little black boys and little black girls will be able to join hands with little white boys and little white girls and walk together as sisters and brothers.

I have a dream today ...

When we let freedom ring, when we let it ring from every village and every hamlet, from every state and every city, we will be able to speed up that day when all of God's children, black men and white men, Jews and Gentiles, Protestants and Catholics, will be able to join hands and sing in the words of the old Negro spiritual, "Free at last! Free at last! Thank God almighty, we are free at last."'

Connecting with others

So often we hear the phrase 'win the hearts and minds' from politicians, company directors and consultants. The attempt is made through speeches or visits and lately policy groups made up of voters, but the responses are thin or short term. Connecting with others is a fundamental part of leadership and like so much we have explained in the *Manual*, begins with you.

> **It is you that has to be communicated as well as your message.**

Communicating is much more than making speeches that someone else has written or saying it using unnatural techniques. We have only to visualise Ian Duncan Smith at the Tory conferences to understand this. The words are much better when they come from your authentic heart because then people see you. They connect your voice and your message. We keep saying it, but it's true: *leadership has to be authentic* and when words and actions contradict each other you lose trust.

Practising Suitcase

What are you telling people? What's your story? What are you asking them to do, to achieve, to be? Are you showing your authentic self? Do you really, deep down, believe in what you're communicating?

Too often in organisations the department head or senior manager relays a message scripted by the board that they possibly don't believe in. Answer the questions in the box above and then write your own script, something you really do believe in and tell people about that. If this challenges your boss then be honest but always be true to yourself. One person who understood this was Gandhi.

Reflective Suitcase

A woman took her son to Gandhi because she was concerned the boy was eating too much sugar and however hard she tried she could not stop the boy from eating it. The woman asked Gandhi if he would speak to the boy in the hope her son would listen and change. Gandhi refused but told her to return in a week. This the woman did, and again asked Gandhi to speak to the boy and try to encourage him to give up sugar. The boy listened and seemed to take notice of what he said. The woman thanked him but before walking away asked Gandhi why he did this today rather than a week ago. Gandhi replied, 'Because last week I was eating sugar.'

To connect with others you need to understand them and that is not achievable through techniques but through knowing yourself and being yourself. When you do this you can empathise (← p. 133). The best way to influence people is for them to see your true character. People will instinctively decide whether to trust you or not. You are communicating not only externally but internally, too, and this is the important difference.

The importance of listening

The most important part of communicating with others is to listen. This means really listening, not pretending to or thinking of what to say next. When doing that you are trying to control or manipulate to win points. Listening is about being in the moment and not thinking of your own agenda. It involves deep concentration and genuine giving to the other person. The outcome of listening is change. For this reason leadership writer Joseph Jaworski wrote in *Synchronicity* that leadership was about 'collectively listening to what is wanting to emerge in the world, and then having the courage to do what is required'.

The aim of listening is to understand not only what the other person is saying but *why* they are saying it. You do this by using not only your ears but your eyes, to pick up body language, and your heart, to feel what they are feeling. Leadership is about asking questions and listening without expecting to know the answer in advance. Listening enables you to fully understand a situation and build trust.

Words are powerful but only a small part of communication: your body communicates, your actions communicate, your attitude communicates and your behaviour communicates. When deciding on a new team member take time with candidates over lunch, for example, and you will see that their performance in a formal interview may differ in a different setting.

At work, leadership is about matching behaviour with your goals. So, for example, if you want to emphasise customer service then spend time with customers and reward those who provide good customer service. Communication is more intangible than we often assume and people pick up *all* the messages. Is the ability to communicate and engage people only available to the few 'charismatic' leaders? To answer this we need to explore charismatic leadership.

Charismatic leadership

There has always been a fascination with individuals who project charisma; organisations often look for this type of person to head them.

Knowledge Bank

To the Greeks, 'charisma' meant a gift given to a person by the gods. It was more recently used as a concept by social scientist Max Weber and has since become part of our everyday language. Weber used it to describe an individual who derived leadership through some unknown gift because they seemed to emerge suddenly. Napoleon was one example and some say Hitler was another.

In its purest sense charisma means the endowment of divine grace, a special gift that few individuals possess that enables them to do extraordinary things. For Weber, charisma was part of the personality. More recent studies proclaim that individuals who seem to have charisma tend to talk fast, touch people when they speak and wave their hands around. At work this type of personality isn't one we often see, so if you are not charismatic, does it matter? Leadership has to be genuine, so that is your goal. When you speak from the heart you will connect with others regardless of whether you are charismatic or not. It is this genuine leadership that is required at work.

Inspirational leadership

'Inspire' means 'to breathe life into'. It can also mean 'to communicate with divine influence'. For this reason inspiration is sometimes regarded as something beyond the merely human that fills us with a purpose or calling. This is important for leadership as there should always be an outcome – a new way of doing things, achieving a goal, fulfilling a vision. What leadership *is not* is living aimlessly: there is purpose to leadership. Neither is leadership isolated: it involves others who are engaged in that purpose.

Inspiration can come from anyone who can breathe life into a project, team, government initiative or country. Therefore we can understand inspirational leadership as having an energy or life-force that can be even stronger than the human body in which it resides. Sometimes it has to be tamed and channelled or a person can become exhausted. Some may say Tony Blair breathed life into the Labour Party, resulting in New Labour, and is trying to do the same in government. However, political reality is not always clear and we sometimes see an exhausted, ageing man. To succeed he has to connect with others, including the public.

Inspirational leadership can move people to act on a compelling vision. Those who express such leadership have the ability to articulate and use language to inspire others to either follow or express their own leadership. They make work and challenges exciting.

If you are ever near Crawley in England you may come across the headquarters of Virgin Atlantic, run by Richard Branson. In the staff restaurant you will hear much noise and feel energy buzzing. There is no doubt that although a natural introvert, Branson is inspirational and encourages ideas throughout his businesses. He excites people and has made this business an exciting place to work. How does he do this and what can you learn from this example?

Branson *listens* to people and if they have ideas, instead of finding ways not to implement them, he *encourages* them to have a go and see if they work. When they do work he asks them to *share that learning with others*. If they don't work, again they can share what they have learned. He encourages everyone to express their leadership rather than try to control. Branson tells his own stories of success and failure. He's *authentic* and doesn't try to be something he isn't. He *speaks from the heart*. How can you implement these steps in your work?

Reflective Suitcase

Here are two examples of inspirational leadership from the world stage. Read them and feel their impact. Do they inspire you to act? Do your talks, memos or reports inspire others to act? Do the meetings you attend inspire action? Why not? What can you do to change this?

In 1940 during the Battle of Britain tired pilots flew time and time again to stop the German forces' advance. Churchill spoke to his people.

> 'If we can stand up to him, all Europe may be free and the life of the world may move forward into broad, sunlit uplands. But if we fail, then the whole world, including the United States, including all that we have known and cared for, will sink into the abyss of a new dark age made more sinister, and perhaps more protracted, by the lights of perverted science. Let us

therefore brace ourselves to our duties and so bear ourselves that, if the British Empire and its Commonwealth last for a thousand years men will still say, "This was their finest hour".'

Sometimes we have to make a challenge for what we believe is right. When Nelson Mandela was locked up he could have become a bitter old man. Freedom came 30 years later when he saw his people vote for the first time. On the day of his election to President he said:

'We understand that still there is no easy road to freedom. We know it well that none of us acting alone can achieve success. We must therefore act together as a united people, for national reconciliation, for nation building, for the birth of a new world. Let there be justice for all. Let there be peace for all. Let there be work, bread, water and salt for all …

Never, never and never again shall it be that this beautiful land will again experience the oppression of one by another and suffer the indignity of being the skunk of the world.

Let freedom reign. The sun shall never set on so glorious a human achievement. God bless Africa.'

Knowledge Bank

Inspirational leadership is as much about language as it is about personality. Looking at the extracts above you will notice the words 'we', 'us' and 'together' are frequently used. When these words become real those individuals become leaders who can engage huge numbers of people. This is threatening to others who want to keep control themselves. The downside to inspirational leadership is that there is a tendency to become a target for those who want to maintain the status quo.

Enabling all to make a difference

Everything we have covered so far in this chapter has a two-way effect. When people are engaged in making a valid contribution your leadership expands. When your leadership expands you act as a role model for others and so help develop leadership in others. However, it isn't easy. During our school years we are encouraged to conform. We then go to work with this learning wired into our heads. Leadership often involves unwiring some of the learning and rewiring it to enable people to be more effective. Dawn is slowly breaking in recognising that the most sophisticated processes are only as good as the people using them and that thinking, beliefs, confidence, self-esteem, emotional intelligence and capabilities are still neglected. The answer isn't training but enabling all individuals to be self-managers or self-leaders.

As a leader your role is to develop these in yourself and help others develop theirs. Most people want to do more than a job. They want meaning and purpose to their work. So how can you make a start?

In the play *Pygmalion* (filmed as *My Fair Lady*), George Bernard Shaw showed that people behave in accordance with other people's expectations of their behaviour.

Knowledge Bank

A professor of linguistics teaches an East End flower girl how to speak in the linguistic patterns and accent of the aristocracy. She passes for a princess and the professor wins a bet, but interesting things happen. She is transformed. Her values, life expectations and behaviours change because people communicated different expectations of her.

Research has shown this happens in work situations and is sometimes called the 'Pygmalion Effect'. People can express their expectations to others in verbal and non-verbal ways. What seems to be important during the communication is not what the person says, as much as the

> way they behave. Indifferent and non-committal treatment communicates low expectations and often leads to poor response. You also know from experience that when someone takes an interest in you it is motivating. This is not the same as making someone dependent on you for motivation. Leadership requires the individual to behave as an adult and to treat others as adults so that support rather than dependency is the outcome.

Each person should be responsible for themselves, for each other and for their learning. This means we have to get away from the belief that a leader does something *to* people and realise that each person should take responsibility for developing these things themselves, with *support* from whoever they regard as the leader at the time. Think of your immediate core team – those you work with the most. What are the relationships? What do you need to see happen? The goal is to develop their leadership and yours so that your core team:

1. Does more than solve problems.

2. Transforms the world around them – where you work.

3. Has the courage to challenge and does not fear failure.

4. Is more interested in its purpose than any hierarchy.

5. Is positive about its goals and believes it can achieve them even against great obstacles.

6. Cares about how it affects others.

7. Remembers to have fun (p. 245 ➜).

Engaging people requires you to think of how you work with all those around you.

In 1990 Vaclav Havel, a dissident writer under communism, addressed the US Congress as head of the new Czech Republic. He said:

'The salvation of this human world lies nowhere else than in the human heart, in the human power to reflect, in human meekness and in human responsibility.'

Now take time to reflect on what you have learned about engaging people.

Message 1. **Leadership begins with you and ends with the achievement of others.**

Action   Write your own scripts;

Be authentic;

Enable others to collaborate and achieve greatness.

Message 2. **The aim of listening is to understand.**

Action   Listen to others;

Use empathy.

Message 3. **Inspirational leadership is felt through the articulate use of language.**

Action   Speak from the heart to connect with others;

Enrich your use of language.

Message 4. **Your expectation of others tends to come true; this is called the 'Pygmalion Effect'.**

Action   Raise your expectations of yourself and others;

Set high goals with individuals' agreement;

Reward hard work.

13

Developing Others

Chapter guide:

- understanding how to release leadership potential;
- being a role model, guiding and enabling others;
- coming to terms with a variety of facilitation and learning approaches.

Contents:

Introduction

This chapter shows you how to help others to learn and practise leadership. The connection between leadership and learning was discussed in Chapter 2 (← p. 27), showing that *leadership learning* is both an individual and a collaborative process.

Some people are natural teachers and we often turn to them either consciously or unconsciously to be our mentors. However, understanding how to help and guide people through the leadership learning process can be learnt.

The following example illustrates how leadership facilitation can make a difference:

We entered a classroom where groups of young people were huddled deep in their work. At the front was their teacher, but her role wasn't to teach by just transmitting her knowledge to them, she worked hard as a facilitator, asking questions and encouraging them to draw out their own views and knowledge on leadership.

We wandered around, joining the groups, listening to them explain to each other why they thought their chosen person expressed leadership in a way they could learn from. They were totally engrossed and the energy levels were high.

In the next room others were planning group presentations and were rehearsing. Each was planning ways of raising funds for worthy causes and putting their leadership into action. The rehearsals included comedy sketches, dancing, music and inspiring words.

Teachers were there to help but not take over. They treated the young people as adults and encouraged them to take some risks by being creative in their presentations.

We were visitors at this school near Washington, there to discuss our research and work with schools in the UK. We could see that a different way of teaching by a few was fundamental to what was happening. It reinforced our findings that very often teaching, lecturing and training is limited in developing others but that the right facilitation is paramount.

Why was this way of developing leadership in individuals so effective?

Practising Suitcase

To develop leadership in others you need the ability to:

- have good personal relationships with others;

- create a spirit of teamwork and support;

- fit the work to their interests and make it relevant;

- challenge them to try new things and stretch their capabilities;

- work alongside them, seeking out problems but not resolving them or taking over;

- offer help and advice when needed;

- give positive feedback and keep up morale.

As a result of the practice above you will be able to empower people to take responsibility for themselves and for each other. This positive approach to helping them learn and develop will be a key factor in encouraging each person to discover their own leadership.

Reflective Suitcase

Make a list of people you would ask to help you develop your leadership. What is it about these people that would enable them to help you? Do you admire their leadership? Have they enabled you to learn or practise any aspects of leadership without you realising until now? What special qualities do they have?

In this chapter you will have the opportunity to:

- understand yourself as a leadership role model;
- develop facilitation skills;

- improve your knowledge of how people learn;

- be able to make accurate observations of people;

- understand how to communicate in a way that promotes learning.

Developing leadership potential

Developing the leadership potential of others requires two important things:

1. A desire to help others grow and develop.

2. The belief that all people have some leadership potential.

This is a test of your leadership as well as others. It involves channelling your ego needs away from yourself into the success of the organisation and the development needs of others. In hierarchical organisations we see too much of ego and chasing status symbols. To develop others the focus has to be on *them*, not *self*.

Promoting leadership learning and practice involves:

- making people feel valued;

- taking time to work with people;

- trusting people;

- giving all people the attention they require;

- being a role model.

Reflective Suitcase

Let's now take a look at how you behave towards others.

How do you relate to others? How do others perceive you? How you answer these two questions will highlight how much you already do to develop others.

Consider your answers to the above while you read the first of two scenarios:

Rebecca is a student who works part time at weekends in a leading high street shop. She is well trained and competent in all aspects of her job. In the summer holidays she joins the full-time staff. She is unknown to many of them and is treated by most as being capable and competent. However one member of staff explains every procedure in great detail without stopping to think about what Rebecca is capable of and trained to do. This annoys Rebecca who feels that she is not given credit for her capabilities or the responsibility she knows she can handle.

Practising Suitcase

Developing others demands that you know and understand what other people can and already do. This may seem obvious, but do you really know? How well do you take notice of and listen to other people?

Find out by watching, varying tasks, setting problems and challenges or rotating jobs.

Examine your communication skills.

Now look at the second scenario.

In the same shop we find Sarah. She works for a variety of line managers and has varying opinions on their effectiveness. For instance, her favourite manager shows that she cares and makes her feel good about herself by praising when appropriate and helping if asked. If needed she will also work alongside Sarah, and she is open with information, passing on knowledge from training courses she has attended. Sarah knows that this line manager is of the opinion that Sarah is competent in all aspects of her job because she has told her so. Whenever she can she challenges Sarah to learn new things and to take further responsibility.

In contrast, another line manager makes Sarah feel as though he has no time for her and that she is a nuisance when asking for help. His communication is very poor; he fails to make eye contact when talking to her and is always making to rush off. He says as little as possible to Sarah and really only communicates when ordering her about.

The first line manager in this example is already helping Sarah to develop her leadership potential – she knows what Sarah is capable of and has communicated this to her. She is also willing to help when needed and Sarah is able to learn from her example. The relationship and communication between them is good.

The second line manager, on the other hand, has failed to establish a relationship and his communication is almost non-existent. Sarah feels that she is not valued by him and that his relationship with her is just to be a manager, to order her about and to be cross if he thinks that she is not working effectively. This manager has no chance in helping her to develop, in fact his attitude may be detrimental to her confidence in her own abilities.

Developing leadership relies upon establishing good relationships and effective communication. It is also about knowing where others are competent and understanding how to release their potential. Achieving this often involves taking risks and allowing people to take responsibility in new or unknown areas. The risks can be reduced by understanding the different ways in which learning can be supported.

Everyone can learn

Enabling and supporting learning is important at different levels:

- individual;
- team or group;
- organisational.

For instance, if facilitation and development is ad hoc, then, as in the high street example, development at individual level will vary in quality and be spasmodic, depending entirely upon the innate ability of individuals. The effectiveness of team or group learning will depend upon the ability of the group to collaborate and support each other. However, if learning and leadership development are valued in the organisational culture then the motivation for individual, team learning and leadership development will be greatly increased.

What if learning isn't valued? Then use your own leadership to change this. Don't allow the feelings of helplessness or a difficult boss to stop you. Leadership involves taking on challenges. If you can create an environment where individuals can tap into conscious personal development, work with a mentor, be encouraged to self-reflect, receive support and use life and work experiences to learn from, not only are you helping to develop their potential and the overall success of the team/department/organisation but you are also developing your possible successor.

Developing your successor

We will briefly visit this as it is a test of leadership. How do feel about the fact that one of your colleagues may end up with your job? Those who express authentic leadership develop others and in doing so identify who will carry on their good work. All too often those in leadership positions in a hierarchy are so concerned with their own reputation they choose successors they know will fail, so that everyone will believe their success was unrepeatable. This is ego rather than leadership ruling. The aim should be to develop people to carry on the work without you because you will be busy working on your next challenge.

Developing leadership in others is not so much passing on knowledge as encouraging an individual to know their own leadership through practice and experience. Your role is to help them make sense of their changes in thinking not through teaching or coaching but through enabling them to experience, reflect on and practise in different contexts. This way thinking, behaving and acting will become consistent following learning.

Leadership and learning at all levels are very closely connected, so how best can an organisation support this? The culture of a learning organisation has to support, allow and trust individuals and teams to:

- make decisions;
- take risks;
- learn from mistakes;
- solve problems;
- take responsibility;
- discuss ideas;
- take time to think;
- give positive communication and feedback;
- truly speak their minds;
- learn alongside each other;
- be innovative and creative;
- develop the cognitive side of their work.

A culture that allows people the freedom to take responsibility is most likely to encourage and support learning and leadership. Creating such a culture frequently involves removing hierarchies and changing structures. Hierarchies can exist in both formal and informal ways and some may be hidden from view.

Reflective Suitcase

Make a note of the hierarchies that exist in your organisation. Do they prevent people from doing any of the following?

Taking risks and being rewarded if the risk succeeds, or evaluating and learning from mistakes if it fails.

Making especially tough or unpleasant decisions.

Taking responsibility and taking the initiative to extend their field of responsibility.

Thinking, being creative and sharing ideas.

Questioning procedures.

Communicating positively.

Giving constructive feedback.

Collaborating.

Mentoring and coaching each other.

Learning and developing leadership.

If your answer is 'yes' to any of these, then take time to consider what it is about the nature of the hierarchy that prevents any of these things from happening.

Challenging the role of hierarchies and their contribution to or distraction from learning takes time. It is not always hierarchies that are detrimental to learning but the expertise of people. In the high street example two managers have very different approaches and success rates in developing their staff. More experience does not guarantee more learning.

What is most important in *auditing* learning and leadership development in organisations is that the views of a significant proportion of the workforce are considered. Developing *learning circles* is one way of collecting this knowledge and providing possible solutions for the way forward. The focus of a learning circle should be 'How can we improve leadership learning and practice?' To answer this the participants need to collect evidence, discuss, reflect and take action. This will be an ongoing process. The term 'circle' is used here because it is the suggested seating arrangement for a learning group. In a circle everybody feels equal as there is no prominent position available and seeing and hearing is equal for all participants.

The success of a learning circle depends upon:

- a well-planned series of meetings;
- a non-judgemental facilitator, skilful in promoting discussion, reflection and problem solving;
- the willingness to implement ideas back in the workplace;
- confidentiality being observed;
- establishing a supportive, non-threatening environment;
- small numbers, 6–8 people maximum.

It is important that the criterion for choosing a facilitator is not solely one of position, power or role as participants of the learning circle need to feel equal and not threatened. This ensures equal opportunity to engage in discussion and take responsibility. Equality promotes dialogue (← p. 30). Apply the principles of dialogue to learning circles.

Successful learning circles can be the catalyst for developing a culture of leadership learning and practice within an organisation. A learning culture requires:

- a focus on shared values;
- open, honest relationships at all levels;
- an understanding of how people learn;

- the opportunity for people to learn from each other;
- an understanding of the importance of leadership development.

Learning is the key to transforming attitudes and behaviour. Without this transformation true leadership development is limited. Although we are suggesting that leadership development is the focus of these circles there is no reason why they can't be used for technical, strategic and other organisational issues. Developing leadership can't always be divorced from day-to-day needs. In fact, it is important that the two become intertwined.

Linking developing leadership in others with work situations is one of the best ways forward. We know that people are more motivated to learn when something is relevant: one learning method is called action research or action learning. Here, learning is connected to day-to-day work issues as small groups support each other through experience, reflection, learning and action. However, like most interventions, action learning depends on how it is run as to whether or not it is effective. Poor action learning practise can demotivate people. We suggest another way to develop the leadership potential of your colleagues that does not need a trainer or anyone else.

First, consider your own learning:

Reflective Suitcase

1. How do you feel when learning seems effortless?

2. What emotions prevent you from learning?

3. Do you learn better in certain environments than in others?

4. Which subjects are your major strengths?

5. How and where do you like to learn?

Understanding your own learning pattern will help you to make a start in supporting others. Through life we learn more than we are aware of in our consciousness – this is tacit knowledge. Tapping into this knowledge requires us to first bring it into our consciousness. Noel Tichy, the leadership researcher and teacher from the University of Michigan, developed the exercise below for managers to tap into their tacit knowledge. This is something you can do with others to help them develop their leadership.

Exercise with colleagues

Take a sheet of paper and draw a simple graph. In the middle of the vertical axis write 'neutral energy', at the bottom write 'negative energy' and at the top write 'positive energy'. Make the horizontal axis a timeline from your childhood to today. Plot on the chart the times in your life when you have felt good about yourself, the times when you were stressed and the times when you were bored. Recall what was going on at those times and think about how those experiences have shaped you to be the person and a leader today. Sharing this with colleagues will create an open, supportive environment for continual learning.

From this you can design opportunities to experience leadership learning. These can include traditional training, although this is limiting; learning assignments that are challenging, as completing these will give a feeling of capability and confidence; and representing the team/department/organisation on a cross-functional project that could be international, as travel and working with different cultures is a huge learning opportunity.

This will develop the self-awareness, self-discipline and self-confidence of individuals to practise their leadership.

As a colleague you are in a position to be a leadership learning role model and it is important that through your behaviour and attitude you can:

- demonstrate that you believe learning to be important;
- admit your mistakes or experiences of failure and tackle them as learning incidents;

- work with others towards shared goals while encouraging them to set individual goals;

- collaborate with others in problem solving, effectively verbalising your thought processes;

- create an environment where motivation rises to the surface;

- encourage peer collaboration and support;

- set the climate for reflection and evaluation.

If you can successfully show that as a manger you value all of these things then your chances of creating the right climate for a learning environment are high. You will be providing a learning ethos that promotes self-belief to learn effectively, recognises that failure is to some extent both inevitable and desirable, and identifies collaborative learning as important not only in solving problems but also in learning from each other.

Understanding learning

Using your expertise to develop others

How people learn is affected by their personality, their preferred way of learning and their history of learning success or failure. For instance, extroverts will be happier in engaging in learning circles and collaborative teamwork. Introverts will probably need more help and understanding to engage in both of these processes but will be happier learning alone using e-learning and reflection.

Knowledge Bank

Understanding learning styles is crucial in enabling others to develop and in having the patience and understanding to give support. The main learning types are:

- the audio learner – aided by listening and talking;

- the visual learner – aided by writing things down;

- the kinesthetic learner – aided by doing and hands-on experience;

- the spatial learner – aided by logical reasoning;

- the musical learner – aided by background music or humming and whistling;

- the confident learner – aided by a positive attitude.

The more knowledge you have of how and why people learn, the more tolerant you will become of their behaviour. Tolerance is an important prerequisite to facilitation. So before we move on consider for a moment the people in your organisation.

Reflective Suitcase

Start by looking around you.

Within your organisation is there a choice of places in which to learn? If so, notice who prefers a noisy environment and who prefers to work by themselves in peace and quiet.

In meetings and other exchanges notice who likes to talk things through and who likes to take copious notes.

Look out for the whistlers, number crunchers and problem solvers.

Notice other ways in which different learning styles are communicated.

Do people have the opportunity to choose how and where to learn?

Do you notice any difference in how extroverts and introverts choose to learn?

Who works in a logical structured way or who is creative and intuitive and able to see the big picture?

What do these observations tell you about people?

The motivation to learn

Developing and maintaining motivation is your key to ensuring that learning happens. Your aim is to develop self-motivated learners who can act upon constructive criticism, return such criticism in an appropriate way, be flexible, creative and critical in their thinking. Let's look at how you can go about achieving this: consider first a simple process that you will be involved with everyday – giving and receiving feedback. Feedback should become a two-way process which helps the participants to trust each other's comments as being valid and meaningful. It is also a useful mechanism for encouraging and extending creative and critical thought. What do you consider to be useful, constructive feedback? Now look at two versions of feedback.

The scenario:

A manager of an important project has overrun on cost. He has taken risks which have not worked but it is possible that there could be other occasions when acting in this way could give the required results. Valuable lessons can be learned from these mistakes. He gets two different types of feedback from his superiors.

One: 'Why did you let this happen, are you stupid or something? I don't accept any of your reasons for taking these risks. If you go over budget again then your days in this company will be numbered.'

Two: 'This overspend is very unfortunate and has come at a time when the company can least afford it. This loss in revenue could be putting jobs at risk. However, we need to learn from this so that it doesn't happen again. We will meet tomorrow morning with everyone involved in the management of the project and review the overspend, why it occurred, and consider if this risk was wise and how we would approach a similar situation in the future.'

Feedback One: will ensure that this manager feels so threatened that he will not want to take any risks again, because the reasons the risk failed were not reviewed and no lessons were learned. A vicious cycle has been set up – do what you know works – avoid change – avoid mistakes – avoid learning.

Feedback Two: has set the scene for not only the manager, but also everyone else involved, to learn from the risk. Creative and critical thinking are being exercised to learn how things could have been different. The manager will not be discouraged from considering taking risks in the future but he may learn how to think the process through in a more informed way. To ensure that maximum learning is derived from this debrief, participants will need to trust each other and be able to be:

- empathic;
- open in their communication;
- positive and constructive, but tough and far-reaching in their criticism;
- willing to put into action the lessons learned;
- creative and critical in their thinking.

How then does creative and critical thinking contribute to learning and leadership development?

Thinking in both a creative and critical way requires not only a will to challenge your own ideas and beliefs, and those of other people, but also an ability to think laterally, questioning and changing ideas and research and testing new ways of doing things. Setting the scene and implementing the process to find out how you can improve demands *the will to change.* It involves effective questioning and reasoning.

Critical thinking is searching for the truth while creative thinking is coming up with new ideas to implement the truth. Creative thinking is linked to intuitive thinking connecting often with the emotional brain. It thrives in a relaxed but challenging atmosphere where trust and empathy abound. That is why Feedback Two in the scenario above is more likely to produce learning and change as the empathy and trust in the debrief will allow the emotional force of thinking and creativity to surface.

As with so many different aspects of leadership development the emotional side of learning and relationships has to be paramount. Developing leadership is about helping people to learn and change:

- emotions trigger feelings, feelings trigger behaviour;
- challenging people to think requires the right approach;
- critical and creative thought is more likely to be generated when feelings are positive.

How you do things to encourage leadership development is more important than *what* you do.

Watching, listening and working alongside others

Are you dedicated to enabling leadership in each person you work with? Do you relate to every person as a human being? If so, then it is important to be aware of how you can use even the briefest of opportunities or encounters to develop leadership.

How you value other people, how fair you are in your dealings with them and how adept you are at exercising empathy (being able to put your self in somebody else's shoes, ← p. 132) all play a crucial role in allowing you to seize unplanned moments for leadership development. The right moments will present themselves if the relationships you have with others are strong and fair.

Reflective Suitcase

To help you deal effectively with unplanned opportunities:

Arm yourself with information on learning styles and the variety of intelligences.

Notice how people around you learn, for instance, prominently visual learners may make notes where as auditory learners may listen and remember.

Understand how people think and communicate, it will be easy to spot the lateral thinker or the communicator who is adept at the creative use of metaphors or similes.

Look out for the negative thinkers, notice how their attitude prevents them from achieving and taking responsibility.

Notice how people's values emerge and either help or prevent them from taking responsibility.

Watch out for people who have stopped learning, you may hear the phrases, 'I'm too old to learn anything new', 'I already know that' or 'I've been doing it this way for ages, why should I change? It works!'

How you deal with everyday leadership development depends upon how well you know other people and the relationship you have with them. Watching, listening, empathising and working alongside others are the key to initiating adaptability, change or responsibility. Giving feedback, recognition and celebrating achievement, if approached in a warm, tough but humanistic way, can play an important part in helping others to develop and achieve and can help to develop good positive relationships that set the scene for maximum learning.

Giving feedback

Knowledge Bank

Giving effective feedback is always easier when information is both positive and constructive. However, the very nature of feedback dictates that this is not always possible. Successful feedback should be fair but tough and constructive. There is little point in delivering feedback that is either negative or so destructive that the receiver feels overwhelmed and unable to act upon the information. Successful feedback depends upon initially having a good open relationship with the recipient and then considering the following issues:

- give feedback as frequently as possible in either informal or formal ways;

- have the recipient identify some areas on which they wish to receive feedback;

- always start with positive statements;

- try to challenge the recipient to think through issues and develop strategies for solving problems;

- identify issues where you see problems and if possible work through these together to plan how they will be tackled;

- follow up feedback especially if it has been difficult. If appropriate work alongside the recipient or offer help; check that you have been understood.

Rewarding, recognising and celebrating achievement are most effective if given in a mixture of formal and informal ways. Involving recipients in choosing how to be rewarded can be effective, for example:

Example   A large global company decides to reward employees for their achievements. The reward, a luxury short break, is in principle the same in every country and is aimed at groups or teams within the organisation who excelled at being effective and productive. Because the break is without their families this reward may be more attractive to employees without children than those with children, who may find it more difficult to be away from home. As a result, some employees may not motivated by this reward. In this case there is a need to give a fairer reward.

Recognising and celebrating achievement needs to be seen as being fair and far reaching. To achieve this a wide range of criteria need to be applied to both processes. Think about the reward system within your organisation:

Who has an input into designing the system for recognising achievement?

How often are rewards distributed? Frequently enough to be motivating?

Is there a limit to how many people can be rewarded?

Does the system allow recipients the opportunity to choose if their reward is to be made public or not?

Do you know if your system is having a motivating effect?

It is fair or appropriate?

Remember that reward, recognition and celebration should not be something that is 'done' to people. Instead it should involve recipients in deciding what shape and form it will take and then maximum motivation, learning and responsibility will be achieved.

Enabling, guiding and being a role model

It is important that we all understand how to help and guide others to develop their leadership. Within your own organisation you can create opportunities to support and encourage each other to develop leadership capabilities. Sharing knowledge and experience and supporting behaviour change can be achieved through establishing 'enabling partnerships'. These can be peer to peer, manager to manager or manager to report.

Enabling partnerships are internal relationships that are constantly proactive, using every opportunity to develop others. The lead in establishing these partnerships needs to be taken by people like yourself. They work best in organisations where hierarchies are diminished and a democratic ethos prevails. They are also the basis for encouraging people to take responsibility for themselves, for others and for their learning. Enabling partnerships are linked to the process of rewarding, recognising and celebrating achievement (cooperative and collaborative in nature) and to the concept of learning circles.

These partnerships enable everyone to take on a supportive role. In an enabling partnership you should be able to ask for leadership guidance from an excellent role model. They then also become your mentor, because you can draw upon their knowledge and expertise. It can also ensure a long partnership if you are both learning together.

Knowledge Bank

Enabling partnerships extend over a variety of:

- job titles
- departments
- learning
- responsibility

- qualifications
- salaries
- ages, races and sexes.

Entering into dialogue lays the foundations for effective and motivating guidance. It opens up ideas and allows an unemotional debate. Listening and speaking with respect promotes intelligent judgement. Both the enabler and the recipient take turns to be leaders, learners and followers. In an enabling partnership both participants are familiar with their environment, able to derive maximum learning from the encounter and able to transfer this learning to other people and situations.

How then can an enabling partnership be initiated? Enabling leadership will be most successful when participants are motivated, recognise a need to learn and have the freedom to choose who will be best suited to be their mentor. This scenario is most likely to happen in an organisation that delegates responsibility as much as possible to all employees. It also requires that those in the enabling process are still learning and that it is not always limited to two participants (but can also be extended to three, to teams and groups).

Enabling partnerships for leadership require an understanding of leadership capabilities and an in-depth knowledge of who you are as a leader and how you express your leadership. Understanding yourself is vital in helping others. For the process to be successful, knowledge and experience of how to guide and encourage people to learn will be advantageous. This should include an understanding of:

- effective listening and the value of silence;
- a variety of questioning techniques;
- reflective and experiential learning;
- participatory power and negotiated needs.

Finally, it requires a new way of thinking about learning – through cooperation and collaboration. Understanding that we all have a part to play in helping others to release their leadership potential will enable you and others to learn – through your ability to be a role model and knowing when it is appropriate to guide others.

Message 1. **Become self-aware in your dealings with others.**

Action   Be a leadership role model – remember your behaviour is always on show;

Interact positively and consistently with others – try to make as many interactions as possible into learning opportunities;

Always be on hand to offer guidance and to work alongside others;

Make opportunities to develop more formal learning partnerships.

Message 2. **Develop an understanding of the different ways in which people learn.**

Action   Take time to understand how people prefer to learn and work;

Extend your knowledge of learning and keep up with recent research;

Work alongside people, observing them carefully;

Give people the opportunity to be open about their learning.

14

Leading Upwards and Across

Chapter guide:

- How to influence upwards;
- How to build a strong peer group;
- How to set an example of leadership.

Contents:

Introduction

One of the biggest issues for people in organisations is that they feel they can control what they do to some extent but wonder how they can influence or lead their boss and peers. This is a challenge wherever you are in the organisation. Julia Middleton, CEO of Common Purpose, says, 'The ultimate challenge is how to lead across, especially at board level.'

Most of us think of influencing people who report to us but sometimes it is necessary to lead peers and bosses. What would happen if you did this more often? What is stopping you? You may sit in a hierarchical structure but that does not mean you are powerless. So here's a test. Read the short story below and write down or say the first thing that comes into your head.

Reflective Suitcase

Consider the following:

Apolinnaire said, 'Come to the edge.'

They said, 'No, it's too high.'

Apolinnaire said, 'Come to the edge.'

They said, 'No, I may fall.'

Apolinnaire said, 'Come to the edge.'

They came, he pushed them ... and they flew.

Did you think – 'Wow!' Or did you think and feel – 'Fools, they could have fallen and died.' Of course he knew that they were equipped with wings to enable them to fly. We have to make sure people are equipped with the right skills and beliefs before they are pushed (← p. 210). Your response will tell you how you think and what you believe.

You have the ability to lead upwards and across just as much as downwards, but you have to believe it first. Remember that this is a challenge for everyone no matter what their role, and it should be part of your leadership practice.

We are all leaders and followers at different times

The idea that someone is always a leader in every situation and never a follower is a myth. Even chief executives, presidents and prime ministers not only have to listen to shareholders and voters but also to follow their lead at times. Examples of this include Mrs Thatcher having to change the council tax after demonstrations around the country and people refusing to pay. More recently chief executives have had to listen to shareholders on issues of pay, especially when directors leave a company.

New thinking in the world is waiting to emerge. Thinking that goes against the present 'order' of hierarchy, control through management and compliance of the many. Control is maintained through targets, statistics and boxes into which people and initiatives have to fit. This is based on the thinking that allowed the Industrial Revolution to happen but today there is a new understanding of the world and with it different thinking is required. The new thinking shows that relationships, trust and openness are important and these require a different structure and way of working. Leadership needs to be spread among people and this threatens the present order. Followers have always had a voice and expressed their leadership in improving the lives of the majority.

Leading upwards

How can you lead upwards? You can influence, act as a lobby or warn against poor decisions. This involves taking responsibility for yourself and asking:

Reflective Suitcase

What do you want to achieve at work?

How are you going to do it?

What do you need from those above you?

What would be the worst thing they could do?

How can you prevent the worst thing happening and still get what you want?

Who will support you?

Sitting passively and allowing someone to dictate to you is not caused by their power as much as by your fear. If you are thinking, 'I couldn't do this with my boss', then follow these steps.

Practising Suitcase

1. What is it I fear? Losing my job, being shouted at or causing conflict? Identify the fear and name it.

2. Write down the worst scenario that could happen if I tried to influence my boss.

3. Write down what you'd like to happen

4. What do *you* have to do to make the above reality? Is it to book time with your boss so you can have their attention? Is it to be better prepared for a discussion? Is it to be more determined not to be dismissed at the first hurdle?

5. Now do it.

If your boss is about to make a decision that you believe to be wrong, would you say anything? If this is difficult try this as an alternative. Instead of suggesting that they may be wrong, take the responsibility for the decision yourself in front of them and question yourself about it. For example, 'Paula, you're about to go into your executive meeting and I wondered if I could make sure that I'm clear about the decision on … Won't it mean …? Now, am I being stupid? Because I'm concerned we could end up with egg on our face, and I'm sure you have thought of this so can you help me here and just clarify how we avoid this.' This action could save an embarrassing situation later but you can sleep, knowing you brought your concern to the fore. This is expressing leadership through influencing upwards.

Leading across

How can you lead across the organisation to peers? The best way is to break the vertical structure and set up team meetings with peers across the organisation. These can be to work through issues affecting different parts of the organisation or to inform them of something you are doing that will concern them. They can be formal or informal and they can be opportunities to set up action learning sets.

If it's a formal meeting:

- set out clear objectives;
- give reasons why the goals are required;
- ask for the concerns of the team and work through them together; and
- show how they can all achieve more if you work together.

A team across an organisation can be leadership in action – as long as the meetings are dynamic and not static. Rather than meetings hold action groups to specifically deal with issues that concern you all. If a member of the team is being disruptive, secretive or negative they can do great harm. The only way to deal with this is to confront them and explain how their actions are affecting everyone – and get everyone to support you in this (← p. 186). You will be encouraging others to take responsibility for them-selves and how they behave.

We are not suggesting that you organise a team meeting and take the view, 'This is the team and I'm the leader'. It doesn't have to be that explicit. The best way to lead across is quietly and humbly acting as a facilitator rather than telling others what to do – which results in either angry colleagues or team members sitting back and not participating.

Followers decide what they want to follow and often it is not so much an individual but an idea or meaningful purpose. This purpose has been called the 'invisible leader'.

Using the invisible leader to help you

'The invisible leader' was first identified and explained in the late 1930s by Mary Parker Follett. She wrote, 'leaders and followers are both following the invisible leader – the common purpose … Loyalty to the invisible leader gives us the strongest possible bond of union' (Follett aand Urwick, 1941).

It is the relationship you create with peers across the organisation that is fundamental to developing your leadership and results in extraordinary outcomes. The invisible leader connects people and builds trust. It engages you and your peers to achieve the purpose of your organisation. It replaces the 'leader from the bridge', who acts autonomously in their position in the hierarchy, with leaders across the organisation who work through their connection based on mutual respect, openness, honesty, trust and empathy.

Together you have a stronger position to influence upwards. Wonderful examples of this can be seen in the way some charities were started. We have to dispel the myth that leadership only happens in business or government. An excellent way to build peer teams is to include individual goals with the team goals. To do this, ask:

- what do *I* want to accomplish in this team?;
- Why do I want to do this?

To this can be added:

- what are the main objectives facing us over the next six months?;
- what are the goals we are going to have to achieve to fulfil these objectives?

This motivates individuals and makes leading across as much about getting to know each other and what each desires as about improving performance because you are working together with new understanding.

What happens if you don't like someone in this group? It will often be the case that you prefer some people to others. However, it is important that you treat colleagues in the same way: often with someone you are not so comfortable with, you just need time to get to know them better. Here is an example:

Jack was working with colleagues but found it hard to gel with Tony, who was quieter than the others. One day another group member broke down and explained that their partner had been diagnosed with cancer. Tony calmed the individual, explaining how his sister had had breast cancer but was now completely well. Everyone looked at Tony differently after that as they realised his quiet way was in fact a reflection of a strong person who would be a rock for the group in a crisis.

Leading across is also leading *upwards*, because the outcome from the group will strengthen your role and you will show a different way of working that achieves success.

Be an example to others

We return to the question at the start of this journey – what sort of leader do you want to be? Now it's time to ask your colleagues the same question. Then agree as a group on the qualities you should all aim to have, for example, honesty or trustworthiness. Diversity is crucial as leadership has to be authentic, but there will be qualities that you all agree on. This will now be your leadership challenge. You have to be seen to express these qualities every day. How can you do this when you have so many other things to think of?

People want to see credibility and trust in leadership more than anything else, as an example of how everyone should behave. Why is this so important? By being credible and trustworthy the behaviour of those around you will change, and is likely to include:

- a sense of team spirit;

- seeing their own values as being more consistent with those of the organisation;

- having a sense of ownership of purpose;

- being proud to say they are part of the organisation.

However, this also works in the opposite direction. If people feel they work with someone who has low credibility the behaviour is likely to include:

- criticising the organisation with others;

- working only when they think they are being watched;

- blaming everyone or the system;

- being motivated only by money – what they can get;

- looking for another job if they think the future is unsure.

So how do you show credibility and trust that results in positively influencing others? First, always do what you say you are going to do. For example, if you say you will read their ideas and come back to them on Friday – do that. So often people feel let down because there is inconsistency between what people say and what they do.

Secondly, it is important for people to see you take the lead in behaving as you expect others to behave. If you want people to be friendly, then be friendly. If you want people to say, 'Thank you, well done' and show appreciation for hard work, then say it yourself when you see genuine commitment.

As Gandhi said, 'Become the change you seek in the world'. So listen, respond, care, respect, challenge, be honest and transform your workplace by being what you want it to be. It is easy to say, 'What's the point?' or find other excuses. It is harder to set the path you want others to follow. This is what makes leadership a learning journey – it's as much about who you are as it is about what you do. Peter Senge wrote, '… leaders are those who "walk ahead", people who are genuinely committed to deep change in themselves and in their organizations. They lead through developing new skills, capabilities, and understandings. And they come from many places within the organization' (1996).

Reflective Suitcase

 If you feel your organisation is large and you are only an individual, imagine what it must be like to try and transform a country. One of the architects of Poland's Solidarity movement was Adam Michnik. He, with others, fought for freedom under communism. His wise words were: 'Start doing things you think should be done, and start being what you think society should become. Do you believe in free speech? Then speak freely. Do you love the truth? Then tell it. Do you believe in an open society? Then act in the open. Do you believe in a decent and humane society? Then behave decently and humanely.'

Message 1. Come to the edge … and fly.

Action Do more than keep your head down;

Walk ahead and set out new and better ways of working.

Message 2. Leading upwards includes influencing, acting as a lobby or warning against poor decisions.

Action Influence decisions that affect you and your colleagues;

Challenge things you believe to be wrong;

Speak up before a poor decision is made.

Message 3. **To work with peers, build a team.**

Action Influence *across* with peers;

Enable peers to be more of a team and be stronger;

Get to know everyone better before you judge them;

Use time with peers to tackle certain issues and resolve them.

Teams

Introduction

In all walks of life we find teams. Understanding how teams work and what differentiates a team from any other group of people provides a basis for determining how to lead teams to achieve high performance. This chapter considers the role teams play in our everyday activities and explores:

- the difference between a team and a group;
- the power of teams;
- what makes a team 'high performing';
- leadership in teams.

Usually we consider a team to be a certain number of people working together and focus inward on the specific members and their activities. Consequently, understanding how a team operates gives an insight into what may determine a team's success or failure. There has been extensive research on understanding the workings of a team and it provides a valuable perspective to help with building and developing them.

While such knowledge is invaluable in understanding teams, we also need to recognise where they exist in reality. For example, arguably where a team begins and ends is far from clear-cut and often we find many that are heavily reliant on each other to be successful. Equally, the ability to individually select all members of a team is rare. Often we join existing teams or inherit new members, determined by the circumstances or organisation within which we operate. Further, while we may not be able to select members, more often than not it is also very difficult to deselect individuals. The end result is a team that may fall well short of the ideal structure, with a mismatch of personalities and role strengths. The theory is great but how do you put it into practice?

How is a team different from a group?

Both a team and a group encompass a number of people doing something together. So what makes them different? By way of a simple example, a group of people at a party are playing a game of charades. The group is divided into two smaller groups and an element of competition is introduced with the aim of winning the game. The emphasis is on having fun, although many of us will have experienced the change in focus and dynamics of the 'group' when a competition is introduced. Clearly the party atmosphere is creating a fun and safe environment in which people may have extra courage. The teams are completely random, yet the players are very supportive and encouraging with people taking part even though they may not be entirely comfortable. When a group of people have a goal, in this case to have a great time and win at charades, you create teams. However, this is only a game and it is not like that in the workplace … or is it? This is an interesting point to consider, as one of the most obvious places to find people performing as teams is in the sporting world. What would it be like if the workplace felt like this as well? If only our office, shop and processing jobs were as much fun as playing a game, just think of how enjoyable work could be. Indeed, the sportsfield is now the workplace for many people.

Knowledge Bank

What makes the difference between being a group of people working together and people on the same side acting as a team:

Target – teams will have a purpose or goal, something that all the people in the team are aiming towards. There will be some leadership which gives direction and coordinates activities towards achieving the goal. Such targets can and do change and the leadership will need to ensure this provides renewed energy and focus, keeping everyone aligned even though circumstances may be constantly changing.

Engagement – people in the team will want to be part of it, will be committed to achieving the goal and actively striving to achieve it through their own personal contribution, performance and support of others.

Action – all activities will be geared towards achieving the target. People will be doing things interdependent of each other, ensuring all actions are coordinated in a 'joined up' way. Individuals will be focused on giving 100 per cent, all of the time, and all directed towards the target.

Maintenance – all teams require nurturing and care to ensure their development and sustainability in the same way a high-performance engine requires oil and frequent servicing to deliver the best results. People within the team can perform a caring role and give considerable support to each other. Giving recognition, valuing individuals' contributions and celebrating success will all be important to maintaining the team.

Synergy – teams should produce far greater results than if the individual team members were working on their own. People will be thinking about continually improving and create a synergy between themselves that delivers more than the sum of the individuals. All team members can lead this and be excited by their outcomes.

Of the above, arguably the most important aspect that differentiates a team from a group is that a team has a clearly defined objective and working together they create synergy – they achieve more than individuals working alone.

Within each element above, people will be involved with giving direction, thinking, doing things and caring. All of these aspects encompass the type of 'team roles' necessary to create a team: none of them is beyond the capability of an existing or inherited group of people that do not currently perform as a team. So what makes turning a group of people into a team something special?

The power of teams

Teams achieve things that individuals could not accomplish on their own. A team strives to magnify the output from the individual member's contribution to achieve an incremental level of performance. Can you imagine making a new car on your own? Even with all the necessary skills, equipment and a kit to make the car, the whole process could take weeks or, more likely, months, if not years in some cases! Whereas utilising the latest technology and employment of skilled teams, a new car can be made within 24 hours. There are almost endless examples of teams that make things happen, which individuals on their own would take substantially longer to do or often would never be able to achieve.

There is definitely extra power in teamwork and, as already considered above, the challenge will be in creating and building the right team. Clearly having the very best people, a perfect mixture of skills and role preferences would seem an ideal composition of a team. However, its power is in the way it magnifies the output from the sum of the individuals, and this can happen with everyone.

A team of ordinary people is capable of delivering extraordinary results.

Perhaps there are some simple lessons we can learn from the animal kingdom … How do geese fly thousands of miles without any help? Answer, by working as a team: Geese fly in formation and as each bird flaps its wings it creates an uplift for the birds that follow, enabling them to fly longer distances. When a goose falls out of formation it soon realises flying alone is more difficult and quickly moves back to join the others. When the lead goose tires, it drops back into the formation and another bird automatically flies forward to take the lead. When a goose falls ill, two other birds will drop out of formation to help and protect it. Geese use honking to encourage each other and ensure those in front keep up with their speed.

In the world of sport, the Tour de France provides a similar example, with teams of riders providing support to each other over incredible distances. In the office, shop, hospital, school, or processing or service industry it is always worth considering:

Together

Everyone

Achieves

More

The key to excelling as a team includes skills, behaviours, values and purpose, which will combine to create high performance.

High-performing teams

For many of us, our challenge is to create and sustain a high-performing team. This must be achieved in a real life environment where the capacity to buy the very best people and offer almost limitless reward to achieve the best results is not the norm. However, even with the very best people there is still a need to focus on the elements that bind them together as a team. In this section we consider the ingredients that can produce a high-performance result by magnifying the performance of ordinary or extraordinary people.

High-performing teams have common elements and by focusing on these it is possible to create a successful team (Diagram 5 below).

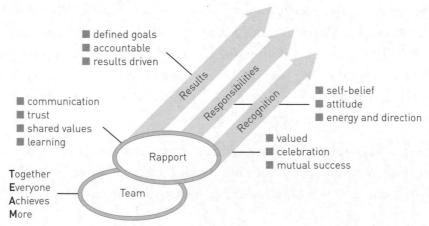

Diagram 5 High-performing teams

Results

Invariably teams will have a common *purpose*. Purpose is different to a goal – purpose has meaning and explains why the team exists. This needs to be carefully defined to identify goals and high-performance standards. The team members' ownership and commitment to these objectives is paramount and they will need to have a burning drive to deliver these results. For this reason purpose comes before goals.

In the service industry the highest standard is frequently changing, as customer expectations and competition performance changes. This applies to all walks of life. So setting a goal based on a clear target measure will not guarantee the highest performance, but it will provide a good starting point.

Most important to team knowledge is knowing where one particular team fits into the bigger picture; this is also important in understanding the ultimate purpose. For example, a team producing a microchip that will be used in lifesaving hospital equipment; or a processing team inputting loan application details that will enable customers to buy their dream home; or a groundsman cutting grass that will produce a cricket wicket that determines the championship. Knowing the end goal can greatly enhance the role and contribution of any team. Defining the true purpose and goal of a team, understanding what this will look like in reality, and what each individual contributes are all very important if high-performance results are to be achieved.

Responsibilities

Within any team each member will be unique and have different skills and attributes. Understanding this and allocating roles and responsibilities accordingly will contribute to high performance.

In the workplace some teams undertake multiple tasks and need a mixture of skills, whereas others are single task and people will need to utilise similar skills to achieve results. In either case, the team members will all possess a different mixture of skills and preferences that need to be considered to achieve the best results.

Whatever a team is doing, the members will have a choice to decide if they wish to be the very best at whatever they are doing. In an ideal team, people will always get the opportunity to play to their strengths and will take ownership and responsibility for delivering a great performance. In reality, however, team roles frequently do not naturally enable this to happen. This simply makes understanding and knowing the people in the team even more important in order to achieve the best results. Each person needs to take ownership and responsibility for achieving the desired goal and while this may be expected as part of the job, to fully engage people will require leadership.

Rapport

The relationship between team members will have a significant impact on performance. In order to develop a high-performing team the rapport between those involved will be supported by:

- clear, open and honest communication;
- mutual trust and respect;
- shared values;
- cooperation, collaboration and sharing;
- a supportive and safe environment which is encouraging and dispels fear of blame for failings;
- an appetite to learn and grow individually and as a team;
- humour.

All these elements will combine to create team spirit. Such rapport will rarely happen naturally at work and teams will undergo a building process during which it has the opportunity to develop.

Recognition

Recognising, valuing and celebrating individual and team achievements will help to encourage high performance. Valuing people for the role they play in a team is important, with praise and encouragement always welcome at every opportunity.

Invariably, valuing an individual will not be achieved from a monetary perspective alone and is often something that we lose sight of during our everyday activities. However, to breed success and confidence such practice needs to be a habit that is second nature and a natural part of being in the team.

Often, individual members of a team may grab the limelight, for example, the best salesperson or the quickest processor. It is important to recognise such individuals and they usually stand out as candidates for praise. However, the players who generate the leads and prepare the items for processing also need to be recognised, but by performing in the background may be forgotten. Everyone has an important role to play and in high-performing teams individuals will regularly be setting new personal bests for the activities they undertake. This needs to be recognised, valued and praised to help build the confidence and assurance of every member.

In summary, for a team to be high performing it needs to focus on results, responsibilities, rapport and recognition and these different dimensions will require leadership to ensure their effectiveness.

Leadership in teams

In most teams, though not always, there will be an appointed leader. This is a critical role, yet simply being appointed is no guarantee of success and often relying on the conferred authority can prove to be a poor substitute for leadership. Equally, at different times, it may be appropriate for the leadership to be held by a different team member who, for example, has the expertise and capability to guide the team through a particular situation.

Whoever has the role of leading, it is useful to briefly consider some of the differences that may be experienced between managing and leading a team (*see* Table 15.1).

Table 15.1

Leading a team	Managing a team
giving purpose	maintaining a given purpose
challenging and questioning	accepting and providing solutions
empowering	controlling
innovating	status quo
risk taking	risk avoidance
supportive and safe	critical and blaming
unleashing people power	task focused
change agent	change resister
performance coach	process controller

At different times there is a place for all the above aspects; leadership and management need to be partners rather than competitors. However, a management approach will only deliver a 'safe pair of hands' result which is satisfactory or at best good, whereas leadership can deliver a dynamic, high-performance result which is growing and sustainable.

Whatever the circumstances the style of leadership will play a significant part in the performance of a team. The leadership will be involved in setting goals, performance expectations, allocating tasks and developing team spirit. In particular, establishing the tone by which the team will work is a key to success. The following provides an example of the behaviours and values embedded in the spirit of one particular high-performing team:

Leadership: we will lead by example, acting and communicating in line with our vision and adapting our style to the situation and person to achieve a winning performance in the greatest workplace environment.

We will inspire our people with a burning desire to win, unyielding support for each other and a passion to learn. We will use coaching to encourage everyone to excel and be an integral part of the most admired team.

We will celebrate every success big and small, recognising and valuing the contribution of everyone with humility and authenticity that will take all our people with us.

We will live and be judged by our vision, results, values and behaviours, making sure these fine words truly mean something.

For this team, the value statements continued by considering the customer, the need to continuously improve, integrity and enthusiasm. The aspirations and standards set were very high, which is where we can all expect the leadership of a high-performing team to focus.

Team exercises

Overview:

Teamwork is always built before the game … invest up front to deliver high performance when it matters!

A great example of team building was achieved over a period of time in a call centre. The management team initiated and facilitated an ongoing series of events to support centre performance through team building with all line managers. The investment in time, taking all line managers away from the workplace during normal working hours to create space for reflection, planning, inspiration, and personal growth proved tremendously valuable. The team sustained a period of continuous high performance and all the staff excelled with the empowerment they enjoyed, particularly on the days the management team was away from the office!

The following provides two simple examples of the type of exercise used to develop a high-performance team:

Exercise 1: Building blocks

This exercise is designed to help with team building and emphasises the message of getting each member 'engaged'. The exercise is competitive and fun and can be undertaken by a single team (6–12 people) or by a large group of teams (50+ people) – the only restriction will be the amount of space available.

Minimal equipment is required: wooden blocks (enough for one per participant) including two which are easily identifiable, for example both painted red; string or rope; stopwatch; and tape measure. Sundry other equipment can be included but is not necessary.

The aim is to create the largest structure possible, with each participant holding on to their own wooden block. There are no restrictions on the style other than it must be clearly joined together. The size of the structure will be measured by the distance between the two identifiable blocks. A time limit chosen by the facilitator will be applied; this will vary depending on team size although, as a guide, allow a maximum of 15 minutes, during which time a number of attempts can be made.

Experience has proven that teams will use a variety of approaches to make the structure, ranging from building a tower from the wooden blocks to making a human chain using the rope. It has always proved tremendous fun and requires the direct participation of everyone.

The message behind the exercise relates to 'team engagement' and can be best expressed as follows:

Everyone – all members must participate.

Now – getting everyone to work together at the same time against the clock.

Goal – a simple and defined goal.

Action – participation is active and you have to take part.

Gripping – captures everyone's attention; responsibility; hold onto your block!

Energy – enthusiasm and energy.

Drive – determination to create the largest structure; improve with extra attempts.

The exercise is light-hearted and will help people come together as a team. Many additional elements can emerge, including: leadership, innovation, comfort zones, team spirit, communication and humour. A skilled observer or facilitator will definitely support the results summary.

As with all such exercises, extracting and reviewing participants' learning and understanding of the message – engagement – are the keys to team building.

Exercise 2: Process pipeline

This exercise was designed to emphasise the importance of improvement to continually produce high-performance results.

In practice, every team will follow a process with different stages that need to be aligned and work together to deliver the best results. This exercise is a simple process involving all team members. The goal is to complete the process in the quickest possible time and maintain quality. Ideally the team should consist of 10–12 people, although it will still work with double this number.

To create a 'process pipeline', one of the simplest adoptions of the exercise requires an object, for example a football or rugby ball, four waste bins and a stopwatch. Place each waste bin an equal distance apart, in a straight line. The goal is to pass the ball down the line, into each bin in the correct order, and through each participant (quality status) as fast as possible (speed). The participants need to be divided equally and to stand between each of the bins.

> The ball and bins can represent anything from a loan application to car production. Whatever the team's activity, the facilitator will be able to tailor the exercise to be more relevant to the people involved.
>
> The facilitator can introduce different rules, for example if the ball is dropped (poor quality) a time penalty is added and a number of attempts allowed (suggest three). The exercise can be successfully completed within 10–15 minutes.

In practice the pipeline process often takes up to one minute at the first attempt and can be completed within a matter of seconds. The latter is achieved, for example, by the team moving the bins much closer together, every team member holding the ball to start with, and one person then placing it in each bin in order. This meets the quality test, with the ball being touched by every participant and following the bin order and certainly delivers some exceptional times!

After the exercise it is important to allow time for reflection and discussion. The exercise is designed to be simple and fun and will invariably demonstrate a competitive drive to deliver a result, creativity, communication, leadership and participation, recognition and celebration.

What if ...

Team building exercises can be great fun, enhance team spirit and help performance back in the workplace. However, time is precious and finding space to take whole teams off the job to undertake exercises can be very difficult. So, even though such an investment in people is considered paramount, what if this is not possible? Such situations arise frequently and it is always worth exploring whether management or leadership operates in the team. In the case of the latter, time will not block team building, whereas for the former it frequently will!

The key elements that feature in high performing teams – *results*, *responsibilities*, *rapport*, and *recognition* – need to be considered and worked on continuously in the working environment. All require communication to take place and even in the busiest of workplaces these elements are integral to the 'way things are done around here' and will engender team building. *As an absolute minimum* a brief daily communication 'huddle' (10 minutes or so) is possible whatever your pressures and this will provide space for supporting team building, including such things as undertaking fun exercises (ice breakers), giving recognition, sharing results, highlighting goals, and asking questions. Equally, do not miss the opportunities that social activities outside working hours can bring to enhancing team spirit.

Bottom line: 'What if there is not enough time?' has no place in the leadership of high-performing teams, even though they will always be busy!

Message 1. **A team will have a number of key elements below:**

Action   Target – ensure there is clarity of purpose and goals;

Engagement – getting people actively involved and committed to the purpose;

Action – energise individuals to give 100 per cent, all of the time;

Maintenance – nurture and care for the team members.

Message 2. **The power of teams is the synergy that results from the combined input of each individual. Remember,**

Together

Everyone

Achieves

More

Action   Results: set goals, measure and profile results;

Responsibilities: allocate roles utilising individuals' best skills;

Rapport: build relationships between all the individuals within the team;

Recognition: celebrate every success.

Message 3. **Leadership of a team will produce high performance, sustainability and growth.**

Action Lead, don't manage!;

Prioritise people and make continuous improvements;

Have team-building exercises.

Part

Purpose and Leadership

16

Organisational Barriers to Leadership

Chapter guide:

- the purpose of leadership;
- the complexities of organisational barriers and how they prevent leadership developing;
- identifying the barriers you face in your own organisation;
- why culture is so hard to change and what to do;
- how structure influences behaviour;
- identifying the behaviour that holds back leadership.

Contents

Introduction

In this final part we will pull everything together, explain the purpose of leadership in organisations and show you how to overcome some of the barriers that are limiting leadership today.

In Part One we showed you that leadership was a lifelong journey of learning and that every experience can be added to that learning to develop your leadership. In Part Two we showed you that every human being has leadership potential and gave you the tools and knowledge to develop your own leadership behaviour. In Part Three we showed you that no two people express leadership in the same way and that the role of followers was dynamic and just as important as leadership. In Part Four we will show you that to enable more people to practise leadership, it has to be transformational, that is, it has to transform you, individuals and the organisation.

The purpose of leadership is to create a future where all contribute. To sustain it, an organisation as well as its people must transform to a more democratic structure and culture of freedom and responsibility. Right now you may be feeling powerless and can't see how you can do this as an individual, but our task is to show you how. Then it is up to you. You and only you can decide how to use your leadership and what beliefs you maintain or change. To help we will share a story that was told by writer Anthony De Mello (*Awareness*, 1990):

'A man found an eagle's egg and put it in the nest of a barnyard hen. The eagle hatched with the brood of chicks and grew up with them.

All his life the eagle did what the barnyard chicks did, thinking he was a barnyard chicken. He scratched the earth for worms and insects. He clucked and cackled. And he would thrash his wings and fly a few feet into the air.

Years passed and the eagle grew very old. One day he saw a magnificent bird above him in the cloudless sky. It glided in graceful majesty among the powerful wind currents, with scarcely a beat of its strong golden wings.

The eagle looked up in awe. "Who's that?" he asked.

"That's the eagle, the king of the birds," said his neighbour. "He belongs to the sky. We belong to the earth – we're chickens." So the eagle lived and died a chicken, for that's what he thought he was.'

Reflective Suitcase

How does this story make you feel? What can you learn from it? Are you now ready to fulfil your leadership purpose?

Leadership isn't just about learning and developing; leadership isn't just about developing behaviour; it isn't just about building collaboration with followers or changing the structure and culture of your organisation: it is about all these things and more. Leadership includes your everyday actions. That is why so many struggle with it and why most training courses do not change much.

Leadership begins with you knowing: who you are, how you are perceived by others, your purpose, and taking responsibility to fulfil it.

Organisational barriers to leadership

Knowledge Bank

At the beginning of the *Manual* we told you that developing your leadership fully would be limited by your organisation in a variety of ways. These include the organisational structure, culture, values, power base; government policies and initiatives; the economic climate; and competition and priorities of the organisation.

Each of these limitations can be a barrier to leadership. For example, a rigid hierarchical structure limits leadership when those lower down feel powerless. Individuals learn to 'play safe' by keeping their heads down, passing the buck, blaming others or the system and producing limited performance and results. In this situation, the organisation may have a set of values it tries to use to change the culture but they are ineffective because what people see is in conflict with those values, therefore little changes.

It is important that you have a realistic understanding of these limitations and we are going to help you make a start at tackling these.

Overcoming barriers to performance is a huge challenge today. Inside any organisation there is an immediate barrier in the form of people's perceptions of how the organisation is doing. There will be those who believe they are taking the right actions to produce results and sometimes feel threatened by anyone outside questioning this. There are those who see potential and opportunity but feel frustrated because they don't believe the right things are being done, and there will be those who feel powerless and disassociated from the organisation. This multitude of perceptions is even more concerning today when other issues are impacting on those beliefs.

The issues affecting organisations include:

- continuous change and complexity. It is no longer proper to say 'seeing the light at the end of the tunnel' because the reality is organisations have to deal with a certain amount of darkness all the time. To deal with this issue organisations have to learn every day and 'refuel while still in flight';

- educated knowledge workers now make up the vast majority of the workforce and what people used to accept about how they were managed is not accepted today. More and more of these employees are leaving not necessarily to join a competitor but to set up their own business. Many knowledge workers want freedom to create, purpose, and to feel fulfilled, not compliance and loss of spirit;

- a world of constant comunication, where even working in public services globalisation will impact on you. People can get information 24 hours-a-day, seven days a week. With this are opportunities to work in different countries and learn from different cultures;

- specialisation that was valued is today only useful if you can link it to others to create value. Cross-fertilisation of ideas, learning, knowledge and solutions means connecting with others in other fields of expertise. The interconnected world is a reality we all need to understand;

- expectations of people are higher and mass communication has meant that no longer can an organisation 'hide' or take too long to produce results. In the private sector this means getting new products out faster while in the public sector services must be seen to improve quickly. Whereas public relations had a role to play in this, now the best words and statistics do not carry as much weight as an individual's personal experience.

All these issues are causing organisations to think and act differently but there is great resistance. We still try to structure and run organisations as if the last 50 years didn't happen, resulting in pain before an organisation tries to respond, but by then it is even harder. Jack Welch once said that when the rate of external change exceeds the rate of internal change, the end is in sight. This is a warning for us all.

What is the alternative to a hierarchy? If we look at the five points above we see the challenges. What structure is best suited to address them? Is it better when the board is shut away on the top floor? Is it only senior managers who can develop strategy? What value do managers bring?

Diagram 6 shows a structure better able to deal with the world in the 21st century. Instead of a hierarchy it is circular; the board is at the centre – the hub from which it reaches out and where it can be reached; around it are self-managed teams who inter-connect with each other at different times. Without this structure there will always be blocks to leadership being expressed and practised. Let us address some of the barriers to leadership.

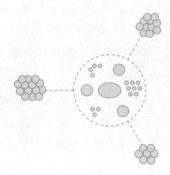

Diagram 6 The Emergence of the Network Organization

You may not be able to change your whole organisation but you can use your leadership to transform your part of it. In doing so, you will send out a message to others who will see what you have achieved. They will need your help to find their courage to follow you.

Not all barriers can be covered here but we are going to explore the major ones, which includes those that are the most difficult to transform. Understanding these barriers and knowing how to dissolve them without damaging yourself is part of your leadership work. This is a complex area and we will help you to identify your *own* organisational barriers, however we are going to be truthful with you and show how some of these barriers do not respond to attempts to change them. This part of your journey has some tough terrain, so the more knowledge you have, the better equipped you will be to deal with it.

Your organisational barriers

The questionnaire below is a simple tool to assess your own organisation. You can use it yourself but we recommend you hand it out to as many people as possible to get a more accurate picture. You may find different departments will have a different picture or you may find the same picture everywhere. There are 10 questions.

Organisation Questionaire

Circle the number closest to your opinion

---

1. *Physical environment.* The amount and quality of space and privacy afforded to people; the temperature, ventilation, noise and comfort levels.

People are cramped for space, with little physical privacy and poor surroundings.

People have plenty of space, privacy and good conditions for themselves.

[1] [2] [3] [4] [5] [6] [7]

2. *Learning resources.* The numbers, quality and availability of books, films, training packages and other resources for learning.

Very few or no resources, out of date and neglected, only technical help.

Many resources/packages, films books etc; up to date and well maintained, helpful training staff.

[1] [2] [3] [4] [5] [6] [7]

3. *Encouragement to learn.* The extent to which the members of the organisation feel encouraged to try new things, take risks, experiment and learn new ways to do old tasks.

No encouragement to learn, no expectations to learn.

Members are encouraged to try new ideas, to extend their skills and knowledge.

[1] [2] [3] [4] [5] [6] [7]

4. *Communications*. How open and free are individuals in expressing feelings and opinions? Is there a free flow of information?

| Members never express feelings, are secretive and give few opinions. Information is hoarded. | People are usually ready to give their views and feelings and ready to pass on information. |

[1] [2] [3] [4] [5] [6] [7]

5. *Rewards*. The extent to which people feel they are rewarded for effort and recognised for good work rather than blamed when things go wrong.

| People are usually ignored but blamed and criticised when things go wrong. | People are recognised for good work and rewarded for effort and creativity. |

[1] [2] [3] [4] [5] [6] [7]

6. *Conformity to norms*. The extent to which people feel they are expected to conform to rules, regulations, policies and procedures rather than being given the responsibility to do their work as they think best.

| People conform to laid-down rules and standards. Little personal responsibility is given or taken. | People do their work as they see fit, there is great emphasis upon personal responsibility in the organisation. |

[1] [2] [3] [4] [5] [6] [7]

7. *Value placed in ideas*. How much are the ideas, opinions and suggestions of people sought, encouraged and valued?

| People are not paid to think, ideas are not valued. | Efforts are made to encourage people to put their ideas forward. They realise the future depends upon people's ideas. |

[1] [2] [3] [4] [5] [6] [7]

8. *Practical help available.* The extent to which people are ready to help each other by lending a hand, offering skills, knowledge and support.

People don't help each other, unwilling to share resources.	People are very willing and helpful. Pleasure is taken in the success of others.

[1] [2] [3] [4] [5] [6] [7]

9. *Warmth and trust.* The extent to which friendliness is considered important in the organisation and the extent to which people trust and like one another.

There is little warmth and support. People don't trust and it feels an isolated place.	This is a warm and friendly place, people enjoy coming to work. There is trust in most places and a belief that good relationships equals good work.

[1] [2] [3] [4] [5] [6] [7]

10. *Standards.* The emphasis placed upon quality and standards and the extent to which members feel that challenging targets are set for themselves and for others.

Standards and quality are low. No-one really cares very much.	Standards are high and challenging, members pick each other up and emphasise work quality.

[1] [2] [3] [4] [5] [6] [7]

Total score _____

If the score is below 40 there is much work to be done. The best way forward is as a team, with support from the right places.

If the score is between 40 and 50 there is room for improvement.

If the score is over 50 it's a good place to work, but don't stop improving.

The rest of this chapter addresses some of the organisational barriers and what can be done about them.

Culture

By far the biggest barrier to leadership is organisational culture. What is culture?

Knowledge Bank

The most common phrase used to describe culture is 'It's how people around here do things'. In this respect, culture determines what behaviour is acceptable and it is in these norms and beliefs that resistance to change most forcibly resides.

As a positive factor culture provides us with a way of identifying with others. Anthropologist Margaret Mead, who spent years exploring and explaining the importance of culture, defines it as 'a principal element in the development of the individual that will result in [them] having a structure, a type of functioning, and a pattern of behaviour different in kind to that of individuals who have been socialised within another culture'.

From about 1950 until quite recently the West took a real interest in how work organisations operated in Japan because their culture seemed to give them an advantage. In Japan the organisation was regarded as a community to which employees belonged rather than a workplace comprised of separate individuals. It was found that Japanese organisations had a collaborative spirit of shared concerns and mutual help. Employees would make a lifelong commitment to an organisation and there were strong links between the individual, the organisation and the nation. This culture of work has developed from the days when the Japanese depended on the collaboration of the rice fields to exist. There were no independent, entrepreneurial pioneers as in the US and we can see this difference today in organisations.

In the US the rise of the individual was supported by the ideas of British-born philosopher Herbert Spencer, who believed in the 'survival of the fittest', where the emphasis was much more on the individual rather than the collective. This difference was noted by anthropologist Gregory Bateson in the way parents were bringing up children in the US during the 1940s compared to parenting in the UK at that time. He observed that Americans encouraged forms of boastful and exhibitionist behaviour in children whereas children in the UK were encouraged to be submissive in adult company and rewarded when they were 'seen but not heard'.

Bateson suggests that these differences produced US adults who were more self-appreciative and self-congratulating and who pushed themselves to be 'number one' in all things. Today we see this difference in work organisations and schools. So culture in organisations is linked to history and to the broader culture of society.

Do you remember the first days of joining a new organisation? Did you spend the first few days listening to the stories and history, what to avoid and the rules that were acceptable? This is how culture occurs. Test this with your own organisation. What is its history? Who were the heroes/heroines? What impact has this had that is still seen today?

When we look at culture in this way we see that it is made up of three levels:

1. The routines, habits and repetitive procedures that people are so often used to they are sometimes unaware of even doing them.

2. The rules, controls, budgets, measurement systems and training programmes which people are aware of as they are affected by them on a day-to-day basis.

3. The more conceptual areas such as creativity, risk, vision, research, initiatives and change.

When going through change programmes, many address only one of these levels, so let's work through all three using leadership. Try this with your team or colleagues. Everyone has a sheet of A4 paper and draws a vertical line down the middle. At the top write 'what we are' on one side of the line and on the other write 'what we can be'. Under the title 'what we are', describe the three levels of your culture. Then ask everyone to describe the three levels of what they would like it to be on the other side. When everyone has finished, share them with each other. Identify similarities and compare differences. Then together agree on what they would like the culture to be and how those behaviours could be rewarded in a non-monetary way. The final step is to ask everyone what behaviours they would expect to see so that they could recognise when they had moved from one to the other. Is this the behaviour they express every day? Are their behaviours more akin to what already exists? Now you see the challenge.

Values and culture

Values are one of the most important elements of culture. It is the values of an organisation that impact on how individuals work together and achieve their daily tasks. Values determine what behaviour is acceptable and remain long after change. Organisations have tried to move forward by writing a set of values and placing them around the walls of the organisation, but employees have little connection with them. They are another cause of cynicism among employees where actions, not words, are believed. It's no good saying teamwork embodies values when what people see is political backstabbing or lack of caring about people. Therefore ask what values are important to your team and make them part of its work.

Values are what you stand for as a group, and should be aligned with each team member's personal values. If your organisation values are in conflict with your personal values, you will feel inner conflict. You have to be true to personal values or feel forever in conflict. So examine your own values and ask:

What sort of organisation do you want to work for?

What do you stand for regardless of situation?

Don't adopt company values or beliefs that you would not embrace yourself. Many value statements have been replaced with an emphasis on short-term results and shareholder return.

The danger with cultural values is that sometimes we regard our own as being universal and judge behaviour negatively if it doesn't conform to our own. With globalisation and the expansion of large organisations this danger is very real, therefore tolerance of different cultural values is a major requirement of all people.

Another issue for values and culture in organisations is gender. Some have suggested that the traditional forms of organisation are often shaped and dominated by male value systems that differ from female ones. This can be seen where emphasis is on linear modes of thought and action, where the drive for results is at the expense of team or community building, or where the emphasis is on masculine approaches to work. In fact, there is strong evidence that many aspects of the corporate world have been trapped within a male archetype and that this approach is no longer working. Attempts to change these cultures are failing, because the glue is too strong for similarly masculine attempts to 'unstick' them.

We suggest a different way of understanding culture and with it a different approach to resolving the issues that also tie in with structure.

The culture we all belong to today

The traditional way of looking at culture is to focus on rites, stories, heroes/heroines and so on. This has a historic link to anthropologists studying different cultures in parts of the world that differed from their own, and has taught us much. However, if we step back there is another way of looking at our organisations that involves culture.

Reflective Suitcase

 Haven't you wondered why it is that everyone goes to work at the same time in the morning and then travels home in the same heavy traffic at the end of the day? Does it make sense? Who are we doing this for?

Political scientist Robert Presthus has put forward the observation that today we live in an 'organisational society' where the organisation is itself a cultural phenomenon that varies according to a society's stage of development. Today we build our lives around the two distinct concepts of work and leisure; follow rigid routines for at least five days every week; live in one place and work in another; spend most of our time performing the same activities, comply with authority; wear uniforms and dress alike, and educate our young people to prepare them for this organisational society.

In societies where homes rather than formal organisations are the basic economic and productive units, work has a completely different meaning. We are seeing a growing number of individuals leaving the formal organisations for the freedom to explore another way of life. French sociologist Emile Durkheim showed that the growth of organisational societies also develops a disintegration of traditional patterns of social order as common ideas, beliefs and values give way to a new society.

In this sense it is possible to say that whether we work in Rome, Paris, London, New York or Tokyo, we all belong to the same culture of organisational societies. If we are bankers we have more in common with other bankers in the world, as teachers have more in common with other teachers. The structure of this society is the organisation, which itself is a cultural phenomenon. The differences between the Japanese worker and the UK worker are breaking down.

Now when we talk about culture we are talking about a process of constructing reality that is self-organising and evolving. This brings culture alive and shows its complexity. Instead of trying to measure it we need to understand culture as a living experience. We can influence that experience but we cannot control it, and this is a frustration for managers. But there is a role for leadership.

Practising Suitcase

Identify the roles, professions and expertise that is valued in your organisation today.

Who represents these at the top of the organisation?

What roles, professions and expertise are valued much less?

Where are you?

What are the roles, professions and expertise that are going to be most valued in the future, as far as you can tell?

What is this telling you?

Your field of influence will depend on this and so its important to know the reality of the situation. You could be stuck at a permanent barrier or in a ghetto! You need to be where your knowledge and capabilities are valued: if you don't value them, why should anyone else? So don't let these barriers prevent you from expressing your leadership. The next barrier is the structure of the organisation.

Structure

During the 20th century the working world spent decades building new and bigger organisations. All were based on a hierarchical structure where power resided at the top. At the end of the century there was a plethora of mergers and acquisitions, management buy-outs and takeovers in the private sector, and a mass sell-off of publicly owned organisations to the private sector. The aim of these organisations was to improve productivity, customer service, cost to the customer and effectiveness. Did they achieve this? At the same time, organisations in the public sector such as the NHS were teeming with managers with the aim of achieving the same objectives. Did they achieve it?

Knowledge Bank

Structure means complex construction. The structure of an organisation influences how people behave because structure is linked to power, communication and effectiveness. A hierarchical structure will always have more power at the top, with people elsewhere feeling more powerless. It attracts individuals who include those whose purpose is to progress up the structure to gain power. Communication will always be limited because a power-based organisation will have layers where information is power in itself, and so those layers will hold onto information. The result is 'Chinese whispers', a 'blame' culture, and people in positions of power whose competence is questionable but are good at promoting themselves.

Many organisations say they have become flatter but in reality they are still hierarchical. Others have tried a matrix a cross-cutting structure containing teams with team leaders, but again it usually ends up below a hierarchy. Research has found the matrix no more effective than the hierarchy because it is not sufficiently different. In addition, a matrix structure ends up with a high-task culture with targets and measures causing pressure. This can result in individuals being unable to cope and playing with the targets to satisfy those setting them, as this is how individuals are assessed. Here you have the worst of both structures and, with it, the single focus of cost cutting. It seems, at times, that today's organisations are in a race to see who can reduce costs the furthest, and in the meantime customers suffer. It clearly shows that the pressure of shareholder value that began in the 1980s has smothered all other initiative, purpose, creativity and values that are now just words.

John Kotter at Harvard Business School found that organisations become bureaucratic over time because of their structure and predominance of more management that slows everything down. (We will pick this up later.) Another US researcher, Jim Collins, studied what made organisations great and concluded that the purpose of bureaucracy is to compensate for incompetence. He argues that organisations build bureaucratic rules to deal with the small number of wrong people who are employees, but that these rules drive away the right people needed to fulfil the objectives, which then increases the percentage of wrong people, which increases the need for yet more bureaucracy to compensate for incompetence and lack of self-discipline, which drives away even more of the right people. With the growth of both the private and public sectors we can see evidence of this. Collins' recommendation is to avoid hierarchy and with it, bureaucracy and replace it with a culture of discipline (which he sees as personal responsibility) and an ethic of entrepreneurship. He believes the outcome from this is sustainable superior performance.

A new structure

If we avoid hierarchy what can we replace it with that is better? A more effective structure is a circular network structure where the organisation and its customers are viewed as part of the whole system (*see* Diagram 6 ←p. 266). It is a fluid structure and can change as needed. The board or executive is placed in the centre where it is seen and accessible.

In this model interconnections and networking communication is dependent on teams of people rather than technology that supports rather than restricts. Power is distributed throughout and a culture of trust is much more easily developed. The back-to-back meetings that fill managers days, with little outcome, disappear. Control is replaced with self-managed individuals and service to the customer becomes a reality while, at the same time, inclusion is a reality for employees and suppliers. Career ladders disappear, making it possible for people to move around and less competent people to be identified more readily, with the aim of supporting their learning. The role of human resources changes dramatically and the need for more and more managers is obliterated. People can bypass the old gatekeepers and access information and share knowledge.

What is interesting is that this new, flat network form of organisation that is emerging to cope with the uncertainty and turbulence of the modern world is a method of working more natural to women than men and is common among the new businesses being built by them. Author Sally Helgesen has written much about this and explains that these women help create cultures where hierarchy gives way to 'webs of inclusion'. Employees are 'in the middle of things' rather than on top of a power structure, building communities based on inclusive relationships characterised by trust, support, encouragement and mutual respect. They produce organisations that are truly 'networked', where the process of doing things based on values is as important as the end result or product.

The world needs organisations that differ from the hierarchies where managers base decisions on a choice of 'either/or'. This will not enable the learning capability required for the future and we are seeing this in the short-sighted decisions being made in organisations everywhere. Let's take as an example the social services department of a local government agency. Here, where jobs are specialised, relationships are formalised and work compartmentalised – knowledge cannot flow freely. The result is enquiries into the deaths of children over and over again, although each year we hear promises that the mistakes will not happen again. The structure of an organisation is vital for learning – hierarchies are not conducive to this.

In contrast to the above, a network organisation is built on two important principles: a structure based on distributed, specialised activities; and a set of relationships based on interdependence rather than dependence or independence. This transformation takes effort but the choices are: to continue as we are; to tinker a bit and see what happens; to have sophisticated plans, talk about alignment and winning hearts and minds but fail; *or* to use leadership and transform the organisation.

In reality it is sometimes hard to pull apart structure and culture because they are interconnected. The problem is that *culture controls just about everything* within an organisation, even how the structure is perceived. So let's see how structure and culture affect people where you work.

Get each of team or colleagues to draw a picture of how they see the organisation. Add words to the drawings. Then compare and discuss. Is this how you perceive the structure and culture? What problems are they causing you and your colleagues? Are you working as a team to address them? If not, then begin to do so, for not only will it enable you to practise your leadership but it will engage your team or colleagues into working collaboratively on real issues that affect all of you. This should be something you all do together on a regular basis.

The last part of organisational barriers to address is the human element.

Behaviour

In an ideal world we would be able to choose the people we work with. However, even if you are starting with a clean sheet of paper, finding the right people is a huge challenge. Some organisations choose on the basis of intellectual ability and try to 'cream off' the top graduates, but does this result in having the best people? Studies have found that one of the issues with highly intellectual individuals is that they have a problem learning at work. This at first appears a contradiction, but psychologists have found that it is an attitude problem among highly educated professionals. It becomes a greater issue as they progress in a career because the outcome of not continually learning is a growing inability to deal with a changing world. How do you resolve this? The way forward is to encourage a shift in thinking about learning. Too many professional people and managers treat learning as problem solving, resulting in trying to control even more. In fact, learning involves much more than solving problems. Individuals need to reflect on their own behaviour, ask how their behaviour and actions contribute to the organisation's problems, and then change how they act. Most importantly, highly talented, intelligent managers need to learn that the way they actually define and solve problems can itself be a source of problems. Examples of this can be seen at senior levels of the civil service, military and BBC.

What are the behaviours that affect leadership throughout an organisation? In a hierarchy, emphasis is on promotion, and this often results in people who are good at promoting themselves failing to cope. Those who try to promote an image of capability that in reality is not what it should be can turn into bullies as a way of keeping people away and stopping them from questioning their right to the job.

The most difficult behaviours to change are based on beliefs that are very limiting but enable the individual to cope in their own way. The first is exhibited by the *apathetic employee* who regards their work as being at the periphery of their life and can perceive it as something they do just to earn a living. This happens often in low- to middle-wage employees, where their focus is on surviving a world that seems unfair at times. However, it can also be seen in older police officers or other workers waiting for early retirement. They may be good at their work but asking more from them will not be successful. Very often they will have a different life outside work and get their satisfaction from this. In this example the organisation has reinforced a belief they may have learned from parents or peers who have consistently told them to just get a job but that living is something outside work.

The second behaviour pattern is found in the *alienated employee* who rejects anything the organisation says or does because they feel that it has rejected them. They feel let down and even angry inside; this can build up and explode. In rare cases we have seen this when an employee or school pupil has turned a gun on others. Here trust has been diminished and replaced with cynicism as a coping mechanism. The problem lies with the organisation, which may not have realised or ignored what has happened to alienate the individual, but should act to resolve the issue because an alienated employee can do damage.

The third form of behaviour is in the *anomic employee* who feels powerless and has no sense of purpose or belonging. They may have very few friends at work, be quiet and feel that they aren't going anywhere and that if they left the organisation tomorrow they would not be missed. With an increase in asylum seekers requiring work where English isn't their first language, this behaviour will become more common unless they are helped not only financially but emotionally as well.

What actions are needed to deal with these three ways of behaving? The apathetic employee is happy when Friday afternoon arrives and they have the weekend to do other things. They need to be treated as worthy, valued human beings. You need to help them change some of their beliefs and a good way of doing this is to move them to work they find more enjoyable. Find out what they do outside work and what their interests are. All work is improved when people move around and try different tasks. Can you set this up in your area?

The alienated employee needs to address their feelings and anger. Find out why they feel this way. What can you help them to do to change this? What effect is this behaviour having on others? Again, move these employees to a fresh challenge with lots of support after they have addressed the anger.

Finally, the anomic employee needs to be better integrated at work. Who would they get on with? Could they work near someone who can bring them out? In all three scenarios the common actions needed are to:

- help the individual become aware of their behaviour without sounding critical;
- find out more about them and why they feel this way;
- help them identify work that they would prefer;
- move people around so they become comfortable with change and new challenges;
- encourage learning, support and listening.

These are just some of the behaviours that present a challenge to developing leadership throughout an organisation. Remember the eagle and the barnyard chickens. The rest of Part Four explores developing your part of the organisation to enable more people to express their leadership.

Practising Suitcase

 How well do you know your team/colleagues? Do you know their beliefs and feelings about work? If you don't then you will never resolve the behaviours that remain blocks to organisations.

Message 1. **The purpose of leadership involves transformation and creating the future.**

Action   Recognise transformation in yourself;

Decide your future;

Take the required steps to start transforming things at work.

Message 2. **Organisations exist in a world of complexity and continuous change that requires new structures and thinking.**

Action   Identify how work has become more complex;

Discuss with your group how to change the structure of where you work in some small ways;

Think and see the world as interconnected rather than as separate parts.

Message 3. **Culture is hard to transform because it has a history.**

Action   Try out the culture questionnaire at work and look for patterns;

Work with others to decide on the culture you would prefer;

Identify the behaviours you want to see and encourage them;

Understand that culture is a process of constructing reality that is self-organising and evolving and as such needs all to participate. Take steps to do this;

Identify the behaviours that block leadership and give people learning opportunities that are relative.

17

The Freedom for Ongoing Leadership

Chapter guide:

- understanding why organisational culture and structure contribute to releasing the freedom to express leadership;

- knowing that freedom equates to responsibility, rather than being the cause of anarchy and chaos;

- being aware of how freedom is the basis for ongoing leadership learning and practice.

Contents:

Introduction

The basis of individual freedom to learn and practise leadership is based upon knowledge of leadership expression, an understanding and practice of behaviour that contribute to leadership, and an ability to interact with and engage others in leadership learning and practice. We have covered all these aspects of leadership development. This chapter shows how organisations can free individuals to take responsibility, challenge each other and work together to provide leadership throughout an organisation.

First, let's consider what we mean by 'freedom'. Freedom has many meanings; dictionaries highlight 'personal liberty', 'power of self-determination' and 'liberty of action' as being the core meanings of the word. For many people the idea of freedom is associated with: not having to follow rules or regulations; the absence of penalties for not conforming; or just being able to do as you please, no matter what effect your actions have on other people. For others, it means freedom from repression, segregation or discrimination. In this chapter the emphasis is on the leadership responsibilities that demand freedom and the role of the organisation in stimulating responsibility.

For some, having personal freedom comes naturally; for others, it is hard work. But on-going leadership requires freedom to develop in an environment that supports and guides thinking, emotional well-being, creativity, dialogue, openness, trust and responsibility. Living and working in such an environment enables growth that can be superior, deeper, longer lasting and more extensive to any leadership knowledge gained on a training course.

Freedom to take responsibility and express leadership can be created throughout an organisation by considering:

- the leadership capabilities and attitudes of those at the top;
- organisational values;
- compliance versus creativity and originality;
- structure and culture;
- communication.

Freedom to express leadership by taking responsibility to question complacency and compliance can come almost naturally to most individuals who find themselves in an encouraging environment. Such an environment will promote transformation of behaviour, being clear and open in its purpose and communication. It will consider leadership learning and practice to be equally as important as its strategic purpose.

Freeing leadership – where to start?

Enabling leadership to freely flourish needs to start with the abilities and attitudes of those at the top. The personal and interpersonal abilities of those concerned with shaping the direction of the organisation must be equal at least to, and ideally more advanced than, those working at other levels in the organisation.

Starting a process of releasing individuals to develop leadership at all levels requires that the senior team be united in:

- passion for freeing leadership;
- knowledge of the importance of everybody expressing and learning leadership and taking responsibility;
- standing back to allow others to lead;
- willingness to experiment in a safe context;
- ability to enter into true dialogue.

Some organisations will be in the position to start the process much sooner than others. Many senior teams will be able to learn and adapt if the passion for the process exists, but for other organisations a change in personnel will be required. If that is the case, how will these new people be chosen? Obviously there will still be a requirement for intellect and technical expertise but additionally they will need to show passion and commitment for the process and display a leadership portfolio of their personal and interpersonal achievements. This portfolio will differ from the present criteria for leadership that tends to focus on strategic achievements and positions held. To understand this, consider the following example, illustrating how two new MDs are introduced to their organisations.

Example   In the first organisation the introduction goes like this …

'Today we welcome Mary Jones as our new MD. Mary has had a distinguished career. Graduating from Cambridge with a first class degree she joined a firm in the City, progressing rapidly to board member. She has held the post of MD in four more successful global companies before joining us today …'

In the second organisation Peter Jones is welcomed as MD. The welcome starts in a similar way, highlighting his education, academic achievements and leadership positions but in addition, reference is then made to his leadership achievements, referring not just to positions held but also highlighting significant events and learning that indicate his values and beliefs and his ability to take responsibility. The introduction continues like this, … 'Peter's leadership learning has been a remarkable achievement. In his own words he started out a person who found communicating with others on an equal level difficult, using a command and control process. He believed that leadership was only for a few. He comes to us today having established leadership learning for all in his last organisation. He demonstrates personal freedom through his ability to enter into dialogue with all those around him, his openness, integrity and creative thinking and his ability to trust others to lead. His role as a follower is appropriate but never passive, always keeping the leader in him alert and thinking, ensuring that he will succeed.'

Practising Suitcase

Start to put together your leadership portfolio. Consider what achievements you have already? What do you need to work on?

Organisations who are committed to allowing and encouraging leadership for all must seek out senior people who:

- can prove the extent and nature of their own leadership capabilities (as opposed to their management capabilities);

- are passionate about enabling others to develop leadership;

- enter into communication in a way that is caring, challenging and helps individuals to learn.

Once the right senior team is in place the challenge then is, 'How can we develop an organisation that will free people to take responsibility and develop leadership?' Before reading further, stop and consider the following:

Reflective Suitcase

 Take a moment to think: 'How many people in my organisation express leadership? What is happening in the organisation that is preventing leadership from being expressed? What ideas do I have for changing this?'

Armed with this evidence, consider how you would go about freeing leadership as you delve into each of the these questions in the light of the following.

Freedom, structure and culture

How important is the structure and culture of an organisation in promoting leadership? According to sociologist Martin Albrow (1997), 'structures are expedient dispositions of resources for someone's purposes, and for whose purpose depends on the prevailing constellation of power. They are therefore subject to the strategic considerations of whoever happens to be in a position to generate structural change. There is an open repertoire of possibilities available at any time, merging, delaying, downsizing, outsourcing, none of which will be "principled" decisions.' However, freedom to practise leadership will focus initially on social relations and the freedom to think, act and be accountable, and give initial direction to a structure that can be fluid enough to change when demanded. Such changes will produce a culture that is capable of enabling transformation of behaviour and establishing leadership relationships. Such relationships help to:

■ build and sustain trust;

■ share and build upon individual knowledge;

■ challenge compliance and complacency;

■ prevent alienation of individuals and their work;

■ improve the performance of the organisation.

An organisation that frees people to develop leadership relationships, however, will need to enrol the entire workforce in a *democratic process* that fuels solidarity. Command and control leadership that serves to ensure that people are disconnected in their thoughts will be replaced with a process that enables everyone to embrace the freedom to feel, think, say and act, and in doing so find their identity and purpose in life. This is essential if people are to fulfil their leadership potential. Individuals enter into the democratic process by having the opportunity to:

1. connect with each other and treat each other as equals;

2. consider and evaluate personal and organisational values;

3. communicate at a level that encourages open debate.

Leadership will then be practiced through individual self-government, self-management and self-determination, encouraging people to cooperate through mutual networks, motivated through their own self-interest to take responsibility. An example of an organisation that employs a democratic process is SEMCO in Brazil. The success of this organisation was initiated through the passion of owner Ricardo Semler. Democratic responsibility allows:

- the company books to be open to all;
- decisions to be made when and where they are needed;
- targets and schedules to be set by those who are working towards them;
- constructive criticism and fairness;
- the asking of 'Why, why, why?'

Semler acknowledges that leaders are required at the top of any organisation but also says that it is important to '[l]et the followers lead' (2003). His is an organisation that encourages leadership learning and practice by allowing everyone to take responsibility and to constantly question the actions and behaviour of others. The success of SEMCO initially depended upon the leadership at the top providing a structure that enabled the democratic process to start and allow people to be free to connect in ways that were not possible before.

The opportunity for people to connect depends on the structure and culture of the organisation and initially this needs to be addressed by the senior team. A structure or culture that is free to promote democracy will not be fixed but fluid and ambiguous, and will change with the needs of individuals, teams and performance.

Reflective Suitcase

Consider how leadership can be released.

The first questions for any senior team to consider are, 'How do we:

Alter the structure and physical layout of the organisation to remove power hierarchies or positional privileges and allow people to feel equal?

Mobilise people so that they no longer consider that their personal space is something to hide behind but feel energised to work where they are needed?

> Ensure that this connectedness involves connecting emotionally and that leadership learning takes place?
>
> Know that self-management by individuals and self-regulation of teams is emerging from this process of connecting and contributing to organisational performance?'

Allowing and encouraging people to move and connect loosens the strings that established and staid groups have on security, complacency and stifling leadership. When people are truly free to connect, leadership learning is expressed through consultation, questioning, challenging, cooperative problem solving and initiative being taken by people who previously felt it was not their place to speak out or act out of position. Relationships are fostered based on knowledge and understanding, not position and power, allowing leaders to emerge and come and go at will. Decision-making is improved by the openness of questioning and challenging assumptions. Leadership role models are free to emerge almost anywhere.

In the following 'before and after' example, consider how a change from command and control leadership to a culture of leadership learning and practice improved leadership behaviour.

Before: *command and control ethos prevails*

A project manager commands and controls his staff to such an extent that employees are bombarded with an array of forms to complete covering almost every aspect of their work. Coupled with this, the manager's behaviour gives out the message 'I am only here to tell you what to do and to make sure you do it' and 'I am not here to advise or help'. His staff comply, filling in their forms by the required date. He is convinced that this is the only way to lead and manage and that the forms provide him with a clear picture of how work is progressing, until one day it becomes apparent to him that one of his staff has been falsifying his forms. When the manager confronts him he finds that his worst fears are correct. When the manager asks why he has behaved like this, the employee admits that he had numerous problems and felt that he could not ask for help and advice because that would have made him seem inadequate.

After: *culture and structure combine to enable leadership relationships to flourish*

A project manager works with a group of 20 people and each week they meet to discuss progress made and to debate any problems that may have been encountered. Openness is valued in these meetings and the frank discussions that prevail ensure that problems are debated fully and solutions found. Questions are raised that probe deeply into every aspect of employees' work. They challenge each other to think beyond the norm in order to improve quality and reduce cost. The need for written evidence of progress is kept to a minimum because every team member, including the manager, is informed about the progress of the team's work. In this culture all team members are taking responsibility not only for their own learning and development and are also willing to support each other. Learning is self-managed and self-directed.

Values and freedom

It is traditional for organisations to publish value statements, the purpose of which is usually to illustrate what the organisation stands for and to act as a guide for employees to follow. Organisational behaviour authors James Collins and Jerry Porras have identified that core values can be a major building block of successful and profitable companies, noting that, '[c]ore values are the organisation's essential and enduring tenets ... they have intrinsic value and importance to those inside the organisation'.

When organisational values are imposed from the top it is important that they equate to developing leadership and, in particular, encouraging people to take responsibility for themselves and other people, and that they stimulate a change in attitude and behaviour. An example of how organisational values connect to leadership is of a large publishing group that has the core values of being brave, decent and imaginative. These connect to leadership in the following ways:

Brave = Courage.

Decent = Integrity.

Imaginative = Vision, thinking of the future.

The challenge in this organisation is to live these values. They will be guiding principles for many, however developing freedom to learn and practise leadership can enhance this and help those who might otherwise struggle with it.

Practising Suitcase

 Think about your own company values. Make a note of how you live those values. Is your thinking and behaviour always in line with them?

Within a democratic culture it is both possible and desirable for values to emerge from the bottom up. Encouraging values to emerge requires:

- open debate;
- equality of communication;
- a culture that encourages trust;
- individual values that are honest, decent and aimed at taking responsibility.

The importance of values and leadership has been highlighted in other chapters. For instance, Chapter 15 on teams shows very clearly how shared values are as important as trust, learning and communication in developing responsibilities. In a democratic process shared values will emerge. They need to reflect the working practices and social responsibility of everyone. Emerging values often have more purpose and a greater capacity to contribute to leadership development than values imposed from the top down.

The process of encouraging values to emerge starts with individuals. The essential personal values for democracy and leadership are:

- integrity;
- honesty;
- truthfulness;
- respect;
- courage;
- perseverance;
- tolerance;
- creativity;
- curiosity.

As democracy allows values to emerge through open communication, enquiry, justification, questions, evaluation and recognition, there is the opportunity for every person to engage in the process of establishing values, to reflect and to change.

The development of individual values in line with those important for leadership and responsibility is an essential pre-requisite for purposeful organisational values. For instance, the freedom to practise leadership demands that employees must be trusted to behave in an ethical way, therefore the communication within an open democratic climate needs to question, challenge and highlight any acts of dishonesty, lies or lack of integrity.

Examples   Mary works in a company that values trust. This value is imposed from the top of the organisation, however the culture does not demonstrate trust. For instance, employees do not have free access to stationery, the result of which is that they hoard more supplies than they need and a proportion filters out of the company for personal use. Because employees are not trusted they fail to buy into the value of trust. Trust breeds trust. (← p. 147.)

In Andrew's company all employees have free access to stationery but they have worked out between them how much each of them is likely to use and this reflects the amount ordered. They also know its high annual cost and understand what the effect of ordering more will have on the company's profitability. They are ready to challenge anyone considered to be abusing the system, but in fact it is rarely an issue as most employees strive to keep their use of stationery down to a minimum. This company's attitude to trust is helping employees to take responsibility.

Reflective Suitcase

Think – how does your organisation help employees to collectively develop values that enable everyone to take responsibility?

Communication and freedom

Finally we come to the most crucial element in allowing freedom to develop leadership – *communication*. Communication must be free of obstacles, in any form, to allow participation to flourish freely at all levels. Communication must be:

- one to one;
- formal group to formal group;
- informal group to informal group;
- teams to teams and between teams;
- department to department;
- organisation to employees;
- employees to organisation.

Freeing communication to operate at varying levels, and to cross and re-cross boundaries will only be possible if the principles of true dialogue are adhered to (← p. 30). Within any communication dialogue demands that there is freedom for all participants to be equal partners and to have equal opportunity to participate. For this to happen any conversation, discussion or communication has to be open, honest and free from domination or any attempt to power play individuals or groups into submission, either by withholding information or twisting the facts.

The essence of true dialogue is that it allows participants to present knowledge and opinions, question, assess, reflect, evaluate and modify. For this to be successful participants need to listen, respect, communicate, rely on their knowledge and intellect, and recognise how they feel about situations and people with whom they communicate.

Example   Every Monday morning Paul calls a team meeting, its aim to reflect and evaluate the progress of the team's work from the previous week, highlight problems and set a new agenda for the week ahead. But every week the same thing happens to stop the effective process of the meeting. The meeting is dominated by John, a powerful, outspoken figure, who fails to recognise or admit that any problems have occurred with his work in the previous week and whose attitude to other people problems is, 'You must be stupid to fall into that trap' or 'Don't you know that?' The result of this exchange is that Paul becomes angry, mainly because he fails to deal effectively with John who makes him feel incapable of managing the group and the meeting. Paul fails to see why his behaviour is a problem and only blames John for sabotaging the meeting.

Developing the art of true dialogue that is at the heart of effective communication relies upon acknowledging, and responding to, true feelings. Paul needs to be able to recognise that the reasons why the meeting failed to reach a satisfactory outcome was not his lack of knowledge or lack of management expertise but his failure to express leadership because he lets his anger get the better of him.

How can Paul rectify this situation? There are two sides to solving this recurring problem.

1. Paul needs to develop his leadership because at the moment he is failing to take responsibility for his behaviour and he is letting his anger get the better of him. Anger management relates to emotional intelligence (← p. 84). First Paul needs to recognise that he feels angry, what the trigger of his anger is, and to understand why his resulting behaviour is inappropriate. Then he has to decide what strategies he will put in place to curb his anger and modify his behaviour. For instance, he could practise becoming more empathic towards John and try to understand why he dominates and sabotages the meeting. Is it really because John feels inadequate or is the job wrong for him? In between meetings he could pay closer attention to John and his work.

2. It could be that Paul's approach to meetings and discussions or recruitment is causing the problem. Let's take recruitment first. If people are recruited to jobs in this organisation purely on technical ability then it is time to include assessment on social and communication skills. Paul could also consider changing his approach to meetings and spend some time introducing the group to the principles of dialogue (← p. 30).

Looking at both these approaches above could help Paul to free himself, and help John and other members of the team to practise leadership. Freedom to express leadership requires the ability to communicate – first by recognising how feelings and emotions can be obstacles and secondly, by learning how to suspend emotions that are blocking our ability to listen, respect others and speak out. Being able to suspend emotions requires the emotional and cognitive brains to be rewired and it begins with an understanding of how emotions affect behaviour. *Entering into true dialogue requires that we change how we feel, think and speak.* Like all changes involving the emotional brain, there is no quick fix, but dialogue is just part of the jigsaw of effective leadership and complements many aspects of this book.

Message 1. **Freeing leadership stimulates personal responsibility to challenge compliance and complacency.**

Action Understand that being compliant may be detrimental to your expression of leadership;

Look around you and recognise where and when complacency inhibits responsibility;

Motivate yourself and others to take responsibility.

Message 2. **Culture and structure can play an important part in either inhibiting leadership or contributing to its advancement.**

Action Understand the cultural or structural barriers that are preventing the taking of responsibility in your organisation;

Discuss with others how these could be changed.

Vision

Chapter guide:

- how vision speaks to the heart not just the head;
- the thinking skills required to develop a vision;
- personal vision is also important.

Contents:

Introduction

During the last 15 years there has been much written and spoken about the role of vision in leadership. Professor Warren Bennis found that developing a vision and communicating it all the time was paramount for leaders at the top of organisations. But what about the rest of us? Is vision a necessary requirement for all leaders everywhere?

The answer is *yes* and it requires more than just looking into the future as it is so often perceived. Vision requires action. We must stop imagining that in itself it will result in change. This chapter explains vision, skills to practise and the requirements for it to succeed.

Too often organisations spend money on 'vision statements'. However, there are more examples of vision not being achieved than being achieved. Why is this? Writing a statement is only a small part of achieving a vision. We will guide you through the process of realising a vision, anywhere in the organisation. Vision has to result in action.

Vision isn't only for an organisation or a nation, it is for an individual. Just as an organisation needs to know where it's going, so too do people. We sometimes ask ourselves, 'Where did the time go? What did I achieve?' We will explore personal vision and its great power.

What is vision?

Vision is more than a catchy idea. Visionary organisations are more successful and enduring than others. Reaching targets is not the driving force of the most successful organisations. They achieve this because of something else – engagement and trust. These concepts are not an issue in such organisations.

Successful organisations have a connection between people and purpose. It is hard to distinguish the values and beliefs of the organisation from their vision. Vision is creating the future, but it is equally about touching people with something they want to be a part of; it is a bridge to the future, worked toward and heard about every day. Vision has meaning and engenders trust as it becomes a reality for every employee.

A good vision should be:

- imaginable – it conveys a picture of what the future will look like;

- desirable – appeals to the long-term interests of employees, customers, the public and stakeholders;

- feasible – comprises realistic and attainable goals;

- focused – is clear enough to provide guidance in decision making;

- flexible – is general enough to allow individual initiative and alternative responses in the light of changing conditions;

- communicable – is easy to communicate and be successfully explained within a couple of minutes.

Vision comes from and speaks to the heart, not just the head. Vision is also a dream and most effective when it belongs to a group rather than an individual. It is not about ambition or profit but something else – a new way of travelling or a new way of learning. Desire to work for something meaningful is achieved when employees are put at the centre of the vision rather than being held down in the hierarchy or out on the periphery.

Management is about control. When managers try to control vision it reduces its potential. Trying to keep 'on top of things' is a way of control. Instead, people should be encouraged to bring their own ideas to the vision. Remember, leadership is working towards a purposeful goal involving collaborative relationships resulting in collective action. People don't need to be controlled to commit themselves wholeheartedly to a vision, but they do need to connect, and they do this with their own ideas.

How does vision work?

Imagine you are in a time machine and you go forward to 2014. You are at home. What would your home look like? What would it contain? What would you eat for breakfast?

You work for the same organisation you worked for in 2004. How do you travel to work? Would you travel to work? What does the organisation look like? Draw it.

How does it feel to work there? What are you doing? What is your role? Describe a typical day. What is the purpose of the organisation in 2014?

What does the world look like? Are people still hungry while others obese? Are there wars? Do children still go to school?

Spend time writing this down or drawing it. How difficult was this? What have you learned?

Using your creativity and imagination is part of the visioning process and you may have found this practice hard. At work we tend to use the left side of the brain, the logical brain. You have just used more of the right side of the brain, the creative, feeling brain. Developing a vision uses both sides of the brain.

Vision works when it connects with *all* employees. It touches the heart and energises people to act. This isn't manipulation because it is authentic. A vision should not only connect to the conscious mind but also the unconscious desire to achieve meaningful work. The vision any leader develops will derive in part from followers' needs, ideas and ideals.

Management analyses and discovers the future; leadership creates the future through vision.

Skills to develop vision

Step 1: Construct a vision

Thinking in the future

This requires the cognitive skill of thinking in terms of time. Many people can think 5 years into the future but very few can think beyond 10 or 20 years. To construct a vision for your team/organisation ask, 'What is my purpose?' 'What am I and others passionate about in this work?' Now extend that 10 years from now and what will you see?

Express the vision

People will test you to see how committed you are to the vision. You must be a living example of that vision in some way. You have to explain the vision by communicating it at every opportunity in ways that are relevant to those listening.

Extend the vision

Use the vision in a wide range of circumstances. Allow it to cut through functions and departments. How does the vision impact on problems, issues, decisions, opportunities, customers, suppliers and so on?

Expand the vision

What can all employees bring to the vision – their ideas and creativity? How does the vision affect every aspect of their working life?

The most important test for your vision is the strength of your personal conviction and whether you believe it can make a difference.

If you do not embrace the vision, why should anyone?

Step 2: Define a team or organisational philosophy or set of principles that supports the vision

Having a vision isn't enough and that is where so many organisations go wrong. It needs to be supported by a set of principles so that it becomes real. For example, a vision about being the best is not effective if people do not care about their work and blame the 'system' when things go wrong. An explicit philosophy with specific programmes to enhance the vision is necessary.

This philosophy must be articulated through action, not just words. It is not enough to have, for example, an equal opportunities statement if it is not implemented. When words and actions are contradictory you end up with cynical people and lack of trust.

Bennis wrote: 'What people want most from their leaders is vision and direction, purpose and meaning, trust and truth' (1989). This takes us to the next part of leadership and vision in organisations.

Step 3: Communicate through stories

Telling stories is a wonderful way to improve your communication skills and connect with others. Providing motivation and plans for action can be done through creating stories. There are three types of stories told in linking vision and leadership. The first are 'who I am' stories. Many can do this and some inspire others through these stories. Others tell 'who we are' stories and you hear these at conferences when people talk about who they are and what they have achieved. But the most important in regard to vision and leadership are 'future stories'. Paint the future with words so that individuals can connect with your vision. One of the best examples of this was Churchill's 'We will fight them on the beaches' speech.

Vision becomes real in companies such as Merck and Hewlett Packard and when you look closely you find they used the story process without realising it. In 1935 George Merck said, 'We are workers in industry who are genuinely inspired by the ideals of advancement of medical science, and of service to humanity.' It was this vision that compelled directors to make the decision to develop and give away a drug to cure 'river blindness', a disease that infected over a million people in Third World countries. They believed that failure to do so would demotivate their scientists, who believed in the vision of improving human life through medicine. Telling stories of the future shows what is possible and gives people the self-belief and motivation to achieve it. There is one final step in using vision to transform or achieve.

Step 4: Be what you want the team/organisation to become

Express the vision every day so that people know you believe in it. Stick to the vision even in challenging times. This does not mean being autocratic or dogmatic or even not listening – it means that you do not allow events to take you off course. One of the frustrations of employees is working towards initiatives that begin but don't end. When you express your leadership through your vision the outcome should be positive people. They should be able to say you listen, trust them, share ideas and make them feel valued as they too work to achieve the vision. Finally, do not be afraid to take calculated risks so that all your efforts can go to achieving the vision. By doing this you set an example to others and create a safe environment for them to sometimes take risks.

With others you can transform vision into reality. An example of this is the company 3M, who live their vision through six principles:

Innovation – thou shalt not kill a new business idea.

Absolute integrity.

Respect for individual initiative and personal growth.

Tolerance for honest mistakes.

Product quality and reliability.

We are in business to solve problems.

How would you feel working in an environment where these were your guiding principles? Can you see that expressing leadership would be easier here than in other organisations?

This is the process for developing vision in your organisation, but what about in yourself? Is vision also something to do with personal leadership?

Personal vision

Vision can crystalise the values and purpose of an individual. This purpose will reflect who you *can be*. For this reason developing your own personal vision is important.

Who we think we are is often coloured by what others have said, for example, the teacher who said you were useless at maths or a parent who said you were lazy. These negative comments stay with us to build a picture of who we think we are and our self-perception can be hugely influenced by this distorted reflection. Using imagination and listening to your inner self, you can develop a personal vision that is about who you truly can be.

A great story that sums up the above is related by Charles Handy in *The Hungry Spirit* (1997). He quotes a verse in the *Bible* that says 'To the one who prevails, the Spirit says, I will give a white stone … [o]n which is written a name, which shall be known only to the one who receives it.' Handy understands this to mean that to prevail we must learn who we truly ought to be and that life is a search for the white stone, we must make ourselves search to find our true selves through our actions.

One action is for you to develop your personal vision to find out your uncharted potential. It should include your dreams and passions while also being anchored in who you really are – not what others think. Listen to your own heart, not others' voices. The standards you set are your own. You may feel a sense of freedom doing this and a release from the constraints holding you back.

Practising Suitcase

Take your time to answer these questions and include work, home, hobbies, interests, etc.

What are you passionate about?

Describe how you'd like your life to be in five years' time

What two things would you like to accomplish in your lifetime?

What would you do on a day that would make you happy?

Write your life as a series of headings.

Who helped you at different times?

What did you learn from these people?

Are there themes or patterns to your story?

What can you learn from this?

What do you want to change so some of the themes don't recur?

When do you feel most focused and energised?

What drives you?

With all this information write a short statement (no more than two sentences) of your personal vision for yourself. This will not be easy but will clarify what you really want and who you want to become. Now *The Leadership Manual* can help you more effectively because you know where you want to go. If you begin saying 'But …', then ask yourself why you are making excuses for not realising your vision. Just as you have to have conviction for an organisational vision, so you must have conviction for your personal one for it to become reality. Have faith and trust in yourself, then others will, too.

Vision is also important at a societal level and is required for those working in the public sector. Economist J K Galbraith said we should focus on the achievable, not the perfect, because the world has constraints but he also argued that a vision must have goals that cannot be compromised. He argued that society should strive for no less than citizens who have personal liberty, racial and ethnic equality, basic well-being and the opportunity for a rewarding life. He saw bureaucracy as failing people and that when democracy fails, society fails.

Message 1. **Make vision something you develop wherever you work.**

Action Assess the vision of your organisation and what it tells you;

Develop a vision for your team;

Practise the skills to improve vision.

Message 2. **Vision works when it connects with all.**

Action Discuss vision with colleagues;

Assess how it connects with everyone or why it doesn't.

Message 3. **Do not be afraid to take calculated risks while achieving your vision.**

Action Have faith and trust in yourself;

Develop your own personal vision to guide you.

19

Transformational Leadership

Chapter guide:

- how leadership can transform individuals, organisations and the world;
- why leadership is needed so much today;
- how to take this journey and transform the world around you.

Contents:

Introduction

At the start of this section we explored some of the barriers facing organisations and here we explain the leadership required to transform them and, if you so choose, the world around you.

Your leadership has remarkable potential but how can you use it fully? Why should you? What does the future look like? Do you believe it will be like George Orwell's *1984*? Will a single corporation control our global communications? Will we resolve the issues of war, poverty, hunger, disease and intolerance? If you and others do not shape the future, who will? What sort of world would you like to see? What are you doing to transform some part of it to make your vision a reality? What is stopping you?

If we are all too busy working and living we preserve the status quo, but what are the consequences for us and the rest of humanity? Can one individual make a difference? What if Gandhi, Mandela, Mother Teresa and others had not taken a leadership role? Why was their leadership so effective that it transformed the lives of those it touched? Can you apply this question to your workplace?

The leadership we are going to work through is called Transformational Leadership because of its ability to transform the individual, followers and the organisation or team. The focus of this chapter is on using leadership to shape the future. It is summed up by American political philosopher John Schaar, who says:

> 'The future is not the result of choices among alternative paths offered by the present but a place that is created. Created first in mind and will, created next in activity. The future is not some place we are going to but one we are creating. The paths to it are not found but made, and the activity of making them changes both the maker and the destination.' (2003)

This sums up the notion of transformational leadership. It begins in our beliefs and values, then in our will to act. It is about creating the future by transforming the present, engaging others in deciding on the preferred future, and together making it real – hence the link with vision. However, we need to give you a warning. There are those who already dismiss transformational leadership, seen in an article in *Management Today*

(October, 2003) saying 'transformational leaders will end up in gaol', or the head of a college saying that schools do not have time for transformational leadership and democracy. A management backlash is taking place; although it often uses the word 'leadership', in reality it is focused on maintaining power structures and cultures that reinforce management rather than transform organisations through leadership.

To give you an example of this, when we talked about the leadership potential in every person at a Chartered Management Institute conference, we were verbally attacked and told that only managers could be leaders. Over lunch, many delegates kept saying the reason for this was that they couldn't get their heads around believing otherwise. This thinking, this paradigm left over from the industrial age, must be addressed.

What is transformational leadership?

Political scientist James McGregor Burns first used the term 'Transformational Leadership' in 1978 when he was studying political leadership in the US. We need to go back to the original work:

Knowledge Bank

Burns found that many leaders used what he called *transactional leadership*. This was based on the exchange of valued things, which could be economic items or the trading of votes. A candidate will give voters what they believe they desire to win votes, for example, keep taxes low or improve education. However, politicians have to show they have kept their side of the bargain to retain votes and this is why statistics departments in government administration have been so active.

In work organisations these transactional exchanges can take the form of contracts of employment and pension plans. If the organisation starts to dismantle these agreements, employees feel no loyalty or obligation to the firm and so transactional leadership may be weakened.

Many people regard transactional leadership as management, because the relationship is often based on exchange. However, the sustainable leadership required today is more than just motivating employees to exchange work efforts for pay. Yet many human resources departments have developed around transactional leadership.

Burns found a rarer style of leadership that contrasted with the above. He wrote, 'Transforming leadership occurs when one or more persons engage with others in such a way that leaders and followers raise one another to higher levels of motivation and morality … transforming leadership ultimately becomes moral in that it raises the level of human conduct and ethical aspirations of both the leader and led, and thus has a transforming effect on both' (1978). He called this 'transformational leadership'.

Do you see anything transformational in those who have a leadership role or title in your work? How do you express your leadership? Is it mainly transactional or transformational?

An example of a company who take transformational leadership to their work is St Luke's, a communications agency based in London. Their philosophy begins with the words: 'We believe that work doesn't have to be like work. It should be a series of great conversations.' The aspirations of the people working there are played out every day in creative challenges. The transformational part of their work is seen in their unique approach with clients. 'When a brand demonstrates a deep understanding and appreciation of its audience, that understanding and appreciation will be reflected back.'

If we change the word 'brand' to 'employer' or 'government' and the word 'audience' to 'employees', 'customers' or 'voters', you can see the moral context of transformational leadership.

Transformational leadership may be perceived as being rather idealistic, but how does it compare to the answer you gave to the question in Part One – what sort of leader do you want to be? Transformational leadership touches our 'human' desire to be worthy. It also has a key feature.

The essence of transformational leadership is that it completely changes the relationship between leaders and followers.

In transactional leadership exchange is based on followers' expectations of reward or avoidance of punishment and the leader expects compliance. In other words, if you fit in and do as I say, you will get your pay and keep your job. Power resides with the manager but employees may be able to exert a little influence in the hope they will receive further reward, if only recognition. Power is regarded as limited and for the transactional leader's own gratification.

We explored charismatic leadership (← p. 202), so how does it compare here? Followers of a charismatic leader exchange work for power or success (like the leader) but very few achieve it because the charismatic leader perceives power as a limited resource and so does not want to give any away. Charismatic leaders often create dependency from others.

Transformational leaders identify their own values and those of people in the organisation to guide their actions, thus developing a shared, conscious way of behaving and acting. Power is distributed because these leaders do not see it as being limited, but extendable. Transformational leaders are concerned with substance and truly empower others. They don't follow the short-termism or shareholder value but that of all stakeholders: customers, employees, shareholders, suppliers and communities. If they focus on shareholders they lose sight of the premise that to be successful they have to serve their customers better than their competitors. Focus on shareholders results in neglected customers, decline of market share and demoralised employees. By looking after all stakeholders, shareholders also prosper.

The challenge is to take Burn's concept and make transformational leadership work in a multitude of organisations.

How does transformational leadership work?

This question was the basis of the work of Bernard Bass, who built on Burns' theory to describe a process that resulted in high levels of performance in organisations where transformational leadership was expressed. He used the concept of charisma in a positive way. According to Bass there are four behavioural components that make up transformational leadership:

charisma,

inspiration,

intellectual stimulation and

individualised consideration.

- *Charisma* is regarded here as the ability to arouse emotions that will result in strong identification of the followers with the leader. This includes the leader providing vision and gaining respect and trust.

- *Inspiration* is based on behaviours espoused by the leader such as communicating high expectations, the use of symbols to gain the focus of followers, and modelling the appropriate behaviour.

- *Intellectual stimulation* includes promoting intelligence and rationality, enabling followers to be creative problem solvers.

- *Individualised consideration* is where leaders give support and personal attention to followers and express appreciation of their work, thus developing their self-confidence.

These behaviours then positively affect followers by elevating them to be the best they can be, motivated by achievement and self-development rather than 'doing a job' that provides security. The drawback with this concept is that Bass still assumes leadership as *position* and omits the moral dimension. Burns regards the latter as an important aspect of transformational leadership: 'The result of transforming leadership is a relationship of mutual stimulation and elevation that converts followers into leaders and may convert leaders into moral agents.'

Evidence has shown that transformational leadership does result in improved performance. It also aligns everyone in a common purpose and has a future orientation. In addition, transformational leadership encourages everyone to challenge and question assumptions and look at problems from new perspectives.

Transformational leadership has its critics, especially from those who want to maintain transactional leadership or management. It has been accused of being manipulative, with a preference for 'servant' leadership as proposed by Greenleaf (← p. 78). We see this as an important part of transformational leadership whereby serving a purpose – first using values to guide you – provides a moral framework. Some researchers have developed psychometric tests to measure transformational leadership but we find that they can be used to justify a model or hypothesis.

Transformational leadership is the key to high performance and motivation when linked to our philosophy of:

> leadership being a lifelong learning process;
>
> every human has some leadership potential;
>
> no two people express leadership in the same way; and
>
> an environment that is democratic and free ensures sustainable leadership development for all.

Why is transformational leadership so vital today?

What do you want to achieve with your leadership? Leadership first has to overcome a social pathology of helplessness and powerlessness that results in knocking those who try to rise above it, risk aversion or passing blame. It also has to overcome beliefs such as:

- if you want a job done right, do it yourself;
- if I'm the boss or head I'm not supposed to make any mistakes;
- if I'm in charge no one should challenge my authority;

- if we do new things they should be my ideas;
- if I'm the head of something I'm supposed to have all the answers.

Transformational leadership begins with different beliefs about oneself and others. The first is that *leadership isn't a job* but a way of being. The second is that whereas in the past leadership meant power and control over others, today it begins with a desire *to enable others* to realise their own power and leadership potential. Third, leadership was based on believing it made people do things whereas today it is about a *mutual relationship* where each participant can rise to a worthy purpose and behave with moral fibre, courage, integrity and trust. What can you do to put these beliefs in action to show others a different way of being?

Practising Suitcase

Actions to encourage transformational leadership:

Put into practice what sort of leader you said you wanted to be. This was your heart speaking. For example, if you said 'fair' and 'honest', be fair to everyone and honest. Become the leader you want to be.

Find out the leadership potential of others and help and support them to become the leaders they want to be.

Finally, help create a trusting environment where you can discuss with colleagues what you regard as the purpose of your work. Encourage openness, honesty and courage to be all you and they can be. You can begin this by saying at the start of the meeting, 'This meeting is going to set the trend for the next six months. We are going to be open and honest with each other and support each other so we can share success.'

We find these actions sadly lacking in many leaders, creating the paradox mentioned in Part One (← p. xvi): we seek leadership but don't trust our leaders. These leaders forget that people believe actions before words and behaviour before promises. The continuous rise in huge financial rewards and perks for directors of companies when employees see cost cutting and job losses has done great damage to the accountability of the business world. In politics convincing a nation to go to war on false intelligence has done great damage to the trust of individuals.

What would you think if you heard of a pilot of a commmercial aircraft being instructed to take off before all the passengers' luggage was on board because a government minister was intent on arriving at a function? How would you view your local police chief if you knew that the local Free Masons had received a visit by police officers warning them in advance that a white van with its windows blacked out would be driving around equipped with radar instruments in the back to catch speeding motorists as a way of raising revenue? This is why there is so much mistrust in our positional leaders who use power over others omitting the moral side of leadership.

Remember Gandhi's words: 'We must become the change we seek in the world'. Leadership is about taking responsibility for ourselves, our learning, each other, and our part of the organisation. Use your leadership for the needs, aspirations and values that are at the core of your organisation to begin the transformation.

Burns believed that

> transformational leaders fundamentally alter the institutions they lead, as opposed to transactional leaders who merely maintain or manage what they are given.

So where will this transformational leadership come from?

The gender issue in transformational leadership

In 1990 academic Judy Rosener published an article in *Harvard Business Review* that showed how her research had found that women tended to be more transformational than men, who tended to be more transactional. She argued that women encouraged participation in power and information and sought to enhance the status of employees. If we look at female entrepreneurs such as Steve Shirley of F1 and Anita Roddick of The Body Shop, a different leadership does emerge from that of many men. However, one study is not enough and others have followed.

Bass went on to develop his four elements into a model with colleague Bruce Avolio, whereby transformational leadership (as they describe it) can be measured. Eighty items were measured to discover if there were gender differences. It was found that women, on average, were more effective and satisfying to work for, as well as being more likely to generate 'extra effort' from their people. Women measured higher on all four of the four elements of the transformational leadership tool, with the difference lowest on intellectual stimulation. Men were better at intervening to correct followers' mistakes.

Bass and Avolio concluded that women were more likely to be trusted and respected and show greater concern for individual needs. The reason they gave for this, after much searching, was in fact the same as Rosener: that women tend to be more nurturing, caring and sensitive than men and that these characteristics are aligned with transformational leadership. Therefore it is correct to say that women tend to be more transformational in their leadership than men, who tend to be more concerned with rules for a hierarchical social order and are more interested in focusing on the failings of their followers rather than caring for them as individuals. Of course this is not the case for all men.

Other studies in transformational leadership and gender since the above have found no significant differences in managers in equivalent positions. Is this because women are now being promoted by taking on male attributes or that men today are changing? We know it is wrong to assume that all women will be transformational. But studies on women in the black civil rights movement in the US and suffrage movement in the

UK found that the majority wanted to use their leadership to transform their world for the good of the majority.

We have found that when gender and transformational leadership is studied, there is a difference between entrepreneurial and corporate women. Female entrepreneurs were more likely to be transformational.

Knowledge Bank

Anita Roddick has challenged the business world with a different philosophy and succeeded in growing a global business that keeps social and environmental dimensions woven into the fabric of everything it does. Burns said that the transforming leader looks for potential motives in followers and seeks to satisfy higher needs. In doing so, the transformational leader engages the full person of the follower. In business this is suppliers, customers and employees, and Roddick has achieved this with her strong message in developing her business.

She writes, 'We communicate with passion … we educate and inform. We do not, for example, train our staff to sell … We prefer to give staff information about our products, anecdotes about the history and derivation of the ingredients, and any funny stories about how they came on to Body Shop shelves. We want to spark conversations with our customers, not browbeat them to buy …' (1991)

Roddick has strong views on leadership:

'I believe that one of our major strengths – leadership – is one of the major weaknesses in other companies. Leadership is not commandership – it is about managing the future … A fundamental shortcoming in much of business today is that the leadership lacks vision and passion – the two most important ingredients to inspire and motivate … Leaders should not be "holier than thou"; they should have flair and a sense of fun, but most of all they should be a Pandora's Box of ideas, offering others the means of taking an idea, opening a door and going through by themselves.'

Her thoughts on leadership challenge others in the business world:

'Leaders in the business world should aspire to be true planetary citizens. They have global responsibilities since their decisions affect not just the world of business, but world problems of poverty, national security and the environment. Many, sad to say, duck these responsibilities, because their vision is material rather than moral.' She continues:

'Authority to lead should be founded on moral vision rather than a desire to create the biggest or the richest company in the world. I don't understand how anybody can be a leader without a clearly defined moral vision.' (1991)

Moral vision is an important part of Burns' transformational leadership and we believe this is why leadership always begins with the person, not the role.

Why is transformational leadership so difficult to develop in organisations?

Many organisations are focused on short-term measures such as cost cutting and targets in a fast-paced world. What is really required is to ask big questions such as 'Why do we educate?', 'What is a healthy life?', 'Is democracy going backwards as fewer people engage with it?', 'What is the purpose of business in the 21st century?'

Knowledge Bank

Many positional leaders are a product of their times. Before the 1980s the requirement was to protect existing advantages in established markets and focus on improving efficiency and developing enhancements to existing products. These leaders learned how to manage incremental change because they had to largely deal with incremental change. In the public sector the skill was to be able to deal with disjointed incremental change as governments changed frequently. This was followed by a longer stay of government that resulted in oppositions taking a less idealistic view and narrowing the differences between parties. Some incremental change continued but there was a shift toward long-term change. However, there appears to be a pattern in politics when one party dominates in that they seem to run out of ideas. Is this also why chief executives in companies now only last a short time?

During the 1990s, as well as 'downsizing', there was a surge of mergers and acquisitions. This created organisational cultures resulting from large dominant players that brought with them the demands of a growing bureaucracy. These in turn need more effort on internal operations rather than adapting to external demands. The outcome has been an emphasis on management processes to keep the existing systems running that has become ingrained in organisational cultures. John Kotter from Harvard University sums up the situation:

> 'After a while, keeping the ever larger organisation under control becomes the primary challenge. So attention turns inward, and managerial competencies are nurtured. With a strong emphasis on management but not leadership, bureaucracy and an inward focus take over. But with continued success … [t]he problem often goes unaddressed and an unhealthy arrogance begins to evolve. All of these characteristics then make any transformation effort much more difficult.' (1996)

Processes end up ruling and these are forced onto people in the form of more budgeting, planning, targets and further and further cost cutting. The result is that individual efforts to initiate transformation are smothered and they hamper the learning and development needed for transformational leadership. Environmental conditions become un-stable and a critical gap emerges between internal capabilities and external demands.

Can you now see why the workplace needs your transformational leadership? So what can you do?

1. Bring back values, purpose and vision to your workplace following the lessons from this *Manual*.

2. Be motivated by these rather than financial reward.

3. Be guided by your personal vision and values, not your ego.

4. Let others see the real you, not who you think you should be.

5. Know what your legacy is. Will you have made a difference in your work?

Transformation needs new perspectives but the present myopic managerial cultures are blocking the learning required. How can you change that in a small part of your work? Kotter concludes, 'The combination of cultures that resist change and managers who have not been taught how to create change is lethal' (1996). Nearly a decade later the requirement is more than change – it is transformation, and this in turn requires learning, not training. Teaching abstract concepts or functional skills is inefficient. So how do you develop transformational leadership in yourself and others?

How to develop your transformational leadership

Large companies and some government departments are realising that a week's training programme is not the answer. Some large organisations are beginning with psychometric tests using Bass's framework and adding other competencies to build competency frameworks. However, research has found that these maintain the hierarchy. Organisations may send employees on a three-day programme while executives spend longer reviewing strategy, but again these programmes are not enough. What is required is an innovative approach to develop leadership: *it requires learning, not training*.

Learning is akin to an adventure where an individual is seeking new knowledge and experiences, quietly reflecting over what they have seen and learned, testing and practising what they have learned, and reviewing how that action has worked. To develop your transformational leadership you need to:

question everything around you;

be open to new information;

challenge the status quo and replace it with new thinking and new ways of seeing the world;

dare to try new ideas; and

learn from mistakes and failure, but always keep learning and trying.

We have now come full circle, as we began with learning and leadership. This *Manual* is not a training course and cannot tell you everything about leadership, but it *is* a guide for a richer experience of work and life. Learning is an active process that begins with the passive action of listening. The more you listen, the more you will learn, and this includes listening to your inner self and allowing it to guide you. Fundamental to leadership is leading by example and encouraging others to take the journey, too.

In developing leaders everywhere you need to be aware to the key factors that prevent learning.

1. Lack of support from senior managers before and after the event is the main reason for lack of change.

2. Long-term learning is more effective than short-term courses. In other words, learning has to be part of everyone's work.

3. Out of context, concepts are not effective. There needs to be a strong focus on context and content relating to the individual's work and organisation.

4. Learning has to include time to reflect.

5. 'Back home' assignments followed by additional learning experiences are effective.

6. Participants need to compare how they see themselves and how others see them, so assessment from others is essential.

7. All this has little impact if the organisation itself and the role of HR remains the same, so organisational transformation must be part of the process.

This final point needs further explanation. Developing leadership that only focuses on the relationship between leaders and followers is not sufficient. There has to be an organisational context addressing structure and culture. Individuals themselves have to decide what is important and what needs to transform. To develop leadership we need to take responsibility for the world around us, including where we work. It is easy to go to work, do a job and go home. Leadership is a challenge and requires the participation of all. In the next chapter, we will explore what form this transformation may take.

Message 1. **Transformational leadership occurs when one or more persons engage with others in such a way that leaders and followers raise one another to higher levels of motivation and morality.**

Action Identify when you are transactional and when you are transformational;

Record for a week how often you give employees 10 minutes at a time of your day. It will show you whether you are making time to engage with them;

Make sure people come out of meetings feeling positive;

Focus on real transformation rather than short-term change.

Message 2. **Transforming leadership ultimately becomes moral in that it raises the level of human conduct and ethical aspirations of both the leader and the led, and thus has a transforming effect on both.**

Action   Establish the ethical aspirations of yourself and colleagues;

Make values and vision part of your work and communicate these with others;

Behave as you want to see leadership in your organisation;

Make work purposeful and meaningful.

The Next Step

Chapter guide:

- how to pull together all your learning;
- where to begin;
- what – and what not – to transform;
- the characteristics of the right structure and culture for leadership;
- what to take with you for further learning.

Contents:

Introduction

This final chapter is going to draw on everything you have read to this point. It will ask you to think, see and act in new ways and this will require courage, self-belief and ability to challenge the status quo – we now want you to express your leadership.

We know that it is useless to send people on leadership programmes if their work environment doesn't change. There is growing recognition that the majority of organisations, whether in the private or public sector, have lost their individual initiative and energy. Instead there is control, bureaucracy, isolation from vital resources, fragmented or oversized structures, inability to focus on the outside world because of internal demands, systems, and procedures that result in thousands of frontline managers needing to find the motivation or incentive to seek out new opportunities or create new ideas.

Many of these organisations recognise the problem but either sidestep or try to resolve it with little success. The answer isn't more meetings, committees, strategic plans, quangos or policy. These are remnants of post-industrial thinking and with them the notion of 'Organisation Man' set in its rational, authority-based, corporate model, framed by the professional management doctrine that makes individuals controllable or at least compliant.

The last 20 years has seen a surge of consultants and gurus, each with what was believed to be 'the solution', but which has resulted in half-hearted initiatives, not always because of the initiatives themselves but how and where they were implemented. Along with downsizing they have left a legacy of fear and distrust in the workplace. Downsizing and, now, the emphasis on shareholder value and a single strategy of cost cutting, has torn apart any trust between employers and employees. Emphasis on targets and tests in the public sector is having the same damaging effect. Is there an alternative way forward?

As early as 1992 John Kotter from Harvard was writing about organisations he termed as 'over-managed and under-led'. He saw that these organisations needed management rather than leadership to cope with the growing bureaucracy and that it was these individuals who became executives or 'advisers'. With their emphasis on structure and process, transformation and employee initiative was stifled. But what do these organisations look like today?

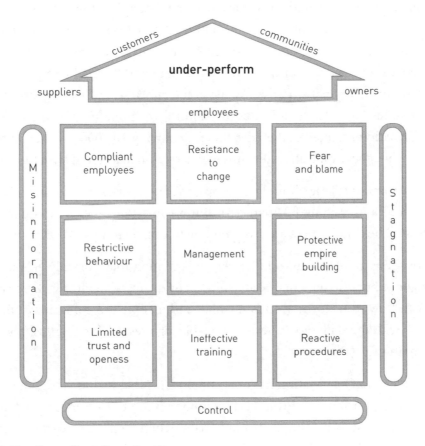

Diagram 7 The Compliant Organisation

From our research over the last three years this is what we found to be the general snapshot of many organisations today (Diagram 7). Of course, there are those organisations where this model doesn't fit completely but there will still be elements of it.

Included in this model are organisations from both the private and public sectors including universities, showing that intellect made no difference. Communication becomes blocked in pockets of the organisation instead of flowing freely. Organisations may have seen change and some have become flatter, but the core of their thinking, power base and behaviour has changed little. Production is low and employees try to compensate by working long hours. To resolve this, many have employed a single-minded strategy of cost cutting to compensate and 'blame' competition or other external causes for their situation. While in the public sector investigation after investigation states 'poor leadership', 'poor training 'or 'poor management'. Yet the real transformation required still eludes them. Removing 100,000 civil servants is not the answer while the organisation remains with a rigid management structure and ethos.

Now everyone is talking about leadership and HR departments are organising psychometric tests and training for managers. But organisations require more than adding a 'leadership box' and expect a week's training to change things. So what can you do?

We are going to introduce you to a new organisation that not only enables leadership throughout but also uses that leadership talent to create a culture where communication can flow; transformation is normal; and, people are committed to a common purpose with the ability to achieve sustainable high results. We call this 'The Leadership Organisation'™ (Diagram 8).

The Leadership Organisation has nine components that include individual and organisational responsibility. Within each component are the 'essences' – what makes up each component. For example, behind accountability will be integrity, openness, governance, ethical leadership, strategic awareness and thinking, corporate responsibility and so on. Whereas behind engagement will be connecting at both heart and head levels, shared aspirations, clear standards and expectations, consistency, tolerance of others, leadership that is relationship led rather then power led and so on.

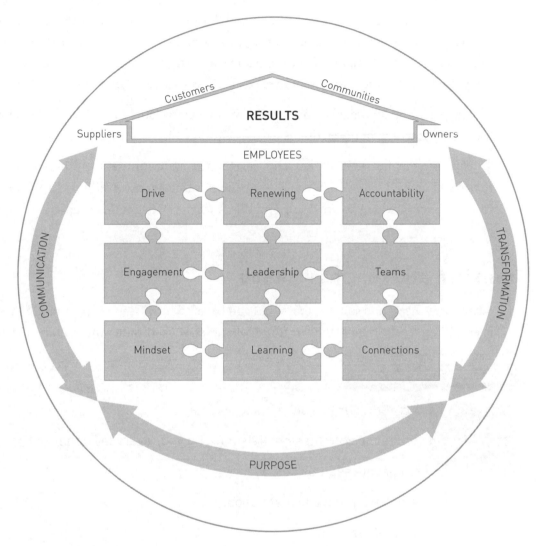

Diagram 8 The Leadership Organisation™

Each component is interconnected to the rest and we have mapped out the essences for each to achieve a high performing organisation with tools to engage and unleash the intellectual capital within. Fundamental to all this is its ability learn an express leadership initiative, creativity, innovation, energy and service.

The Leadership Organisation can be a school, hospital, professional business, entrepreneurial company, police constabulary, prison, government department or large corporate organisation. What is important is the outcome of the transformation. The tools to achieve this are available to those who want to make this journey and details are at the end.

As one person in an organisation where can you begin? How can you now put all your leadership learning into practise?

To express your leadership today and develop the environment for others to express theirs will take all your courage and self-belief. In fact, success will only happen if you really believe in what you are doing and this is where we begin this chapter.

Transformation begins with you

Search your heart and soul for the values and beliefs that will guide you and use these to keep you on track. Then with your team/colleagues, work through this exercise together.

Practising Suitcase

What four or five beliefs do you share?

What effect do these beliefs have on your everyday behaviour?

Do people see this behaviour?

What are you passionate about?

What drives you?

What can you offer the world?

At what can you be the best?

Is this the focus of your work?

These questions go deep and need time to be answered properly, but they are important and should be answered before embarking on creating the right environment for yourself and others. You have the power to transform your workplace – regardless of your role – because *you begin with transforming yourself*, and only you can do this. Do you believe this? It is important that the community you work with also has the opportunity to answer these questions and share the answers.

The will to act

Inside you is a force, an energy, that is unique to you. For some people it is very dynamic and to those around them they may appear driven. The key to such a strong force is to learn how to channel it and calm it down at times. For others, the force has been smothered by negative feelings of hopelessness, powerlessness and cynicism. These beliefs have to be challenged and changed for the energy to flow. But everyone can tap into this energy. Are you aware of your energy force? You are going to need it.

You are also going to need courage, focus and commitment: the outcome will be action. The will to act begins by accepting our humanity: we only grow from our own efforts while maintaining the will to act. What is the purpose of your action? To know your purpose is to know who you are. When all this is clear you can focus on the task ahead – to develop an environment for leadership to thrive. This may be inside an organisation, a community, hospital or school. *The Manual* will guide you but it cannot answer all your questions – you have to answer some yourself.

What – and what not – to transform

Preserve the core values and purpose of your organisation and team/department. To do this you must first know them. Then transform the cultural and operating practices, specific goals and strategies, and negative beliefs holding things back.

Remember that transformational leadership draws on the values and beliefs from the organisational community and then acts to make them explicit so that they become conscious beliefs and goals. If the culture has created negative beliefs then you have to tackle these first. You can begin by establishing the desired beliefs of the workforce. You are now responsible for the transformation.

Responsibility

Freedom to act, courage and integrity are only part of this challenge – responsibility runs alongside freedom. Never waiver from responsibility: but this doesn't mean carrying the weight of the world on your shoulders, it means you are responsible for your actions and their consequences. How can you have leadership where individuals who decide strategies and policies do not take responsibility for their outcomes? You can't. Whether in business, politics or voluntary work, responsibility has to be included in leadership.

Knowledge Bank

What are the characteristics of a structure and culture that enables leadership?

- inspiring individual leadership and initiative requires people to feel a sense of ownership in what they do and this is achieved best in smaller rather than larger units;

- the sense of ownership needs to be complemented by a strong sense of self-discipline so you need to build a culture around freedom and responsibility within a framework of self-discipline. This is achieved through performance standards that come from each individual, not from above;

- filling the culture with those who are willing to go all the way to fulfil their responsibilities; helping people reach this point;

- respecting the individual in a supportive culture that is open in communicating, listens to questions and tolerates failure. People will then be more likely to take risks and be innovative;

- sustainable transformation tends to follow a pattern of build up and breakthrough. It requires effort from everyone in a consistent direction and is always more than a single action or programme. There is no need to run a 'managing change' programme, 'motivate the troops', or use short-term pressures to excuse failure. Enable momentum to build and let people be part of the success.

Developing ownership

The more regimented the processes, the more people see that their ideas are not taken seriously, that they are not included in discussions or decisions, that their concerns are not listened to, the more they will disengage from work. Therefore the opposite is required to reengage people, and this works best in small, flexible, fluid units such as those shown in a network structure (← p. 277). Our research has shown that structure has an effect on behaviour, whether in a school, company, hospital or government department. The ideal number for each unit is about 150 people, within which are smaller teams who mix and match for different products or services. An individual may be in one or more teams.

Rather than have someone tell people what team they are in, allow the team members to decide and practise using their own responsibility for what they do. For those wondering if chaos will reign, losing control *is* an uncomfortable feeling, but the bottom line is whether you trust people to make the right choices and act sensibly. You can either control through the hierarchy and lose initiative and motivation, or you can allow initiative and ownership of success to flourish in a different structure.

Self-discipline

The context of discipline is very different from the culture of control and compliance. In an environment of freedom people go beyond following directives and conforming to policies; they take responsibility for their decisions and actions. You can actually see this because you will notice that people turn up on time for meetings, keep their promises, return phone calls promptly. So how do you build discipline into the organisation?

Practising Suitcase

There are three actions you can take.

The first is to work with your team/department/colleagues to *establish standards of performance*. These are not targets and our research on teams has shown that people working to different standards is a destructive element of teamwork. The workforce need to establish the standards that they all adhere to and they themselves should address an individual they feel is letting them down. There is no doubt that the more everyone communicates expectations, the freer an organisation can be, and it doesn't have to be down to one person but a part of everyone's role.

The second action is to *make information available to everyone*. Maintaining the hierarchy is achieved with privileged access to information. In a democratic organisation information should flow. Your leadership role is to challenge the information systems. At present managers provide information that is then used to control the workforce, whereas information systems should be designed to assist them. Information such as reports should be available to everyone at the same time. We still have to get away from the notion that those at the top of a hierarchy can make better decisions than everyone else.

The third action is to *develop an environment that challenges* through regular reviews among peers. These are not the same as meetings but where people can focus on achieving their own targets and check that they are following their values and beliefs. Each of these contributes towards a culture of self-discipline and responsibility. Not only are you developing your own leadership in achieving this, but developing theirs, too. The next challenge you face is to build trust.

Creating an environment of trust

Where information has been a source of power it is difficult to suddenly decide to share information without the consensus of the majority, so this is something you must gain. This transformation cannot take place smoothly in an environment of transactional management where rewards and avoidance of punishment is on a contractual basis, leading to teams protecting their own interests.

An environment of trust requires an organic approach where everyone is committed to their part of the whole for agreed standards and where emotions are honest. In this environment people will take risks in suggesting creative ideas and challenging issues, because they know they have support around them. When this occurs ordinary people do extraordinary things.

The recipe for healthy organisations is not very different from the recipe for healthy relationships outside the workplace: openness and honesty in how things are done, a sense of equality and fairness in decision making, and a shared set of core values to live by and to which everyone agrees. In addition, how people are selected, integrated, treated and rewarded has to be included. People need to feel they can challenge or disagree without damaging their career.

If you are open and act out of integrity you are setting an example of what is expected, whereas if the focus is on performance targets, strategic objectives and budgets the result is cynicism and sometimes underhand behaviour. Instead, focus on your shared values, what the team stands for and not only is trust developed but you also attract employees to join the team because people want to do more than a job. They want to be part of something exciting, where there is a sense of unity and an environment of trust.

How do you know when you have achieved this? Identify what this environment will look like, feel like and produce, and then work towards these elements. Remember the story of Dunblane and the Snowdrop Campaign (← p. 18) where individuals *did* make a difference. Never doubt your power or leadership capabilities.

The leadership journey continues

To help you on the leadership journey the Institute of Leadership provides further learning for those who want to explore, develop and question their leadership in organisations globally. You can keep in touch via our website and e-learning network. The journey of learning leadership continues by clicking onto www.iofl.org.

Souvenirs

At the end of this journey you will want to take with you some souvenirs and so we have compiled a list of books for further leadership learning in *Recommended books* (p. 344 ➜). Let us give you some words for final reflection. They are words we use at the Institute to guide us and we'd like to share them with you. Whenever you feel frustrated at work or find large boulders on your path in trying to bring about transformation or in expressing your leadership, they may comfort you.

Final reflection

'Each time a person stands up for an idea, or acts to improve the lot of others, or strikes out against injustice, they send forth a tiny ripple of hope, and crossing each other from a million different centres of energy and daring, those ripples build a current that can sweep down the mightiest walls of oppression and resistance.

Few are willing to brave the disapproval of their fellows, the censure of their colleagues, the wrath of their society. Moral courage is a rarer commodity than bravery in battle or great intelligence. Yet it is the one essential, vital quality for those who seek to change a world that yields most painfully to change.' (Robert F Kennedy)

Trust your leadership and let it take you to new places while taking others with you. Be the best you can be and express your leadership fully. Good luck.

Message 1. **Our blessing that you succeed.**

2. **The hope that we meet you at some part of your journey.**

3. **The wish that you in your turn will support others to express their leadership.**

Action Make time to reflect on what you have read here and elsewhere;

Make learning and leadership part of every day.

Leadership and 500 managers

Issues and questions they want answered.

What can we do to help leaders emerge?

We need leadership that makes change happen at middle levels.

How can we develop leaders who communicate a clear sense of direction to everyone?

How do we 'walk the talk'?

Are we effective in selecting our leaders?

What are we going to do with those leaders we identify?

Are followers responsible for making leadership effective?

How can we help the management board become leaders?

How can leadership be taught or learned?

How can we build teams of leaders rather than individuals?

How can we enable all people to make a difference?

How can we support leaders to achieve targets?

As leaders, what are we frightened of, and what is holding us back, e.g. risk or intimacy?

How do we change whole organisations?

What behaviour gets in the way of leadership?

Why is the visibility of leaders so important and how do we do it?

What is leadership?

What makes a good leader?

How do I know I'm being a good leader? What will I see in my team?

Is leadership genetically programmed?

How can leadership motivate people?

Can we believe everyone can be a leader?

Is leadership a trendy word for management?

How can you turn staff at all levels into leaders?

What is being done to enable leaders to be leaders?

Who is our role model for leadership?

What can we do about senior managers who can't or don't want to be leaders?

How can we keep creativity in leadership?

How can we get leadership away from ticking boxes?

How can we learn from experiences of bad leadership?

What is the contribution of a leader?

What is the difference between leading large and small teams?

How do we recognise successful leadership from the viewpoint of being led?

How do you build a team of equals?

What is the transition from being a manager to being a leader?

How do we cope with the isolation/loneliness of being put in a leadership role?

How do leaders handle overlapping responsibilities?

Are the right people being elected as leaders?

Who have been the greatest leaders in the past and what can we learn from them?

How do you lead from the middle?

How do we tackle our less able performers in the team?

How do we show we actively listen to ideas?

What makes a leader rather than a dictator?

How do we value leadership?

How do you lead poor and good team members?

What do leaders do wrong?

How do you manage the expectations of all those who want to be leaders?

How do you lead a matrix organisation when boundaries are blurred?

Do we bring leaders in at the expense of internal talent?

Does good leadership add value?

How do we cope with bad leaders and what can we learn from it?

Is leadership compatible with being open?

What is EI and what has it to do with leadership?

How do you lead different sorts of people?

How do you turn bad leaders into good ones from underneath?

How do we create leaders who desire to serve people rather than expect people to serve them?

Recommended books

The Leader of the Future – Drucker Foundation, ed Hesselbein, Goldsmith & Beckhard (Jossey Bass)

Servant Leadership, Robert Greenleaf (Paulist Books)

Shackelton's Way, Margot Murrell and Stephanie Capparell (Brealey)

The Fifth Discipline, Peter Senge (Century Business)

The Female Advantage, Sally Hegesen (Doubleday)

The Art of the Long View, Peter Schwartz

A Peacock in the Land of Penguins, by Hately & Schmidt (Berrett Koeller)

Why Leaders Can't Lead, Warren Bennis (Jossey Bass)

Synchronicity, Jo Jaworski (Berrett Kohler)

The Soul at Work, Roger Lewin & Birute Regine (Orion)

Achieving Emotional Literacy, Claude Steiner (Bloomsbury)

The Autobiography of Martin Luther King, ed. Clayborne Carson (Abacus)

In Search of Leaders, Hilarie Owen (Wiley & Sons)

Unleashing Leaders, Hilarie Owen (Wiley & Sons)

Emotions Revealed: Understanding Faces and Feelings, Paul Eckman (Weidenfield & Nicholson)

Emotional Intelligence, Daniel Goleman (Bloomsbury)

Seven Day Weekend, Ricardo Semler (Century Random House)

Good to Great, Jim Collins (Random House)

Man's Search for Meaning, Viktor Frankl (Simon & Schuster)

Executive EQ, Robert Cooper and Ayman Sawaf (Corion Business Books)

Crossing the Unknown Sea, David Whyte (Michael Joseph)

Ghandi, David Arnold (Longman)

On Becoming a Leader, Warren Bennis (Perseus Publishing)

Geeks and Geezers: How Era, Values and Defining Moments Shape Leaders, Warren Bennis (Harvard Business School Press)

Index